If Gravestones Could Talk

Stories from the Churchyard

of St. John's Camden

Janice Johnson

Camden Historical Society

Published by Camden Historical Society Inc.
40 John Street, Camden, NSW 2570
(SAN: 908 3002)

www.camdenhistory.com.au

Published with funds from the Estate of the late Janice Johnson, who died in 2017.

© 2022 by the Camden Historical Society Inc.

All rights reserved. No part of this publication may be used or reproduced in any manner whatsoever without written permission, except in the case of brief quotations in critical articles and reviews. Contact the Camden Historical Society PO Box 566 Camden NSW 2570 Australia for more information. (secretary@camdenhistory.org.au)

All photographs in the publication are part of the Camden Historical Society's collection or are used with the permission acknowledged in the text.

First published in 2010
Revised November 2014.
Second Edition January 2022.

2nd Edition

ISBN: 978-0-9875820-4-1

Front cover: St John's Anglican Church, Camden. The aerial photo was taken from a balloon in 1994: Photographer – Rosemary Gibson.

Back cover: Draped urn – Ferguson family grave – Section C002.

Contents

Contents	iii
Illustrations	ix
Acknowledgements	xiii
About the Author	xv
Introduction	17
St. John's and the Churchyard	21
Aborigines and Islanders	31
Guribunger	32
Susan Sophaline Barrett	32
Richard Barrett Jnr.	32
Mary Matilda Barrett	32
James Barrett	32
John Solomon	33
Jiminy	33
Henry Kaffie	33
They Came in Chains - The Convicts	35
Richard Barrett	35
Richard Boyd	35
George Coker	36
James English	36
Thomas Herbert	37
Jonathan Wood	37
Free Settlers – Landowners, Storekeepers and Tradesmen	39
Henry Grattan Douglass	39
Commander Alexander Martin	43
Eliza Pearson	47
Edward Thompson Palmer	48
Mary Edith Allan	49
Maximillian von Zglinicki	50
Garlies Allinson	51
John Benson Martin	51
John Lakeman	52
Alfred John Bayley	54
Susannah Butler	55
Henry Thompson	55

Contents

Thomas Dawson	56
George Poole	57
Jessie and Mabel Sidman	57
A New Beginning – Bounty and Assisted Immigrants	**59**
Sophia Cox	60
Thomas Dockery Richardson	62
William Fairall	62
William Rofe	62
Jesse Dunk	62
Francis Ferguson	64
Henry Pollock Reeves	64
Fanny Wheeler	65
Joan Vaux	65
Eliza Jane Rapley	65
John Leonard Monk	65
Oliver Hinde	66
John Thomas McMinn	66
Richard Hawkey	67
Samuel Ellis	68
First Fleet Connections	**69**
Philip Gidley King	69
Philip Parker King	70
Philip Gidley King (the younger)	70
Robert Lethbridge King	70
Rev. Cecil John King	71
Rev. Copland King	72
Australian Born – The First Generation	**73**
Jessie Carron	73
Henry Thomas Close	73
Philip Benjamin Hodge	74
Charles Hopson	74
George Edward Kettley	75
Ellen Rosetta McMullen	75
Edward Lomas Moore	75
Henry Clarendon Hughes	76
William Rapley	77
Joan Stuckey	77
William John Taplin	77

George Wheeler	78
The Young Ones	79
Elias Thorn	79
Jonathon Spice	79
Robert Veness	79
William Gibson	80
Alice, Florence and William Boyd	80
Ethel May Anderson	80
Maggie Blow	80
Leonard Ross Cranfield	81
Reginald George Gardner	81
Unnamed Infant	81
William James Barry	82
Following Generations	83
George William Armour	83
William Alfred Ernest Biffin	84
James Kinghorne Chisholm	84
Mary Jane Dawson	85
Emma Dengate	85
Richard George Hindes	85
William Henry Hopson	86
Agnes Elizabeth Lowe	86
Rev. Arthur George Rix	86
Ellen Stanner	87
Charles John Sutton	87
William George Watson	88
John Edward Veness	89
Francis James West	89
Francis William West	90
Milton Brettel Ray	90
Tragedy at the Home Farm	93
Lives Lost Too Soon	97
Jeremiah Martin	97
William Boyd	97
Elias Casson and his family	98
Thomas Watson	98
John Tickner	99
Benjamin Weeks	99

Contents

Jennings Starr	100
William Hall	100
Thomas Cranfield	100
Robert Henry Druitt	101
Dorothea Campbell	102
Richard Mitchell	102
Thomas Bryant	102
James Small	103
George Frederick Heighington	103
Keith Angelo Tornaghi	103
William Leslie Critchley	103
Thomas James Rossitter	104
Frederick Nixon	105
Gladys May Shoobridge	106
Bertie Stewart Gunn	106
William Arthur Channell	107
Lest We Forget	109
Boer War	110
Francis Arthur Macarthur-Onslow	110
James William Macarthur-Onslow	111
Carlton Smith	112
World War I	112
John George Adams	113
Percy Sidney Raymond Brain	113
Alexander Brien	113
Cecil Clarence Butler	113
Hilton John Chesham	113
James Coleman Clarke	114
Edward John Dengate	114
Vivian Charles Gardner	114
Victor Louis Bosker Haigh	115
Richard John Hawkey	116
Wallace Conrad Rofe Jenkins	116
William Calbraith Livesey	116
Eric Lyndon Lowe	116
George Griffin Roy Mills	117
Essington Moore	117
Arthur William Macarthur-Onslow	118

George Macleay Macarthur-Onslow	118
Astley John Onslow Thompson	119
Frank Henderson Paul	120
Rev. Thomas Giles Paul	120
John Lambert Richardson Poole	123
George Quigley	123
Robert Alfred Sidman	123
Hector Small	123
Reginald (Rex) Sydney Smith	124
Cecil Claude Wheeler	125
John Edward Williams	125
World War II	125
Astley Arthur Cranfield	125
Robert Bruce Ferguson	125
Ernest Henry McGrath	126
Norman Thomas McLeod	127
Ivo Garnett Perry	127
Edwin Morton Rapley	127
Roy Sawyers	128
Colin Tate	128
Ernest Leon Wade	128
Last Flight of the Dragon	129
Radiant Light	133
The Stained Glass Designers	134
Frederick Pellatt – Pellatt & Co	134
Clayton & Bell	134
Alfred Charles Handel	134
Powell & Sons (Whitefriars) Ltd.	134
Stephen Moor	135
Kevin Little	135
The Original Windows	135
Rev. Cecil John and Copland King Memorial	136
War Memorial	138
Rev. Henry Tingcombe Memorial	140
Lancet Windows	142
East Window – James Macarthur Memorial	144
Captain Arthur Alexander Walton Onslow	147
Elizabeth Macarthur-Onslow Memorial	149

Contents

Brigadier General George Macleay Macarthur-Onslow Window	151
John William Clinton and Alice Wilson Clinton	152
Bertha Victoria Brien	155
Written in Stone	157
Plans	213
Bibliography	219
Index	223

Illustrations

Adams, Catherine Jane	129
Allinson, Garlies – coffin grace	158
Armour, George	83
Belgenny Farm – knock-off bell	107
Boyd – children grave	80
Brien, Bertha & Michael	155
Bull, Ann	76
Cemetery from the eastern side of St John's	213
Cemetery rules	28
Chesham, Lance Corp. Hilton – grave	113
Chisholm, James	84
Clarke, Lance Corp. James	114
Clinton, John William	153
Coker, George & Hobbs, Thomas – grave	38
Cranfield - Book of Life - D063	18
Cranfield, Bertha Victoria	155
Cranfield, Leonard	81
Cranfield, Thomas	101
Crookston, Dr - house	108
Dawson, Thomas - A129	20
Dawson, Thomas – farm	56
De-Havilland Dragon	129
Douglas, Hester	42
Douglass – Cottage	41
Douglass, Henry Gratton	39
Doyle, Sergeant Douglas Brian	130
Doyle, Sergeant Frances Joseph	130
Druitt, Rev Thomas Henry & family	108
Dunk, Jesse - medal	63
Dunk, Jesse	62
English, Herbert	26
Ferguson, Robert Bruce	126
Ferguson – grave - C02	234
Fuller grave - E051	19
Gardner, Reggie – plaque	81
Grattan, Henry	42
Grave, Douglass – plaque	43
Graves Management	30
Harley, Frances	76
Hawkey, Richard	68
Hinde – family memorial	66
Hodge, Phillip	74
Johnson, Janice	xv
Kaffie, Model hut	34
King – grave	70
King, Rev. Cecil John	71
King, Rev. Copland	72
Lakeman, John	52

Illustrations

Lester, Flying Officer Geoffrey	130
Leuckel – children's grave	213
Lowe, Lance Corp. Eric Lyndon – memorial plaque	117
Lowe, Lance Corp. Eric Lyndon	116
Macaria	56
Macarthur-Onslow, Brigadier General George Macleay – memorial plaque	109
Macarthur-Onslow, Capt. Arthur William	118
Macarthur-Onslow, General James William	111
Macarthur-Onslow, George Macleay	118
Macarthur-Onslow, Lt. Francis Arthur	110
Macleay, Sir George	142
Martin, Alexander – property map	45
Martin, Alexander – tombstone	44
Martin, Alexander	44
Martin, John	51
McGrath, Private Ernest	126
Memorial, Dragon	132
Moore, Edward	76
Moore, Lt. Essington	117
Nixon, Frederick and his team	105
Onslow Thompson, Lieut Col. Astley John	120
Onslow, Captain Arthur Alexander Walton	147
Overgrown graves	28
Palmer plaques	49
Palmer, Edward	48
Palmer, nee Robinson	49
Patrick, Rev. Alan	29
Paul, Frank Henderson	120
Paul, Rev. Thomas Giles	120
Plan – Royal George steerage	61
Post Office, Camden	47
Ray, Milton	90
Reeves, Henry	64
Roll of Honour	109
Sidman, William	57
Small, Lance Corporal Hector	123
Smith, Carlton	112
Smith, Reginald Sydney	124
Smith, Rex, Amelia & Ida	124
St Johns	87
Stewart, James – grave	96
Stewart, James	96
Stuckey – store	77
Stuckey, Elgar	77
Stuckey, Joan	77
Sutton, Brett	30
Table grave	158
Tate, Flt. Sgt. Colin	128
Tickner, Edward	99
Tingcombe, Rev. Henry	140
Veness, Edward	89
Watson's bakery	88
Weeks, Benjamin	100

West, Dr Francis William – funeral procession	90
West, Dr Francis William – grave	92
West, Dr Francis William	89
West, Dr Francis William	92
Window – Bertha Victoria Brien memorial	156
Window – Brigadier General George Macleay Macarthur-Onslow memorial	152
Window – Capt. Arthur Alexander Walton Onslow memorial	148
Window – Elizabeth Macarthur-Onslow memorial	150
Window – James Macarthur memorial	146
Window – John William & Alice Clinton memorial	154
Window – King memorial	137
Window – Lancet	143
Window – Original	133
Window – Tingcombe memorial	141
Window – WWI memorial	139

Acknowledgements

In November 2007, I began researching the Cemetery at St. John's with the intention of preparing an updated list of the graves. I soon became distracted by the many stories I began to uncover and realised that I needed to put these down in some order.

I was encouraged in this endeavour by local resident Shirley Rorke who reminded me that many of the early pioneers had stories to tell. Not just the prominent landowners, but many others like the labourers also had stories that should be told. It was not until I began to delve further into the Cemetery listing that I realised how right she was.

Richard (Dick) Nixon (1919-2008) was the church historian for many years, and his card index also provided useful information. The work done by the Patrick family in the 1970s also needs to be acknowledged. The late David Patrick (1955-2009), together with Stephen Wedd, transcribed many of the headstones in Sections A, B, and C, some of which are now extremely difficult to decipher or are no longer in existence.

I appreciate the wealth of information and encouragement, and advice given by John and Julie Wrigley, Ian Willis, Annette Macarthur-Onslow, Len English, Peter Hayward and others.

The Camden Historical Society is pleased to publish this second edition of Janice's book and thanks Fletcher Joss from Egarag Pty Ltd for his significant contribution in preparing the book for publication.

About the Author

Janice Johnson had an ongoing interest in local studies and was a member of the Camden Historical Society and Camden Family History Society. She had a particular interest in the people and events that helped shape Camden and in the history of St. John's Anglican Church, Camden.

She was the author or editor of:

Janice Johnson

- *Camden's WWI Diggers: 1914-1918*
- *Camden – Unlocking the Past* (Co-author with Brian Burnett)
- *Part 1 Pioneer and Federation Index* (e-Book)
- *Reminiscences Early Camden* (Editor)
- *Reflections on Old Sydney and Colonial Days* (Editor)
- *They Worked at Camden Park* (Co-author of 3rd, 4th, and 5th editions)
- *We Do But Sleep: The Cemeteries & Columbarium of the Camden & Menangle Anglican Parishes* (e-Book)
- *Camden Through a Poet's Eyes 1847 to 1854 – Charles Tompson (Jnr.)*
- *Camden Soldiers of King and Queen 1788 to 1913*
- *Camden Stories of Service in World War II*

For a time, Janice worked in the office of St John's, where she kept the cemetery records, assisted people searching the cemetery and gave regular tours. Janice died in 2017 and bequeathed money for the completion of her work. This included her outstanding books and installation of plaques to preserve the inscriptions on some of the more important graves in St John's cemetery: E82 – Gumbleton; B22 – Haigh; A103 – Lakeman; A102 – Lakeman; B91 – Zglinicki; B17 – Stewart. Camden Historical Society acknowledges her valuable work as a researcher advancing our understanding of the history of the Camden area.

This book is the way Janice wrote it. If readers find corrections they would like to suggest, they should put them in writing and submit them to the Secretary of the Camden Historical Society, Mrs Lee Stratton, PO Box 566, Camden NSW 2570, or email secretary@camdenhistory.org.au.

Introduction

If gravestones could talk what stories they could tell of those who lie beneath, stories of the people who helped shape the township of Camden as we know it today. Of good times and bad times, of tragedies, accidents, of those who had helped build the town and had been part of the community. Of those that had triumphed out of adversity, of the people who worked to build a new life in a colony on the opposite side of the world from where they were born; people of many nationalities. Some had come in chains, others had fled poverty in the hope that the new land would give them opportunities to prosper.

Varying circumstances had brought them to this land. Some had been transported as convicts, and others had come as part of the military establishment. Poverty in the land of their birth had encouraged others to face the dangers of a long sea voyage and seek a new life in the Colony. Some had been engaged by landowners such as the Macarthurs because of the skills they could provide.

Late in 2007, I began to prepare a comprehensive listing of those who were buried in St. John's Cemetery using the old Burial Registers and a plan of the Cemetery. It was not until just before Easter 2008 that I began to understand how important it was to know not only the names of those buried there, but who the people in each of the graves were.

One entry in the Burial Registers had intrigued me — *"Nanny"* who was described as *"an Aboriginal Nanny from Camden Park."* At the Camden Show in 2008 I ran into John Wrigley and asked him *"Who was Nanny? Did Nanny have any connection with Nanny Barrett?"* He laughed and referred me to the gentleman on his left — Len English; the answer, they are one and the same. Len English had been trying to locate "Nanny's" grave for a number of years without success, so in identifying just where the grave was located, I learnt a lot about Nanny and her descendants and began to unravel the many other stories in the Cemetery.

Tantalising comments in Burial Registers and on gravestones encouraged and challenged me to unlock the stories behind them, *"Fell from a window at the Plough and Harrow;" "Run over by own bullock team;" "Killed by a maniac at Camden Park"* were just some of the examples. The stories began to emerge from old newspapers and other documents; the gravestones began to speak.

This is primarily about some of those buried in the churchyard, about the formation of the town of Camden and building the church. Of people from England, Europe and the Pacific islands who were brought here in chains or undertook the perilous journey to a new life. Of their descendants, many took up the challenge and prospered, others did not meet their full potential as a result of accidents. Others cherished the freedom this land offered and paid the ultimate sacrifice by defending this land in time of war.

Resources for the stories are old newspapers, coroner's inquests, letters held in the State Archives and memorials within the church or churchyard. Whether it is in the stained glass windows of the church, on the gravestones in the churchyard, or in tantalising comments in the Burial Registers, the lives of many are told here. Less than half the graves have gravestones or memorial plaques, and many of those are slowly fading and the stones crumbling. All known inscriptions have been recorded and are included.

So often, we neglect our old cemeteries looking on them as faded, crumbling stone that have no relevance in our modern world. The people in the cemetery at St. John's may have been forgotten, but their stories give us a fascinating insight into our early history and the people who formed this

Introduction

township. Their descendants still call Camden home and are proud of their heritage and what their forebears achieved.

It was inevitable once the original book was published that additional information would be provided as interested descendants imparted new facts. This version incorporates corrections and this additional information. For instance, whilst searching Trove on another matter, what happened to William Buchan, the stonemason, was discovered. Additional information has also come to light on Victor Louis Bosker Haigh, as well as the intriguing story behind the Sutton grave in Section E. This, therefore, is an extended story of Camden's forebears, and I am sure there are still many stories yet to be told.

Book of Life – Cranfield grave in Section D063

Fuller grave in Section E051 – note amendment of name from Sharlet to Charlot for Frances Charlotte Fuller

Introduction

Grave of Thomas Dawson in section A129 with the Masonic symbol at the base.

St. John's and the Churchyard

In the early 1830s Governor Sir Richard Bourke approached John Macarthur and asked him to surrender 320 acres (129.5 hectares) of his land to allow for a town to be built on the western bank of the Nepean River. Macarthur refused, fearing the effect it would have on his *Camden Park* estate. After John Macarthur's death in 1834, his sons, James and William, favourably considered the request for a town to be established, and in 1836 the area was surveyed with land offered for sale in 1840. Elizabeth, John's widow, or relict according to the terminology of the day, chose the hill overlooking the town as the site for an Anglican Church in line with Governor Lachlan Macquarie's instruction

> *"all ticket of leave holders are to attend church at least once each week, failure to do so would mean that such a convict would have to resort to Government work."*

The site chosen for the church included a 1¼ acre (5058.5 m2) site for a cemetery, school and rectory plus space for a small farm to provide a living for the incumbent. This was in order to comply with the directive issued to Macquarie and other early governors —

> *"that you do by all proper methods enforce a due observance of religion and that as near to each town as possible you set apart land for the building of a church and four hundred acres adjacent thereto allotted for the maintenance of a Minister."*

Before work on the building could commence, the ground had to be "stumped." This involved the removal of trees and shrubs and their stumps/roots. Earth was shovelled away from around the stumps, and they were then hauled away to help in the burning of the more stubborn ones, with the work done using axe, mattock and shovel. A letter from Mrs. Macarthur dated 10th July 1836[1] indicated that some clearing had already taken place on the proposed church site and the hill leading to it.

The foundation trenches for the church were dug during the winter of 1836 when the site was cleared and levelled by six ex-convicts, employees from the *Camden Park* estate, who were paid 4 shillings (40 cents) per day for the work, which took about 206 man-days. The group known as Patrick Sullivan and Co. included Patrick Sullivan, John Carroll, James Christy, Joseph Cumnock, Joseph Liversay and Owen Kennedy. None of the men from the Stumping Gang are buried in the churchyard as they apparently left Camden shortly after. By the time land sales took place in October 1840, the church site for the new town of Camden had already been cleared.

The hilltop at the top of John Street is double-humped with the church on one prominence and the rectory, built in 1859, on the other.[2] Plans for a classical style church were prepared in 1836 by the Diocesan Architect, James Hume, who was paid £25 ($50). The plans were only utilised[3] for the foundations and building work below window level. The building design has long been attributed to Mortimer Lewis, the Colonial Architect; however, the decorated gothic stone tracery was something entirely new to the Colony and to Lewis' previous work. Other authorities believe Lewis only acted as supervisory architect, and the design should be attributed to John Cunningham from Liverpool, England[4].

Very little work appears to have taken place after 1836 until 1840 due to the need to source

---

[1] Macarthur Papers A2906
[2] "St. John's Hill and John Street Urban Conservation Area" A. Strachan, S. Sky, D. Saunders – February 1977
[3] "150th Anniversary Laying of Foundation Stone, November 3rd 1840" The Crier 24th October 1990
[4] "Gothick Taste in the Colony of New South Wales" Joan Kerr and James Broadbent

tradesmen from England. James Macarthur was in England during 1837, at which time tradesmen such as Basden and Wheeler were recruited. In 1838 James wed Amelia Stone (known as Emily) and returned to Sydney on the *Royal George* in March 1839.

The stone foundations were laid in 1840, and work commenced on the brickwork. The foundation stone was laid by Bishop William Grant Broughton on 3rd November 1840, probably on the eastern wall of the building, as the stone has not been seen for over 136 years. It is believed to have been covered over when the chancel was extended in 1874 and to now lie under the floor of the chancel.

It would appear that shortly after the foundation stone was laid, work on the church ceased for a short period. Emily Macarthur, who had picturesque tastes, is thought to have contacted her sister Mary Egerton (previously Lady Mary Marjoribanks), the wife of Rev. George Egerton, rector of the eighteenth-century church of Middle in Shropshire. Mary sent tracings of Cunningham's gothic revival style design for alterations planned for the church at Middle to Emily Macarthur, and the design features remarkably are similar to St. John's *"particularly the decorated gothic tracery and the multiple stepped buttresses."*[5] Undoubtedly Mortimer Lewis modified the design to include a loftier tower and removed embellishments to the buttresses.

Morton Herman is reported as declaring St. John's as *"perhaps the finest example of early Gothic Revival architecture in Australia"*[6] and Bishop Broughton agreed with him, declaring it *"was one of the handsomest churches in his See."*[7] In 1845 he commented that *"it was in a correct style of decorated architecture with a lofty tower and spire, and even in its unfinished state forms a most striking feature in the landscape."*[8] The original plan was to stucco render the external facade, but after seeing the finished building, and the pleasant tone of the bricks, and due to financial constraints, the trustees decided to leave the mellow tones of the brickwork visible.

The responsibility for much of the building work lay with Richard Basden, born in Brighton, Sussex, England in 1795. Basden had been a bricklayer in England, and as there was a need for an experienced bricklayer to work on the new church, and the numerous other buildings proposed for the new town. He came to Camden as a bounty immigrant on the *Augusta Jessie* and arrived on 11th October 1837. The Macarthurs provided him with a small brick cottage, rent-free[9], but he was not a good businessman and constantly experienced financial difficulties and was declared bankrupt in 1851. He managed to trade his way out of his difficulties and built the Rectory in 1859. He died aged 75 years on 23rd January 1870 and is buried alongside his wife Theodosia in Section A145.

The 386,000 bricks used to build the church came from the brickworks operated by James Lacey, trading as Lacey & Co. The original brickworks located on the western side of what is now known as Macquarie Grove Road,[10] about 100 metres to the north of the junction with Exeter Street, on land leased from the Macarthurs, were referred to as the Old Kiln.[11] Lacy employed a number of men, probably 4 or 5 brickmakers as well as 2 or 3 labourers. The brick makers would generally make about 1,000 bricks a day.

Work on the building recommenced when bricks were delivered to the site on 11th May 1841. Lacey continued to supply bricks for the 18 months it took to complete the brickwork. When the clay deposit at the Old Kiln was depleted, he moved to a new site at the northern end, eastern

---

[5] Ibid
[6] Ibid
[7] Ibid
[8] Ibid
[9] "Camden" – Alan Atkinson
[10] This area is part of what is now known as the Camden Town Farm
[11] "Locations of Brickworks" - Richard (Dick) Nixon

side, of Argyle Street and established the New Kiln. The Old Kiln ceased operation in April 1841, but bricks from its stocks were in use up until 8th July 1841. During this period, he supplied bricks to other customers, including for the building of the Camden Inn, Thompson's Flour Mill and for Lieutenant Thomas Woore's *Harrington Grove*.

William Buchan, a sculptor and stonemason from Edinburgh, Scotland, did most of the stonework on the church. Buchan was born in Edinburgh, Scotland, on 2nd February 1805, the son of Alexander Buchan, a stonemason. On 15th May 1825 he married Margaret Henderson nee Walch, the daughter of Alexander Walch and Elizabeth Bell.

Buchan, his wife and four children sailed from Greenock on the *Duncan* on 11th January 1838 and arrived on 30th June, 1838 after an eventful voyage from England via Cape Horn. The *Duncan* had almost foundered during a storm which had carried away the rudder and compelled the captain to make for Rio de Janeiro for repairs.[12] The family lived in Parramatta for two years, and where Buchan purchased land. Financial difficulties forced him to leave the land in 1840, and the family came to Camden, where Buchan worked on the church and other buildings.

The stone for the building came from the quarry at *Denbigh* and was used as flagging in conjunction with timber flooring under the pews. The stone flagging was described on 2nd July 1849 by the Sydney Guardian as *"the very best piece of work of its kind in the country."* In 1852 the timber flooring was found to have suffered extensive damage from white ants; Buchan replaced it with stone flagging. He also made, and presented the stone baptismal font *"a handsome gift from a poor tradesman."*[13]

The font was originally located in the northeast corner of the aisle but in 1869, the third rector, Rev. Henry Tingcombe, relocated it to the traditional position at the entrance of the church. The Buchan family, possibly his wife Margaret, protested thinking William Buchan's gift was not conspicuous enough and Bishop Frederic Barker persuaded Rev. Tingcombe to move it to a position at the front of the then central pews.

We know that William Buchan was in Camden in 1851 as he was appointed Bailiff of the Small Debts Court in Camden in October 1851, but he had relinquished this position by May 1852 and left Camden, possibly to seek his fortune in the Victorian goldfields. His family was unaware as to where he could be located as an advertisement was placed in the Sydney Morning Herald, on Tuesday, October 24, 1854 -

> *"MR WILLIAM BUCHAN - If this should meet his eye, he is earnestly solicited to communicate with his family. Supposed to be at some of the Port Phillip diggings. Any information from any persons will be thankfully received by address a letter to Mrs. BUCHAN, Camden, N.S.W or Mr. Alex. BUCHAN, Balmain, near Sydney".*

After failing to make his fortune in the goldfields, Buchan moved to Ulladulla, where he worked for a short time before his death there on August 24, 1854. It was some months before the family learnt of his demise.

The chancel was extended in 1874, but it is not known who was responsible for the stonework as both William Buchan and his son Alexander were both deceased.

William Buchan's wife Margaret was a dressmaker and kept a store on the corner of Argyle and Oxley Streets until shortly before her death on 4th October 1897. The grave of Margaret Buchan

---

[12] Obituary – Mrs. Margaret Buchan – Camden News 7th October 1897
[13] "Camden" – Alan Atkinson

and her infant son William are to be found in section A149 alongside her daughter Jane's parents-in-law (Ebenezer Simpson and Sarah Clarke).

In 1895 the fifth rector, Rev. Cecil John King, had the font moved back to the traditional location at the entrance of the church.

Another craftsman that worked on the new church was John LeFevre, a native of Jersey in the Channel Islands. He was the craftsman responsible for the carpentry and joinery. LeFevre crafted the shingles for the roof of St. John's, and many other buildings in Camden and at *Camden Park*. It is understood that part of the work on the roof took place away from the Church site as in July 1842 Spencer Whiteman and Joseph Goodluck received payment for "*drawing roof to church.*"[14] LeFevre declared he was insolvent on 9th February 1844[15] when the depression that had gripped the Colony resulted in no work being available. He was able to trade his way out of his difficulties when work recommenced on St. John's in 1847, and he did the copper work for the church windows and fitted them in place. He died on 19th May 1879 and is buried in an unmarked grave alongside his wife Georgina in Section C057.

Jonathan Wheeler was born in Bisley, Gloucestershire, England, on 4th September 1791, the son of Nathaniel Wheeler and Sarah Fowler and married Jane March, a house servant, on 4th January 1813. Wheeler had been a labourer, but according to the 1815 baptismal record for his second child Hester, he had also been a soldier. There are no records to show in which combats he was involved, but as the major battle in 1815 was the Battle of Waterloo, and as others from Bisley were involved in that battle, it is possible he was in the same regiment.

After 1815 Wheeler returned to Bisley and worked as a weaver. Widespread destitution soon occurred as the small clothiers who employed spinners and weavers in their mills were replaced by cloth manufacturers and the factory system. Many were forced out of work and faced being sent to the poorhouse. On 21st June 1837, the Bisley Parish submitted a list of 68 people selected to travel on 8th September 1837 to the Colony on the *Layton* as assisted immigrants.

The Wheeler family were amongst this group and spent approximately five weeks on board the *Layton* prior to their departure where they were visited by James Macarthur. The Wheeler and Butt families were selected to work at *Camden Park*. The voyage was tragic for many when a measles epidemic broke out; the Wheelers' two youngest children were to die at sea. The *Layton* arrived at on 19th January 1838, and the Wheeler and Butt families made the journey on foot to *Elizabeth Farm* at Parramatta before continuing the journey to *Camden Park*.[16]

Jonathan Wheeler was employed at *Camden Park* as a sawyer, and his sons followed the same trade. He later opened a sawmill at North Cawdor on Mataylor Creek, and it was here he cut the timber sourced from Crocodile and Monkey Creeks[17] for the Camden Inn, which was erected in 1841 at the corner of Argyle and Elizabeth Streets.

Jonathan felled the ironbark trees and shaped the timber used to construct the roof of the church, with the logs being brought from Bargo, The Oaks and Bob's Range. Jonathan and his sons were each granted 100 acres (40.5 hectares) of land at Mount Hunter; each joining and bordering on Westbrook Creek. He died on 19th May 1855 after falling from his wagon whilst he and one of his sons were carting wheat[18] to Junee, and is buried in Section D004.

---

[14] Macarthur Papers 7th, 8th and 11th July 1842 – payments A2995
[15] "New South Wales Government Gazette" Friday February 9 1844
[16] "Camden News with Record of Dates Commemorating the 50th Anniversary of the Municipality of Camden" Camden News 2nd March 1839
[17] ibid
[18] "The Wheelers of Camden" by Linda Anne Powell

The chancel was extended by 26 feet (7.9 metres) in 1874 from a design prepared by the eminent Gothic Revival architect Gilbert Scott of London.[19] The work, which included a small vestry, was carried out by Edmond Blackett of Sydney using bricks from the nearby old Thompson's Flour Mill no longer in use as a result of the devastation to the wheat crop in 1860 due to rust disease. As the original brick pits had been covered over, this source of bricks was essential to ensure the new blended with the old. Samuel Edward Albert Wheeler, the son of Jonathan, was engaged to do the timber work; he is buried in Section D196 alongside his second wife, Annie Richards.

By 1841 the walls had been completed, and work had commenced on the roof, and the external work on the building was largely complete by 1842. A sketch by Lieutenant Thomas Woore, RN dated 1842, shows that the tower and spire of St. John's Church then dominated the countryside. A comment in the newspapers in 1842 stated –

> *"The Church at Camden has been roofed in for some time, and may be shortly expected to be fit for the celebration of Divine Service. The land which this building occupies was the gift of Mr. James Macarthur, who has likewise subscribed a handsome sum towards the erection of the church."*[20]

The girth of the spire is 44 feet 8 inches (13.4 metres) and the height 57 feet (17.4 metres) from the tower. The height of the tower is 70 feet (21.3 metres), making a total height of 127 feet (38.7 metres) to the top of the spire.[21]

The church would not be completed and consecrated until 7th July 1849 due to a shortage of funds as the result of the agricultural depression in 1843[22] and the Bank of Australia closing its doors[23] when John Terry Hughes and John Hosking became insolvent over failed land deals and were unable to pay the $310,000 they owed. This was compounded by James Macarthur facing financial difficulty over a mortgage on the Australian Newspaper whose proprietors were George Moss and the Rev. William M. Hesketh. In 1843 Moss pulled out of the partnership with his share being transferred to Joseph Compton Potts; with Hesketh in financial difficulty the newspaper was facing bankruptcy. As Potts had been introduced to James Macarthur by his wife's family James Macarthur was reluctant to push for payment, and the financial drag on his purse increased.[24] In 1844 Potts was declared insolvent, and his possessions went to auction.[25] In 1844 the Australian Newspaper was taken over by Thomas Forster and Edwin Henry Statham relieving the financial drag on James Macarthur's purse even though he continued to hold a financial interest. The agricultural depression caused hardship for many, including the Macarthurs, Macleays and tradesmen, with the difficulties compounded when investors in Britain stopped exporting their capital and endeavoured to recover investments[26] as best they could.

In April 1843 Rev. Robert Forrest was appointed to Camden, and whilst the Burial Registers date from that time, building work possibly prevented burials within St. John's churchyard until June 1844. It would appear that no work was done on the church from 1844 until 1847, enabling the cemetery to be used.

The stained glass for the church windows was not fitted until 1847, with the clock and bells not installed until 1897 when Mrs. Elizabeth Macarthur-Onslow presented the clock and eight bells.

---

[19] Church Windows – Camden Crier 26th April 1988
[20] "Country Intelligence- Berrima" Sydney Gazette & N.S.W. Advertiser – Tuesday, 22nd March 1842
[21] "Centenary of Consecration of St. John's Camden" Camden News 2nd June 1849
[22] "A Macarthur Role in Church" Chronicle 6th November 1940
[23] Bank of Australasia v. Bank of Australia, Judicial Committee of the Privy Council, 15 February 1848 - SMH 23rd June 1848
[24] "James Macarthur Colonial Conservative 1798-1867" John Manning Ward
[25] "New South Wales Government Gazette" Friday, February 9 1844
[26] "Illustrated History of Australia"

On seven of the bells are inscribed the names of various members of her family, whilst the large tenor bell is inscribed with the words of the doxology.

The early records of Burials, Baptisms and Marriages that took place at St. John's appear to have been given in the mid to late 1960s to the late Miss Llewella Davies. It is known that by the end of 1969, the early records were no longer being held by the church. Miss Davies, who was active in the Camden Historical Society, showed the Registers to Nancy Phelan, a travel writer, about this time and told her, *"But they gave it to me. They don't seem to value it."* [27]

Nancy Phelan's book, which was published in 1970, recalled the meeting with Miss Davies. Horrified and embarrassed by the disclosure Miss Davies managed to have the book banned for a period from Camden Library.[28] After this revelation it appears Miss Davies handed the Registers to Richard (Dick) Nixon OAM, also a member of Camden Historical Society, and the Church's historian. Dick Nixon guarded the Registers fearing they may again be thrown away; the Registers were returned to the Church after his death in 2008.

Herbert English at work

Herbert English

The Lych Gate was built in 1912 as a memorial to Mrs. Elizabeth Macarthur-Onslow who had died in London on 2nd, August 1911. The gate was designed by Mr. Kent, an architect from Sydney, and built by Herbert Thomas English known as Herb. Herb was born at *Camden Park* in 1886, the son of James English and Eliza Tripp and a great-grandson of Richard Barrett and Guribunger.

In 1907 Herb married Lilly Woods at Mosman, and from 1910 until the 1950s they lived at the *Home Farm*[29] where he held the position of Head Carpenter. As well as the Lych Gate he also built many of the cottages and other buildings on *Camden Park*.

During the depression years of the 1930s the architect Cyril Ruwald, a frequent houseguest of Edward and Winifred Macarthur-Onslow, sketched a plan for an old style coaching inn. According to information given by Herb to Annette Macarthur-Onslow,[30] Ruwald did not supply a finished plan but merely an artist's impression. It was left to Herb to work out what was required and to complete the building originally known as the Camden Vale Inn.

---

[27] Some Came Early Some Came Late – Nancy Phelan
[28] John Wrigley - Camden Historical Society
[29] Belgenny Farm
[30] "Recalling Camden Vale" by Annette Macarthur-Onslow, Back Then, The District Reporter 26th April 2005

Herb sourced the best Blackbutt timber from a firm in Parramatta, but was horrified when asked by Ruwald to roughen it in order to give it a rustic look. According to his nephew Len English, his uncle Herb laid deep foundations, ensuring the building's longevity. The Inn opened in 1939 and provided milkshakes and Devonshire Teas for visitors to the area. Today it is known as the Camden Valley Inn. Herbert Thomas English died on 12th April 1958 and is buried in Section C036.

St. John's and its adjacent lands reflect the development and growth of the Camden Township as well as the lives of the people who have lived and worked in the town. The cemetery site is on sloping ground with some very steep sections. The soil is highly reactive clay, which constantly moves with ground moisture changes. This has caused nearly all memorials to suffer damage over the past 166 years—sometimes minor in nature, but frequently major. Falling tree limbs have also caused extensive damage to some graves.

There are 900 gravesites/plots and 1,862 burials, ashes and/or memorials within them. The first burial took place on 29th June 1844, 5 years before the church building was completed and church and cemetery consecrated in 1849. During the early years the cemetery was the only one in the town, and as a result people of different nationalities and other denominations such as Methodists and Roman Catholics are buried here, including the well-known Primitive Methodist, Sivyer Rootes and the children of Christian Leuckel and Margaret Haas. Five of the Leuckel children were buried here between 1859 and 1888 but the parents are buried in Camden Roman Catholic Cemetery.

As the churchyard was regarded almost as a general cemetery it is not surprising that in March 1894 the Church Committee expressed concern they would run out of burial plots within two years. By the beginning of 1894 there were only 184 of the 900 burial plots unsold. Those already sold ranged in size from the standard 3 feet (0.9 metres) up to 21 feet (6.4 metres) with provision made for the first coffin to be buried deep to enable another coffin to be placed on top.

In March 1895 representation was made to the Government for the creation of a General Cemetery, and whilst a Progress Report was later received on the "new burial ground" it was not until the 8th October 1898 that the Lands Department notified the Church of the "Declaration of the General Cemetery." In the meantime the rector, Rev. Cecil John King, together with the Church Committee, restricted the sale of burial plots to members of the congregation. This ensured that a few plots were still available until 1956 when the last grave plot was sold to Milton Ray.

St. John's and the Churchyard

We have no clear indication as to the charges that applied from 1844, but on 27th June 1895 Rev. Cecil John King inserted an item in the Camden News[31] detailing the Cemetery Rules and charges applicable.

In 1972 when the new hall was built it was decided that a columbarium would be erected on the eastern side behind the church. The columbarium initially consisted of four walls identified by their compass points. Later a wall abutting onto the West Wall, facing the church, known as the St. John's Wall was added. A freestanding wall, known as the Kernohan Wall, was also added a short distance from the East Wall. Amongst others it contains the ashes of Dr. Elizabeth Kernohan, her parents and brother.

From the time of World War II it appears regular maintenance of paths, weed control, etc. was not carried out. When Rev. Alan Patrick and his family moved into the Rectory on 27th January 1976 they found the cemetery a wilderness of feral shrubs and trees (African Olive, Chinese Elm, Privet, etc.). Many of the old gravestones recording Camden's earlier days had become overgrown.

Rev. Patrick's son David was fascinated by the cemetery and thought it would be an interesting project to try and clear it, and record the location of the graves marked by headstones. A friend of David's, Stephen Wedd who lived in Forrest Crescent, was also interested. Together they de-

Cemetery rules from the Camden News 27 June 1895

Overgrown graves 1976

Overgrown grave of Commander Martin in 1976

cided to see what they could do. Work started on Saturday 13th March 1976, and continued on

---

[31] See S.John's, Camden. (1895, June 27). *Camden News (NSW : 1895 - 1954)*, p. 6. Retrieved December 30, 2021, from http://nla.gov.au/nla.news-article133278992

and off on Saturday mornings for the next nine months. They usually worked together, assisted by Cindy the Patricks terrier-cross dog, but as the work continued others became involved. John Newhouse, a member of the choir, gave regular help and Rev. Alan Patrick assisted when he could, between weddings and other Saturday duties.

Alison Patrick helped pull the weeds and push the wheelbarrow and Percy Dawson one of the churchwardens made a significant contribution to the task. Mrs Helen Patrick supplied the refreshments for the workers at morning tea and often also at lunchtime.

The work proceeded at a steady pace. During April and May there were many heavy tasks to be done. The largest privet bushes were removed, their roots dug up and the ground levelled. Many hidden gravestones were discovered, and grave plots cleared of undergrowth. Some old stones that had fallen face down, had to be turned over to record the details. In some cases it was possible to stand them upright again.

Rev. Alan Patrick with the cemetery plans in 1976

It soon became apparent to the energetic workers there were many historic graves in the cemetery, with many early Camden pioneers and their families represented. In May 1976 David and Stephen began recording the graves, and commenced drawing up a plan of the cemetery based on what was being found. Gradually they began to make some headway. On 24th July they cleared a section of D row and it was then possible to see right through the cemetery from one side to the other for the first time in many years.

By October it was necessary to start mowing the sections that had already been cleared due to new growth as the weather became warmer. The whole task was completed on Saturday, 4th December 1976. The cemetery had been cleared and the accumulated debris and undergrowth of many years removed. A few weeks later Stephen Wedd completed the plan, and after David had completed the indexing of the Burial Registers the great task was over.

After the Patrick family left Camden the cemetery again became overgrown, though not to the same extent as previously. In 1987 a group from Work for the Dole undertook the clearing of the weeds and using the plans and listing prepared by David Patrick and Stephen Wedd, together with the assistance of Dick Nixon and Stanley Ames (a surveyor), they prepared a typed cemetery listing but many of the graves remained unidentified. The plans and lists proved to be invaluable when I prepared the current listing of the "Cemeteries of the Camden Anglican Parish" in 2008, and entered all available information into a database. This helped identify all but 6 of the occupants of the graves and therefore the same number without a grave. The original Burial Registers, the 1888 Cemetery Register and the work done in 1976 and 1987 helped immensely.

St. John's and the Churchyard

Additional work was carried out in 1995 with the assistance of Brett Sutton and a team from Graves Management. Since that time the cemetery has been maintained by a dedicated group of men from the church who regularly mow and remove the weeds.

Brett Sutton and his team from Graves Management in 1995

Aborigines and Islanders

The arrival of the First Fleet in 1788 and white settlement had an adverse impact on the traditional inhabitants of this new land — the aboriginal people. Traditional hunting grounds were cleared for settlement around Botany Bay and Sydney Cove, but the settlement soon moved west and south as land was cleared for farming and towns were established.

The cattle that arrived with the First Fleet, 2 bulls and 5 cows, had escaped a short time after the settlement was established and were not heard of again until the winter of 1795 when aborigines reported a herd of approximately 60 cattle grazing 60 kilometres to the south west of Sydney. In November of that year a party, which included the second Governor John Hunter, visited the area which he named the Cowpastures. The aboriginal people who lived in the Camden area were subsequently referred to as the "Cowpastures" tribe. They were in fact part of the Dharawal (Tharawal) group whose territory covered a region from Botany Bay south to the Shoalhaven River and inland to Camden.[1]

In July 1803 the third Governor, Philip Gidley King, issued an edict forbidding anyone to cross the river to the Cowpastures without his permission. It appeared regular settlement of the area was unlikely and the cattle were reasonably safe except from selective slaughter to provide meat for the Colony. In 1805 John Macarthur returned from England with an order for Governor King from the Right Honourable the Earl Camden, Secretary of State for War and the Colonies that Macarthur be granted 5,000 acres (2023.4 hectares) in the Cowpastures as Lord Camden believed the area was ideally suited to sheep.

The aborigines who lived on *Camden Park* were of the Cubbich Barta Clan, the name being derived from white pipe clay which was used as body paint for ceremonial events such as corroborees.[2] The Cubbich Barta maintained good relationships with the local farmers but the 1812 drought, which continued until 1816, led to large numbers of the neighbouring Gandangara coming into the area searching for food. The good relationships that had developed between the local Aboriginals and Europeans were disrupted as tensions developed between farmers and the Gandangara people resulting in a number of deaths on each side. These tensions ultimately resulted in the bloody massacre that took place at Appin in the early part of 1816.

Despite tensions in nearby areas the relationship between the Macarthurs and Cubbich Barta remained cordial. From memorandums made by the Deputy Surveyor General James Meehan to Governor Lachlan Macquarie in 1818, we know that on the evening of Thursday, 5th March 1818 he recorded —

> *"Having had instructions from his Excellency the Governor to mark out a small piece of land for John Macarthur esquire whereon his present residence stands — as also a piece of land to be assigned to some black natives who wish to reside on it under the protection of W. Macarthur."*[3]

This portion of land at the request of John Macarthur, and sanctioned by Governor Lachlan Macquarie, was marked out for the Cubbich Barta to live on under the protection of the Macarthur family[4] and was referred to as Boodbury's Paddock. By 1821 the Macarthurs regarded

---

[1] "The Dharawal and Gandangara in Colonial Campbelltown, New South Wales 1788-1830" Carol Liston
[2] "My recollections" — William Russell (of the Gandangara)
[3] SR N.S.W. Sz1046; Fiche 3276
[4] "A History of the Aborigines in the Camden Area" - Dan Tuck

Boodbury as the leading aborigine in the Camden area; Boodbury is believed to have been still residing there as late as 1860.[5]

Guribunger

Among those buried in the cemetery at St. John's are an aborigine woman and members of her family. "Nanny" or Guribunger a member of the Cubbich Barta Clan was born c.1816. Guribunger first appeared in European historical records in 1827 when she was listed among the 21 men and 19 women and children who received blankets and slop clothing from the Cawdor bench. In this instance her European name was recorded as Nanny, but on later records both her aboriginal and European names were acknowledged.

In 1830 she formed a relationship with a convict, Richard Barrett, who had arrived at Camden in May 1830; their first child Susan Sophaline was born in 1831. Guribunger and Richard had 5 children, 2 boys and 3 girls but their births were never officially registered. When their daughter Margaret died in 1906 the Burial and Death Registers show the father as Richard. On the death of Mary Matilda both Annie and Richard are shown as the parents (Annie being the name Barrett used for Guribunger). The Baptismal Records for the youngest son James note he was born 12th January 1856 and baptised 11th March 1856 with the parents being Richard and Nanny.

Guribunger died 17th February 1870 of a chronic inflammation of the lungs and general debility. Whilst the Burial Record only lists her as "Nanny" the Grave Record indicates that Mrs. Barrett was buried in Section D070 on 18th February 1870 and that the Macarthur family provided the plots that contain the graves of Nanny, Richard and their children.

Susan Sophaline Barrett

The eldest daughter, Susan Sophaline Barrett, was born c.1831 at *Camden Park* and died 30th March 1915. She is buried in Section D072, with the church records referring to her as "*Black Susan — the last of the local aborigines.*"[6]

Richard Barrett Jnr.

The eldest son, Richard Barrett Jnr., was born c.1839 at *Camden Park*, died 28th May 1887 and is buried in Section D072.

Margaret Barrett

The second daughter, Margaret Barrett, was born c.1840 at *Camden Park* where she worked as a house maid. On 27th July 1871 she married George Drummond Gunn at St. John's. Margaret died 17th January 1906 and is buried on top of her mother in Section D070. Her husband died in 1909 and is buried in Section D064.

Mary Matilda Barrett

The third daughter, Mary Matilda Barrett, was born c.1845 at *Camden Park* where she worked as a seamstress. Mary married James Joseph English at St. John's on 23rd September 1869. She died 27th September 1912 and is buried in Section D068. Her husband died 9th November 1927 and is buried on top of her.

James Barrett

James Barrett was born on 12th January 1856 at *Camden Park* and was christened at St. John's on 10th March 1856. He died on 13th December 1912 and is buried in Section D071.

---

[5] "Journeys in Time - Profile - Bootbarrie - Macquarie University -lib.mq.edu.au/all/journeys/people/profiles/Bootbarrie

[6] Burial Register for St. John's Camden

John Solomon

Another aboriginal buried in the cemetery was not of the Dharawal (Tharawal) people. Little is known about John Solomon other than he was born about 1873 and died 5th February 1895 at the age of 22 years. The Burial Register simply states *"aboriginal kanaka."* Aboriginal kanakas were generally Aborigines from Cape York coerced into being labourers in the cane fields of Queensland. How John Solomon came to Camden is unknown, but at the time of death on 5th February 1895 he was working at *Moreton Park*.[7] He is buried in Section B119.

The cemetery is also the last resting place also of two islanders. It is known that at least one of them had come to Camden from Queensland, but whether he was originally a kanaka is unclear. From about 1860 native, non-European labourers for the sugar cane fields of Queensland were "recruited" from Vanuatu, Papua New Guinea, the Solomon Islands, New Caledonia and Cape York Peninsular, to undertake hard manual work. To say they were "recruited" is not correct; they were coerced, and kidnapped into indentured servitude and in many cases forcibly transported to the Queensland cane fields.

It is understood that during this period some 62,000 islanders and Aborigines from Cape York were working in the cane fields. This process was generally referred to as "blackbirding" and the men and women thus "recruited" referred to as "kanaka." The term "kanaka" is derived from the French equivalent "canaques" which is still used in some parts of Melanesia today.[8] Queensland was a self-governing British Colony until it became a State of the Commonwealth of Australia in 1901

According to some references, the violent kidnapping tended to relate to the first 10-15 years of the trade (i.e. from 1860 to 1875). When Queensland became part of the Commonwealth of Australia the majority of those that had survived were repatriated during 1906-1908 under the *"Pacific Island Labourers Act 1901."*

Jiminy

Whether Jiminy who was born in Fiji c.1859 and died at the age of 13, on 31st August 1862 was a kanaka is unclear. Surviving records do not indicate who purchased the grave, only that the Burial Register reads *"a Fiji Island boy"* and he is buried in an unmarked grave in Section D048. It is possible he was working for William Stoneham Morgan, a merchant from Levuka, Fiji, who is buried in Section A068.

Henry Kaffie

Henry Kaffie was born c.1833 and died 1st September 1918 aged 75 years. Henry's Burial Record indicates at the time of his death he was a *"servant to Murray Blandon of Mander."* It is well known that Henry had also worked for the father of Dr. West, Francis William West, who died 4th February 1912. It is understood that Francis James West brought Henry with him from Toowoomba, Queensland in December 1911 when he came to Camden to visit his son. Francis William West died in 1912 and was buried in St. John's. Kaffie purchased a grave nearby so that he

---

[7] Moreton Park was originally a grant of 2,000 acres given in 1822 to Jean Baptiste Lehimas De Arietta. This property was in the area later known as Douglas Park

[8] "Blackbirding" - Wikipedia; and "Kanakas in Central Queensland" - Toni Philipoom - CQ Family History Association Inc

Aborigines and Islanders

"could be close to his master" and is buried in Section B 127. The model of a hut in Camden Museum, which was at one time in Dr. West's office, is believed to have been made by Henry Kaffie.

Model of a hut which at one time was in Dr. West's office and is purported to have been made by Henry Kaffie. Model is now in the Camden Museum

They Came in Chains - The Convicts

In 1788 eleven ships which formed the First Fleet, landed in Botany Bay carrying about 780 convicts. Most of the offenders were ordinary working-class men and women and the majority first offenders. About 75% had been convicted of petty larceny or of receiving stolen goods and were usually given sentences of transportation for 7 years, 14 years or life. About one quarter of the convicts had been sentenced for *"the term of their natural lives,"* and a proportion of these had reprieves from the death sentence.

Between 1788 and 1823 the Colony was comprised mainly of convicts and marines and their families and was a penal settlement under the control of Governor Philip. Governor Philip instigated a labour system whereby the convicts were employed according to their skills with the majority working for free settlers.

Transportation to the Colony continued until 1st October 1850 despite growing dissatisfaction at the practice from the population. There were by then enough bounty and assisted immigrants to undertake the work previously done by convicts. The convicts had served their purpose and the Colony could now sustain itself.

A number of ex-convicts are buried in the cemetery including Joseph Aldridge, Thomas Avery, James Butler, Lazarus Chapman, Samuel Johnson, John Lock, Henry Sharp and others.

Richard Barrett
Richard Barrett was born in Wales about 1800 and arrived in Sydney on 12th May 1830 aboard the *Nithsdale* and was assigned to John Macarthur of Camden. The Macarthurs insisted that their assigned convicts serve their full sentence and never permitted them to marry during that period. Soon after his arrival at Camden, Barrett became involved with Guribunger, an Aboriginal woman from the Cubbich Barta Clan known as "Nanny" whom he called Annie.

As with many such relationships in the early years of the Colony no formal marriage appears to have taken place, but Nanny/Annie was recognised as his common law wife. The three eldest were born prior to the church being built and there are no records of their baptism at St. John's. Richard died aged 60, on 8th December 1856 and is buried in an unmarked grave in Section D071.

Richard Boyd
Another convict was Richard Boyd, the son of William Boyd and Mary who was born in Lanarkshire, Glasgow Scotland about 1800. Richard was about 5 foot (1.6 metres) high, with a ruddy complexion, black hair and brown eyes and at an early age had been apprenticed to a brush maker. At 15 years of age he was caught stealing 6 silver teaspoons from the residence of shipmaster George Johnstone in Greenock, a busy industrial and shipbuilding city on the Clyde River.

Records of Boyd's trial[1] which took place at the Aberdeen Court of Justice on 28th September 1816, and documents signed by him, indicate he had received some education. He was sentenced to 7 years transportation and held in Greenock Gaol until on 9th April 1817 when he together with other convicts and paying passengers (including John Macarthur and his sons James and William) sailed for the Colony on the *Lord Eldon*. The ship arrived on 30th September 1817, and James and William, on behalf of their father, petitioned for 10 of the convicts to be assigned to them. Boyd was amongst the 10 taken to *Elizabeth Farm* at Parramatta.

---

[1] From Tartan to Wattle the descendants of Richard & Sarah Boyd"- compiled by Val Garner & Jeanette Robertson

Boyd later moved to *Camden Park* where he remained until he received his absolute pardon on 16th October 1823. He continued working at *Camden Park* as a groom and saddler and on 18th July 1824 married Sarah Higgins at St. Peter's Campbelltown. Sarah, the daughter of Sergeant Robert Higgins and Lydia Blair, had prior to her marriage to Richard been in a relationship with George Griffin. A son of that relationship, Edward, was born 21st January 1821 and died aged 25 years on 24th March 1846. He was buried as Edward Boyd in an unmarked grave in Section D052.

The Boyds' 6 sons and 5 daughters were all born and worked at *Camden Park* where Richard continued to work until his death on 13th January 1859. He is buried in Section E066. Sarah died on 6th December 1870 and is buried on top.

After the tragic murder suicide at *Camden Park* in January 1872,[2] all but one of the surviving children left Camden. Elizabeth was the only one to remain in the area, her third husband James Watson, was verger at St. John's. They are buried in Section A009.

George Coker
George Cuckow was born in Kent, England in 1808 the son of Thomas Cuckow and Oliff Floyd and baptised on 2nd April 1809 in Boxley Parish, Maidstone, Kent England. On 8th August 1829 George and his father were tried in the Lincoln Court, Lincolnshire for stealing a cow and given life sentences. They were transported to Australia on 2nd December 1829 on the *Mermaid*, arriving in 1830. Both were assigned as labourers to the Macarthurs at *Camden Park* and received their pardons in 1843. Thomas Cuckow died on 30th June 1843 aged 81 years and is buried at St. Thomas's Cemetery, Narellan.

George Cuckow married Mary Dawson the daughter of John Dawson and Mary Hockney at St. John's Parramatta on 12th April 1843 and about this time changed his name to Coker. The Macarthurs gave him a lease south-west of Camden which he named *Matahli Farm*. As well as farming George worked for a time as a teamster, but after his crops failed he fell into debt and the stress that resulted affected his health. He died on 31st October 1846 aged 36 years, leaving a widow and 2 young children and is buried in Section A108.

Mary Dawson then married a widower, Thomas Hobbs, and they had 8 children. After Hobbs died on 21st February 1862 he was buried in the grave next to George Coker, Section A109. Mary died and was buried in Cootamundra on 13th April 1892.

James English
James English, born c.1806 in Ipswich Suffolk England, arrived as a convict on 9th November 1830 on the *Royal Admiral*. English was described as being of ruddy complexion with pitted skin and a diagonal scar in the centre of his upper lip with dark hair and blue eyes. He was a bricklayer by trade and was able to both read and write. On 15th January 1830 he was tried in Ipswich for stealing cloth and sentenced to transportation for 7 years.

On his arrival in New South Wales he was sent to Port Macquarie as a labourer for the Board of Works but after completing his sentence moved to Campbelltown where on 16th April 1839 he married Eliza Tripp at St. Peter's Campbelltown. They had 9 children and the family prospered. His son James Joseph was the first of the family to work at *Camden Park* as a carpenter. James English was later employed there as a bricklayer. He died at *Camden Park* on 14th September 1877 aged 71 and is buried in Section D066.

---

[2] See chapter "Tragedy at the Home Farm"

Thomas Herbert

Thomas Herbert, the son of Thomas Herbert senior and Jane, was born in Holborn, London on 8th January 1770. Herbert became a postillion for the Duke of Chandos, but after the death of the Duke on 29th September 1789[3] was unemployed.

On 12th January, 1791 he was indicted in the Old Bailey for burglary and sentenced to death which was commuted in April 1791 to transportation for life. He arrived on the *Pitt* on 14th February 1792 and was assigned to John Macarthur at Parramatta. He worked as a stockman at *Elizabeth Farm* Parramatta but was later transferred to *Belgenny Farm* Camden, and rose to the position of overseer.

In 1811 Governor Lachlan Macquarie gave him a grant of 100 acres (40 hectares), west of Narellan. The grant was later known as *Herbert's Hill*. On 22nd May 1815 he married Catharine Campbell at St. John's, Parramatta. Catharine was the daughter of Thomas Campbell, a convict who had arrived on the *Sydney Cove* on 21st October 1807. Herbert died on 17th October 1846 aged 77 years and is buried in Section A044. After his death Catharine moved to *Redbank* Picton where she died and was buried in 1871.

Unfortunately Thomas Herbert's grave, together with those of other members of his family, was accidentally covered over about 1980 when some work was done on the roadway around the church. The only exception is the grave of Kezia Herbert nee Mitton the wife of Herbert's stepson Thomas Kelly who changed his name to Herbert. Kezia died on 1st June 1872 and is buried in Section A046 her 3½ year old granddaughter Rosannah Moses is buried with her.

Jonathan Wood

Jonathan Wood, the son of Thomas Wood a wool sorter from Northamptonshire, England was born in 1805. He is described as being 5 foot 4 inches (1.524 metres) tall, with a ruddy complexion, brown hair and grey eyes.[4] Jonathan worked as a ploughman until on 28th February 1824, during the Lent Assizes in Northampton, together with his accomplice James Richardson he was tried for housebreaking. Both were sentenced to death with the sentences later commuted to 14 years and transportation. Jonathan arrived in the Colony on the *Asia* on 22nd February 1824 and was sent to work for Mr. Campbell at Bringelly.[5]

Jonathan had apparently not learnt from his first encounter with the law as on 7th February 1831 he was tried by the Bringelly Bench for stealing from a dwelling house and transported to Moreton Bay for 3 years where he worked for a Mr. Pope. He received his Certificate of Freedom on 2nd March 1841. He married Harriet Haynes on 17th April 1843 at St. Peter's Campbelltown.

By 1854 he had obtained a clearing lease from the Macarthurs at Menangle where he died on 23rd March 1881 aged 76 years. He is buried in Section C034. Harriett married George Dabinett and continued to live at Menangle until Dabinett died on 28th October 1883. Dabinett is buried in an unmarked grave in Section A093. Harriett then lived with her son at Moss Vale where she died on 10th July 1916 and was buried in the Bundanoon Cemetery.

By a strange coincidence Jonathan's accomplice, James Richardson, arrived as a convict on the *Mangles* on 6th July 1824. He died on 22nd July 1854 aged 66 years and is buried in Section C019.

---

[3] "Thomas Herbert's World 1770-1846" — Jeanne Cheadle Stacey.
[4] Certificate of Freedom 41/293
[5] NSW & Tasmania, Australia Convict Muster 1806

They Came in Chains – The Convicts

Graves of George Coker and Thomas Hobbs - courtesy John Wrigley

Free Settlers – Landowners, Storekeepers and Tradesmen

Many of our earliest settlers were retired Army and Navy officers and as such were highly regarded in the Colony. Prior to 1832 land grants were given to all persons who could give satisfactory proof of having means of support. After that time land was sold by auction with retired Army and Navy officers given remission in the purchase money proportionate to their service rank. Being accustomed to the management of bodies of men these officers were regarded as conservators of the peace and many were appointed as Magistrates.

The retired officers in the Camden district included Captain John Macarthur of *Camden Park;* Major Henry Colden Antill of *Jarvisfield* Picton; Lieutenant Thomas Woore R.N. of *Harrington Grove*; Captain William Hilton Hovell of *Narellan Grange*; Commander Alexander Martin, R.N. of *Camperdown*; Lieutenant Thomas Shadforth of *Ravenswood*; Colonel Henry William Breton; Captain John Oxley of *Kirkham* and *Elderslie*; Lieutenant McAlister of *Clifton*; Dr. Henry Grattan Douglass of *Hoare* and Captain George Molle of *Molles Main*. Of these only Commander Martin and Dr. Douglass are buried in St. John's Cemetery.

Not all unassisted immigrants were retired Army and Navy officers and their families, and as the Colony grew many saw business opportunities in the new colony. Settlers intending to buy land in the Colony, or to invest a small capital in trade, were not eligible for a free passage.

Henry Grattan Douglass aged 22

Henry Grattan Douglass

One settler, who rose to prominence, was Henry Grattan Douglass, born in Dublin, Ireland in 1790, the son of Adam Douglass an apothecary,[1] and Ann Edwards. In 1809 Britain was engaged in war against Napoleon, and experienced surgeons were in short supply. The Government employed young men who had completed the first stages of their medical studies and Douglass, a 19 year old medical student, was appointed as an Assistant Surgeon with the 18th Regiment during the Peninsular War in 1809-10[2] and in the West Indies in 1811.[3]

Whilst in the West Indies he contracted Rheumatic Fever and returned home. The date of his return was fixed upon his memory by the entrance of one of his sisters into his bedroom the morning after his arrival, to tell him Prime Minister Spencer Percival[4] had been killed by an

---

[1] Apothecary is a historical name for a medical professional who formulates and dispenses medicines to physicians, surgeons and patients — a role now served by a pharmacist. In addition to pharmacy responsibilities, the apothecary offered general medical advice and a range of services that are now performed solely by other specialist practitioners, such as surgery and midwifery.

[2] The Peninsular War began in August 1808. In 1809 the battle concentrated mainly in Portugal around Corunna, Oporto and Talverna.

[3] In 1811 the British Navy captured Guadeloupe, the last French Colony in the West Indies.

[4] Spencer Perceval, KC (1 November 1762 – 11 May 1812) was a British statesman and Prime Minister. He is the only British Prime Minister to have been assassinated.

Free Settlers – Landowners, Storekeepers and Tradesmen

assassin's bullet.

In 1812 Douglass married Hester Murphy, the daughter of Arthur Murphy the chief of O'Murrough in County Wexford, and Margaret Rooney and accepted a civil appointment as Medical Superintendent of the Fever Hospital and Infirmary at Cahir, Tipperary. In 1815 he was admitted as a member of the Royal College of Surgeons of England. He returned to Ireland in 1817 during a typhus epidemic and later published a thesis which he submitted for the Doctorate of Medicine at Trinity College, Dublin. In 1819 he was licensed as a Physician at the King's and Queen's College of Physicians of Ireland; in June 1820 he was elected to the Royal Irish Academy.

About this time he became interested in prison reform. Among his friends were prominent Quakers - the Frys,[5] Hoares,[6] Gurneys,[7] and Allens - who had combined to improve the condition of prisons, and soften the rigor of the penal laws which sent a woman to the scaffold for stealing from a counter a few yards of calico, and consigned hundreds of human beings to a similar fate for a crime which would now result in a short term of imprisonment.

It was towards the end of 1820 that Douglass accepted a colonial appointment. With his wife, son and 2 daughters he arrived in Sydney on the *Speke* on 18th May 1821 with a letter of introduction from Earl Henry Bathurst to Governor Lachlan Macquarie. As Douglass had good connections at home and was very highly qualified Governor Macquarie reported back to Earl Bathurst:-

> *"I have just made necessary arrangements for placing Dr. Douglass in charge of the Colonial General Hospital at Parramatta (which particular station he prefers to every other) where he will have considerable private practice and other advantages besides being placed in the centre of a fine rich populous district. I intend immediately to appoint Doctor Douglass a Magistrate at Parramatta and to build him a good, comfortable barrack, the present one for the medical officer at that station being in a state of decay and almost uninhabitable. I shall consequently be under the necessity of hiring a good house in the meantime, for the residence of Dr Douglass and his family until a Government quarter can be built for them.*[8]

Governor Macquarie left the Colony soon after sending this letter but Douglass became very friendly with his successor, Governor Sir Thomas Brisbane, who arrived in November 1821 and became a regular visitor at the new Governor's residence. This association brought him into conflict with his senior colleagues on the Parramatta bench, but the friendship stood him in good stead in the troubles in which he became embroiled.

In 1822 Douglass received a grant of 800 acres being Portion 7, Parish of Camden, which he called *Hoare* as a compliment to his friend Samuel Hoare. The original grant had two of its boundaries on the Nepean River and Harris Creek and was registered in the name of his young son Arthur. When the rail line to Goulburn was constructed in the 1850s a small township named Hoare Town[9] was built on part of his property to house the construction workers.

---

[5] Within Britain, prison reform was spearheaded by the Quakers, and in particular, Elizabeth Fry during the Victorian Age. Her father, Joseph Gurney, was a partner in Gurney's bank. Her mother, Catherine, was a part of the Barclay family, who were among the founders of Barclays Bank.
[6] Quaker banker Samuel Hoare came over from Cork and set up home in Heath House in 1790. He was concerned with the anti-slavery movement
[7] Joseph John Gurney was a banker in Norwich, England and an evangelical Minister of the Religious Society of Friends (Quakers). He was also the brother of Elizabeth Fry.
[8] From copy of letter in the "History of Parramatta Hospital to 1988" - catalogue.nla.gov.au/Record/569670
[9] The area was later renamed "Douglass Park" after objections from the local womenfolk. The dropping of the second "s" is thought to have been a clerical error.

The first clash between Douglass and his fellow magistrates – Rev. Samuel Marsden, Hannibal Hawkins Macarthur and Dr. James Hall - came in August 1822 over a convict girl, Ann Rumsby, who had been assigned to him as a servant. Dr. Hall had been surgeon superintendent of the *Maria Ann* on which Rumsby had been transported and had met her again on a visit to the Douglass residence.[10] Misunderstanding a comment from Rumsby he placed the matter before Marsden and Macarthur alleging that Douglass was behaving improperly with her.

The three magistrates summoned Douglass to appear before them but when he failed to appear they had Ann Rumsby[11] arrested. When Rumsby denied the allegations against Douglass she was charged with perjury and sentenced to imprisonment at Port Macquarie. Governor Brisbane intervened, gave her a free pardon and threatened to remove the Parramatta magistrates who had not only refused to sit with Douglass on the bench but also called a secret general meeting of Justices to support their action, and complained to London.

Douglass could fend for himself. In April 1823 he brought an action for libel against Dr. Hall[12] claiming damages of £5,000 ($10,000) but was only awarded £2 ($4) and costs. The following month, together with William Lawson, Douglass fined Samuel Marsden for allowing one of his convict servants to be at large. When Marsden[13] refused to pay Douglass and Lawson had his piano seized and sold. Marsden promptly sued him for damages of £250 ($500), but the court awarded him only the amount of the fine which resulted in Marsden complaining to Charles James Lord, Bishop of London, that Douglass was preventing inmates of the Female Factory from taking their infants to church for baptism.

Douglass's Cottage at Hoare Town

Marsden also connived with Hannibal Macarthur to send a letter to Sir Robert Peel at the Home Office charging Douglass with drunkenness, torture of prisoners and other disreputable official conduct. The letters, forwarded to the Colonial Office, brought orders for an inquiry which exonerated Douglass but provided a loophole for Hannibal Macarthur as foreman of the Grand Jury to publish further complaints against Douglass in the Sydney Gazette. Brisbane's reports extolled his virtues with increasing warmth after each attack and in February 1824 he nominated Douglass as Commissioner of the Court of Requests and sent him to London to consult the Colonial Office on the functions of the new court.

In addition the Governor suggested Douglass be appointed as Clerk of the Legislative Council, but changed his mind when Douglass was censured for a gross breach of military discipline. It

---

[10] K. B. Noad, 'Douglass, Henry Grattan (1790 - 1865)', Australian Dictionary of Biography, Volume 1, Melbourne University Press, 1966, pp 314-316
[11] The problem had initially arisen when Dr Douglass insisted that Ann Rumsby marry William Bragge, despite her reluctance. After receiving her pardon Ann agreed to marry Bragge and they were married by Reverend Thomas Hassall at St. John's Parramatta on 3 February 1823 and they had 7 or 8 children. Ann is buried in the church-yard of St Anne's Anglican Church, Ryde
[12] Dr Hall was himself later found guilty of kissing female prisoners after having had them flogged, and was removed from office. Charles Bateson, 'Hall, James (1784 - 1869)', Australian Dictionary of Biography, Volume 1, Melbourne University Press, 1966, p. 503
[13] It is interesting to note that Samuel Marsden himself was known as "the flogging parson."

was revealed that he had left England in 1821 without permission from the War Office. Douglass was recalled for service in March 1825 but sailed for Sydney without apology or explanation.

In May 1828 Douglass again sailed for England. This led to Robert Howe, the Editor and proprietor of the Sydney Gazette, publishing an article on 9th May 1828 which, whilst not mentioning Douglass by name, made comments such as *"ex-civil officer"* and *"to save his political reputation from being blasted in Downing Street"* and made reference to *"inflicting illegal punishment on prisoners in the Colony."* On 24th December 1828 a case of libel against Howe was held in the Supreme Court before Mr. Justice Dowling. Despite Douglass not being present, the Jury found in his favour and Howe found guilty of libel, and Douglass was awarded £50 ($100).

Later he heard that Governor Ralph Darling who had arrived in December 1825 had cancelled his land grant at *Narrigo* on the Shoalhaven River. This land and his son's farm at Douglass Park had been leased in 1828 to William Charles Wentworth for three years. After the Douglass Park lease ended a small cottage was built on the site. This was used by his widowed sister Elizabeth Taylor and her children. Elizabeth looked after the family interests until her death in 1864.[14]

In 1839 Douglass sought compensation from the Colonial Office, but after long correspondence his claim was rejected; in spite of a letter of support from Sir Thomas Brisbane. Governor Sir George Gipps could trace no record of Douglass's authority to the *Narrigo* grant, although he did unearth proof of a 17 year old debt to the colonial government of more than £700 ($1,400).

Douglass remained in England until 1848. Records from 1835 indicate Douglass was a physician attached to the King William IV's household, but shortly after he left England for France. In Paris his knowledge of infectious disease was valuable during an epidemic of cholera, and his services won commendation and a medal from the government of King Louis Philippe 1. In a suburb of Le Havre Douglass founded a Seamen's Hospital and directed it for 12 years.

He returned to Sydney in October 1848 as Surgeon Superintendent of the emigrant ship *Earl Grey*. The follow year he became an Honorary Physician at Sydney Hospital and was one of the first teachers of clinical medicine in Australia. In 1854 he was appointed a Director of the hospital, but resigned after two years to take a seat in the first Legislative Council under responsible government.

Grave of Henry Grattan & Hester Douglass

---

[14] Elizabeth Taylor is buried in the churchyard in Section C178 but has no gravestone.

Dr. Douglass initiated, and followed up, several important reforms. He introduced into N.S.W., before it was adopted in England, the Law of Limited Liability in commercial partnerships. He also obtained the abolition of public executions which he hoped would lead to the abolition of capital punishment. One of his Bills was to regulate the qualifications of practitioners in medicine, surgery and pharmacy but this was laid aside in 1860. He also resumed his philanthropic activities becoming a Vice-President of the Benevolent Society, and helping Charles Nicholson to revive the Philosophical Society, of which he was the first Secretary. This society was later renamed the Royal Society of N.S.W. He was also a member of the Royal Agricultural Society.

Douglass helped to introduce child welfare by sharing actively in forming a Society for the Relief of Destitute Children and in establishing an orphanage at Randwick for their care. There are few of our educational or charitable institutions in the organisation of which Dr. Douglass had not a distinguished part including in a project for taking better care of the blind.

He also played a part in the founding of Sydney University. In 1849 Douglass badgered Francis Lewis Shaw Merewether who was at the time clerk of the Legislative Council and of the Executive Council, seeking his influence for the establishment of a University. He was advised to seek the assistance of William Charles Wentworth, who had already shown interest in such an establishment. Wentworth was successful in establishing the University, but Douglass was not appointed to the first university senate. He was however elected to fill a casual vacancy in 1853, and was a member of the Medical Faculty Committee and remained a senator until 1865.

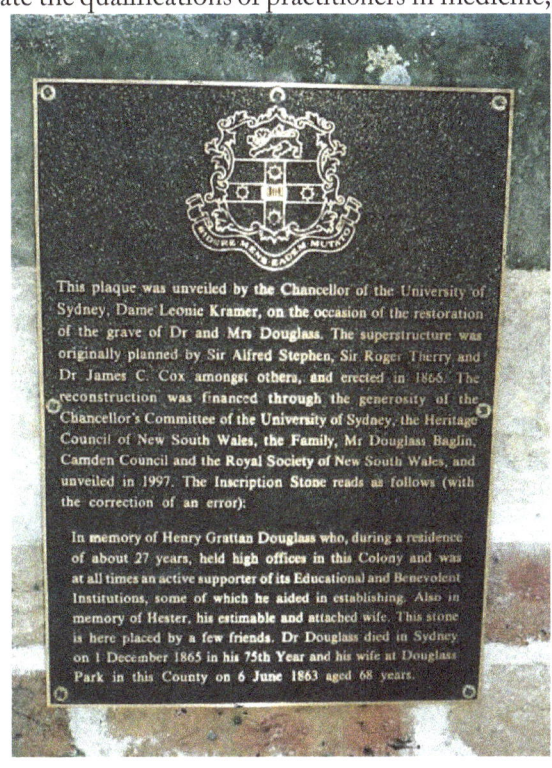

Plaque commemorating the restoration of the Douglass Grave in 1996 by Sydney University

Henry Grattan Douglass died at Woollahra on 1st December 1865 and is buried alongside his wife Hester, who had died on 6th June 1863, in Section A047. He is commemorated at Sydney University by his coat of arms in stone on the south side of the entrance to the Great Hall, and in a stained-glass window in the south porch of the main building. The University was also instrumental in repairing his grave in 1996.

Commander Alexander Martin

One retired naval officer was Commander Alexander Martin who was born in Portsea, Hampshire, England on 2nd September 1784, the son of John Martin and Mary. Nearly all his relatives were connected with the Navy, or involved with the dockyards, or shipping and his father also had seen service in the Navy. He was 11 years old when he joined the Royal Navy as a first-class volunteer in 1795 on board *HMS Triumph 74*[15] serving under Captain Sir Erasmus Gower and later under Captain William Essington. Shortly after joining he was involved in a battle which became known as "the retreat of Cornwallis."

---

[15] A number after the name of the ship indicated the number of cannons on board

Admiral Sir William Cornwallis[16] and his fleet of 4 ships of the line and 2 frigates were cruising near Brest on 16th June 1795 when they were sighted by the French fleet of 12 sail of the line and several large frigates. Admiral Cornwallis was attacked on both sides, but turned to support his rearmost ship, the *HMS Mars*. This convinced the French that the Admiral had other ships in easy reach and they gave up the pursuit.

Martin also took part in the action near the Dutch coast off Kamperduin[17] (north of Haarlem and north-west of Alkmaar). The Battle of Camperdown was fought at 7:00 am on 11th October 1797 and both the battle and victory were obviously important to him as he was to later name his property, near Theresa Park, *Camperdown*.

In January, 1799 Martin transferred to *HMS Formidable 98*, under Captains James Hawkins Whitshed, Edward Thornbrough, and Richard Grindall. In that ship he served in the Channel,

Alexander Martin's tombstone

Commander Alexander Martin c.1860 wearing medal - courtesy J Wansey

Mediterranean, and West Indies until September 1802 and towards the end of this period was promoted to Midshipman. He was with Captain Grindall again in 1808 on board *HMS Prince 98*, and was for about three years sailing in the Channel, and off the Port of Cadiz.

Aboard *HMS Prince 98* he was involved in the Battle of Trafalgar[18] which took place on 21st October 1805. This famous sea battle was fought between the British Royal Navy and the combined fleets of the French and Spanish Navies during the War of the Third Coalition (August-December 1805) of the Napoleonic Wars (1803-1815). The battle was the most decisive British victory of the war and was a pivotal naval battle of the 19th century. Twenty-seven British ships

---

[16] Admiral Sir William Cornwallis was the brother of the 1st Marques Cornwallis, General Charles Cornwallis. encyclopedia.jrank.org/Cor_Cre/Cornwallis_Sir_William_1744_181.html">Sir William Cornwallis (1744-1819)
[17] Also spelt Camperduin and more popularly as Camperdown
[18] "Commander Alexander Martin R.N. – Memoir by one of his Sons" – Camden News 25th August 1898 and 1st September 1898

of the line led by Admiral Lord Nelson aboard *HMS Victory* defeated thirty-three French and Spanish ships of the line under French Admiral Pierre Villeneuve off the south-west coast of Spain, just west of Cape Trafalgar. Martin was later awarded the Naval General Services Medal with clasps for Camperdown and Trafalgar but the medal was not authorized until 1847, and then only awarded where the recipient was still living.[19]

He later sailed on *HMS Glory 98*, under Captain William Albany Otway, and on *HMS Prince 98*, the flagship of Rear Admiral John Child Purvis, both stationed at Cadiz. In December 1807 he was promoted to Acting Lieutenant of the *HMS Terrible 74* under Captain Lord Henry Paulet, and was part of the force employed in the Mediterranean.

In February 1810, he joined *HMS Alacrity 18*, under Captain Nesbit Palmer. In May 1811 that vessel was captured by the enemy, but Martin at the time was absent from the ship as he was in charge of a Greek prize vessel. On 29th October 1811 he was promoted to Lieutenant and was from 2nd November 1811 until 8th January 1815 employed on the Leith Station[20] in *HMS Nightingale 16*, under Captain Christopher Nixon.

After the end of the Napoleonic war most of the ships were out of commission, so Martin was compelled to look about for means of adding to his income. He leased a wharf at Chatham, Kent, engaged some Sunderland colliers, and started business as a coal merchant. On 2nd September 1816 he married Henrietta Maria Fullagar, the daughter of John Smith Fullagar and Rachel Smart, in Chatham, Kent. Shortly after the Navy informed him that it was against navy regulations for an officer to engage in business, so he was forced to close the business.

Having one relative in London who was a sugar refiner, and another who was a sugar planter, and

Map indicating location of Alexander Martin's property

member of the Legislature in Jamaica, he took to the sea again; this time trading to Jamaica and St. Kitts, in the West Indies. He next entered the employ of Green, of Blackwell, and was involved

---

[19] "Spinks Standard Catalogue of British Orders Decorations & Medals" – A.R. Litherland & B.T. Simkin
[20] Leith Station was located in the harbour in Edinburgh, Scotland

in transporting convicts to the Colony. He placed his eldest son, Alexander Smart Martin, under the tuition of the Royal Engineers, to learn field surveying at the Brompton & Chatham lines as his brother-in-law, Smart Fullagar, was a designer in the Chatham Dockyard and he hoped this profession would prove lucrative for his son in Australia.

Martin and Henrietta had three sons between 1816 and 1821. Sometime prior to 1823 Henrietta died and Martin married her sister, Sarah Smith Fullagar on 23rd June 1823 at St. Pancreas, London. Their first child, Sarah Henrietta Maria Fullagar was born in Chatham on 26th October 1824, and their son Robert Jonathon Martin was born in Chatham in 1826.

Martin was favourably impressed with the Colony, and, after one of his voyages on the *John* in September 1829 (when one of the passengers was Archdeacon, later Bishop, William Grant Archdeacon Broughton was given control of the Church & School Corporation whose offices were then in Macquarie Place. As the paperwork was in need of urgent attention, the Archdeacon offered Martin a temporary position as a clerk. After he had completed his work he made Liverpool his headquarters. As the Courts of the time were composed of the military officers of the garrison and half-pay officers of either service, he was soon placed on the court list. He attended the Assize and Quarter Sessions Courts, but also travelled about to see the country as he intended in the future to apply for a grant of land.

After seeing much of the country and acquainting himself with the regulations respecting land grants, he returned to England to bring out his family, expecting to obtain 1,000 acres (404.7 hectares) for himself and 640 acres (259 hectares) for each of his children on their coming of age, or marrying.

As there was very little commerce with N.S.W. at this time, he had difficulty in obtaining passage. His delay in returning was further exacerbated when one of his sons was smitten with brain fever. The delays were to completely destroy any hope of his obtaining a land grant. He was finally able to secure a passage on the barqué *Caroline* and sold off some property and effects. The family went into lodgings, awaiting notice to join the ship; but many weeks elapsed before they departed Gravesend in August 1831. Arriving in the Colony on 2nd January 1832 they learned that Governor Sir Ralph Darling had returned to England, and had been succeeded by Major General Sir Richard Bourke, who had arrived just a month before. They then realized the consequences of their having failed to arrive earlier, for an Order in Council had reached the Colony with Governor Bourke, abolishing free grants and substituting sale by auction.

Martin appealed to the Governor, who promised to submit the matter to the Home Authorities. He also had his Navy agent in London Mr. Stilwell present a petition to the Secretary for the Colonies, showing that he had sacrificed everything in a bona fide effort to become a colonist, in full expectation of obtaining a liberal grant of land; which had been frustrated by the unexpected change. The reply to both petitions was that he had no valid claim as he had not given notice of his intention when leaving the Colony, nor at Downing-street, before finally leaving England.

The family first resided at Parramatta, and later on their property of *Camperdown*, which Martin purchased in 1832. The property consisted of 640 acres (259 hectares) situated below Camden on the left bank of the Nepean River. The neighbouring properties were those of Hannibal Macarthur – *Westwood*;[21] James Terry Hughes - *Theresa Park*; and Alexander Macleay[22] - *Brownlow Hill*; across the river was William Charles Wentworth's property *Vermont*.

---

[21] Hannibal Hawkins Macarthur (1788-1861), was a pastoralist, politician and businessman. He was born on 16th January 1788 at Plymouth, Devonshire, England, son of James Macarthur, the elder brother of John.
[22] Hon. Alexander Macleay MLC FLS FRS (24 June 1767 – 18 July 1848) was born on Ross-shire, Scotland, eldest son of William Macleay, provost of Wick.

Martin has been described as being of a cheerful and affectionate disposition. Bishop William Grant Broughton held him in high regard, and he was a frequent guest with the Bishop and his family on his visits to Sydney. In 1837 the Bishop placed Martin in charge of the Female Orphan School at Parramatta.[23]

As Martin was still in effect a serving naval officer he had to apply every two years for a fresh leave of absence. During the China Opium War[24] there were concerns that he might be recalled to service, but on 1st April, 1853, he was retired on the rank of Commander. He died in Camden on 7th September, 1868, aged 84. His wife Sarah died on 2nd October, 1884 aged 96, and they are buried in Section F003. By early 2014 this grave was in desperate need of restoration as the base of the grave had collapsed. We are grateful to the Narellan Men's Shed who undertook the restoration of this important grave.

Etching of Camden Post Office and Shop circa 1841

Eliza Pearson
Eliza Doodey was born in Liverpool, England c.1798 the daughter of Roger Doodey and Mary Bourne. She was christened in the Oldham Street Presbyterian Church on 25th February 1798. On 16th October 1822 at St. Nicholas' Church, Liverpool she married James Pearson who had been born in Liverpool c.1798. He was the son of Rev. Thomas Pearson, rector of St. Nicholas' Church Liverpool where he also ran a seminary. The Pearsons, together with their daughter Amelia, arrived on the *Deveron* in July 1824 and lived at 16 Pitt Street where Pearson taught music. He later opened a shop in Market Street selling drapery brooms, sheet music, etc. Pearson took out advertisements in the Sydney Gazette and Australian Newspaper describing himself as a Professor of Music and offering lessons. After 1828[25] the family were living at 22 Castlereagh Street, and in 1831 their address was 84 Pitt Street.

Pearson was appointed Organist at St. James, King Street, Sydney in October 1827 and was the first to hold that position. The finger organ at St. James had been built in London by John Gray. It was installed by Pearson in late October 1827 and he received £26 ($52) a year as teacher of the choir and organist at St. James.

On 15th July 1831 James resigned as organist. He had come into conflict with one of the members of the choir, possibly over churchmanship, and was dismissed by Archdeacon Thomas H. Scott, despite Rev. Hill the rector of St. James standing by him.[26]

Shortly after his resignation Pearson was employed to erect an organ at St. Luke's Anglican Church, Liverpool in late July 1831. Pearson continued to teach music and to be involved in installing organs in other churches. In January 1833 he erected and tuned the organ for St. Anne's

---

[23] "A Giant for Jesus (The Story of Silas Gill)" – Eric G. Clancy
[24] The First Opium War or the First Anglo-Chinese War was fought between the British East India Company and the Qing Dynasty of China from 1839 to 1842
[25] 1828 Census
[26] "Historic Organs of N.S.W." – Graeme D. Rushworth

Ryde.[27] The family moved to Cawdor in 1836 and Pearson was appointed to the position of Clerk of Petty Sessions at Cawdor and Postmaster. In May 1841 due to a lack of permanent water at Cawdor, and the establishment of Camden Village as the centre of administration for the district, the Court, was transferred to Camden. The family moved to Camden where Pearson was to maintain his position as Clerk of the Bench and as Postmaster for the district. The Pearsons opened a small drapery business in conjunction with the Post Office but James was to die on 13th July 1841;[28] he was buried at St. Paul's Church Cemetery Cobbitty.

Eliza Pearson then became postmistress for Camden from 1st July 1841 until 1879. On 21st August 1841 she provided the required bond, naming as sureties James and William Macarthur of Camden. Eliza did not receive any stipend for the duty but the Macarthurs had provided a house, at what is now 61 Argyle Street, rent free and she continued to run a small business selling stamps, drapery, cabbage-tree hats and other items.[29] Upon her death on 25th May 1879 she left £600 ($1,200) to be divided among her five daughters. Her son Alfred's daughter Amelia succeeded her as Postmistress in 1879. Eliza is buried in Section F004.

By early 2014 this important grave was in a state of collapse. It was being held together by star pickets and it appeared that the side and foot of the grave would shortly collapse. The Narellan Men's Shed undertook the restoration of this grave ensuring its survival. We are indeed grateful to the work carried out by these men.

Edward Thompson Palmer

Edward Thompson Palmer was born in Kings County, Ireland on 31st March 1812 the son of Thomas Palmer and Anne Thompson, and grandson of a Captain of the Dragoon Guard. Palmer arrived in Hobart, Tasmania as a free settler on the *John Denniston* on 7th June 1835 with his brother Thomas Wellington Palmer and sister Letitia Palmer. Letitia stayed in Hobart but by 1836 Edward and Thomas had settled in Wollongong N.S.W. where Edward owned a property called *Springfield* at what is now the southern end of Figtree. He also had a general store in Market Square in the centre of Wollongong. When he advertised the store for sale from April 1839 to July 1840 he stated that he was selling such items as wine and spirit, fabrics, saddles etc.

Edward Thompson Palmer - courtesy of Essie Moffatt

The sale of the store was probably prompted by his wedding plans. On 16th January 1840 he married Jane Emily Robinson much to the delight of her father who wrote home boasting *"my eldest daughter has just got married to the most respectable, well-conducted, and rich young man in all Wollongong and vicinity."*[30] Palmer's father arrived in Australia on the *Portland* on 11th March 1841 and joined him at *Springfield*, but the reunion was to be short lived as his father died on 12th April 1841.

On 28th February 1854 Palmer purchased 350 acres (141.6 hectares) of farming land from Charles

---

[27] St. Anne's Ryde has also been known as The Field of Mars Church and Kissing Point Church.
[28] SMH 28th July 1841
[29] "Camden" –Alan Atkinson
[30] Clougher Record "From Fintona to Wollongong, 1838"

Campbell for £1,721 ($3,422).[31] This land had originally formed part of John Oxley's *Elderslie* estate and included the river frontage in an area boarded by what are now Macarthur and Springs Roads, next door to *Galvin's farm*. In 1856 he sold *Springfield* and settled at Elderslie serving as a Magistrate and Coroner in Camden until his death due to bronchitis on 19th April 1879. (Palmer was the Coroner at the inquest into the murder/suicide on the *Home Farm*, at *Camden Park* on 5th January 1872).[32]

His sons Edward (Ned) and James were educated at Camden Grammar School at Macquarie Grove by William Gordon but were later attracted to Queensland by Sir John Robertson's "Plains of Promise." In 1865 after searching for country all-round the Gulf in far North Queensland they decided to occupy an area where the Dugald, Corella, and Cloncurry Rivers form a junction and called it *Conobie*; sheep were placed on the run in May 1865. Edward (Ned) Palmer married Clara Susan Betts, a granddaughter of Rev. Samuel Marsden, and became a Member of Parliament for Cloncurry. Ned later wrote a book titled "Early Days in North Queensland." Edward Thompson Palmer died on 19th April 1879 aged 67 years and is buried in Section B009.

Jane Emily Palmer nee Robinson - courtesy of Essie Moffatt

Jane, Edward Thompson Palmer's widow, sold the property on 18th January 1886 to Charles Thomas Whiteman and moved to Darling Point, Sydney where she died on 4th December 1900 and is buried at South Head Cemetery.

Mary Edith Allan

Mary Edith Palmer, the daughter of Ned Palmer and Clara Susan Betts was born in Parramatta on 28th December 1879. After her father's death in 1899 his property, *Conobie* was sold and her mother returned to Sydney to live at Hunters Hill with one of her sisters.

Mary Edith married George Allan of *Thrunsli*, Central Queensland, in Sydney in 1913 and at the time of her death on 19th April 1939 they were living in Boundary Street Roseville. Mary bequeathed £50 ($100) towards the seats in the choir stalls in the church with a request that plaques commemorating her father and grandfather be attached. When the choir stall seats

Plaques in memory of Edward Thompson Palmer and his son Edward (Ned) Palmer – note year of death for Edward Palmer is incorrect, he died in 1879

---

[31] "Camden" – Alan Atkinson
[32] See chapter "Tragedy at the Home Farm"

were moved the plaques were relocated and set into the marble flooring near the Communion Table in the Chancel.

Mary is buried beside her grandfather Edward Thomas Palmer in Section B009.

Maximillian von Zglinicki

Settlers came to the Colony for many reasons. Maximillian von Zglinicki was born in Poznań,[33] Poland in 1828, the elder son of Count Boguslaw von Zglinicki and Henrietta von Fitzwitz. After Napoleon's defeat, Poznań had become part of Prussia and functioned as the capital of the autonomous Grand Duchy of Poznań. At the time of Maximillian von Zglinicki's birth Poznań was semi-autonomous, but by 1846 this autonomy had been revoked.

By the early 1840s Zglinicki was in active service in the Austrian Army and had been promoted to Chief Lieutenant. However he became involved in the political troubles which would lead to the first of the two uprisings in Poland. Zglinicki made some incautious political statements which brought him to the attention of the authorities and when warned by a faithful servant that he was to be arrested he fled to England.

He worked in London for a period teaching languages with some success; and then decided to come to Australia, arriving on *The Peru* on 23rd December 1852. Zglinicki worked hard teaching French and German but had limited success in finding pupils. On 21st January 1862 he married Bridget O'Hare, from Newry Ireland at St. Mary's Cathedral, Sydney. After his marriage he visited the gold fields of Victoria and *"there gained colonial experience."*[34]

Zglinicki was described as *"a man of great stature,"* and this combined with his military training led to him be induced to join the Queensland Police. Despite the high praise he received from the Queensland authorities, Queensland did not live up to his expectations and he returned to N.S.W.

The N.S.W. Police in Sydney immediately employed him as an interpreter with the rank of Sergeant. When troubles arose in the gold fields he was sent to try and quell the trouble. On another occasion several prisoners were being conveyed from the Sydney Gaol to Berrima. One of the prisoners managed to undo the chains and leg irons fastening the prisoners in the coach in which they were travelling. The prisoners endeavoured to escape, and in the scramble one managed to grab a constable's revolver. Sergeant Zglinicki struggled with him and disarmed and recaptured him.

Zglinicki was then appointed to Camden and Picton, and later to Scone where he resided for five years; becoming Governor of the Port Macquarie Gaol. He was then promoted to be in charge of the gaol at Campbelltown but after a prisoner escaped whilst enroute to Sydney he received a rebuff from the authorities. After this he was for many years a sergeant in the Mounted Police. On his retirement he was awarded a substantial pension for his meritorious service.

During the latter period of his life he resided in Camden where he was a well-known figure. He was one of the thirteen foundation members when Abbotsford Lodge[35] was consecrated on 10th of August 1894. He died on 18th January 1898 and was buried in Section B091 with Bro J. D. Rankin conducting the graveside ceremony together with Rev. Cecil John King.

---

[33] From the 2nd partition of Poland in 1793 until 1806, Poznań was in South Prussia (part of Prussia). From 1806 to 1815, Poznań was part of the Duchy of Warsaw. – "History of Poznań" - Wikipedia
[34] "Obituary – the Late Mr. Max Zglinicki" – Camden News 27th January 1898
[35] Abbotsford Lodge changed its name to Camden Lodge no. 217 in 1916. Rev. Cecil John King was also a member

Garlies Allinson

The reason why some settlers came to Australia, and to Camden, is not always clear. One such is Garlies Allinson who was born in Whitehaven, Cumbria, England c.1828, the youngest son of Joseph Allinson and Ann. His father was an ironmonger, and spade and edge tool maker. Some time prior to 1855 Allinson moved to Singapore where he worked in a trade. It was in Singapore that he met and married Agnes Caroline Scott born c.1855. Agnes was the daughter of Robert Scott and Catherine Maughan. Her grandfather was James Scott the trading partner of Captain Francis Light[36] during the early days of the settlement in Penang; and she was a distant relative of Sir Walter Scott. Sometime after the birth of their daughter Harriet in 1857 the family moved to Camden where Garlies is described as a gentleman merchant. On 7th February 1859 he died aged 31 years. Just 5 days later his youngest daughter Annie Caroline was born on 12th February 1859 and the bereaved family returned to Scotland.

The grave of Garlies Allinson is probably one of the more unusual ones in the cemetery; it is quite ornate and resembles a sarcophagus. The grave can be found under a large Bunya Pine in Section CO33.

John Benson Martin

John Benson Martin the son of Alexander Martin and Henrietta Maria Fullagar was born in Rochester Kent 20th December 1818. He arrived in Sydney with his father, stepmother and siblings on 2nd January 1832 on the barque *Caroline*. John was 13 years of age when he arrived in the Colony but as his father had always been at sea there had been limited contact between father and son. During the first three years in the Colony he was again separated from his family as he was left in Sydney for three years and then sent to a station in the interior, where he remained for some years and was for some time a government clerk.

Martin was appointed Clerk of Petty Sessions for Campbelltown, Picton and Camden, on 31st August 1852, leading to another separation from his family. He was to hold this position for over 50 years until 1887; 35 years as Clerk of the Court and Registrar at Camden Courthouse.

In 1856 he married Honor Orchard at All Saints Sutton Forrest, and they lived in a large shingle-roofed house, known as *Alpha Cottage* on the corner of John and Mitchell Streets, Camden.[37] Martin was a literary student and writer, and a prominent supporter of the Camden School of Arts; his book "Reminiscences" was published in 1883.

It was said at the time of his death that *"the history of Mr. Martin is practically the history of Camden."*[38] He was a frequent correspondent to the Camden News, simply identifying himself as J.B.M. His articles gave a clear

John Benson Martin c.1890

---

[36] Captain Francis Light (1740 – 25 October 1794) was the founder of the British colony of Penang (in modern-day Malaysia) and its capital George Town in 1786
[37] "The Best of Back Then" – by John Wrigley
[38] "Obituary" Camden News 5thNovember 1908

insight into what was happening in Camden and the Burragorang during his time. He was also the first to advocate a weir for Camden, and lived long enough to see the weir completed. He died on 2nd November 1908 and is buried in Section B019.

John Lakeman

One settler who was to have an impact on Camden was John Lakeman who was born in Westminster, London on 3th September 1811, the son of Eleazer Lakeman and Elizabeth Burbage. Lakeman who had been trained as a domestic servant married Catherine Elizabeth Gibbs at St. George the Martyr, Southwark, Surrey on 26th February 1838. According to Lakeman's Death Certificate they arrived in N.S.W. in January 1839.[39]

John Lakeman

John had been working as a waiter at the Red Cow in Parramatta[40] until 1843 when he took over from Joseph Goodluck as the Innkeeper at the Camden Inn.[41] It is not clear from where he managed to obtain his initial capital, but it has been suggested that he may have obtained it from an inn-keeping relative,[42] namely Edward Lakeman the landlord of the White House Inn at Parramatta. John was a good landlord, unlike Joseph Goodluck, and the hotel prospered under his management, so by 1846 he was able to purchase the property outright.

Lakeman also purchased other property in Argyle and Mitchell Streets and was regarded as a respected and prosperous landlord, but credit must be given to his wife Catherine who was a meticulous bookkeeper. He was also landlord of the slaughterhouse and the local butcher; and widely unpopular in the town. In July 1855 his world was to come crashing down around him, when he was indicted for having "*violated the person of one Mary Ann Woods.*"[43]

Mary Ann Woods was the wife of Joseph Woods; the couple being bonded servants of Lakeman. The Woods had arrived as bounty immigrants in May 1855 on *HMS Victory* and had been taken by Lakeman to Camden. Joseph attended to the outdoor work, such as looking after the cow, etc., and Mary Ann was engaged to do the work of a general servant. Mary Ann told the Court that on the Sunday her mistress had gone to church and she was making the beds when Lakeman had come into the room and raped her. When her husband returned home after completing his duties she told him what had occurred and requested that Lakeman be punished. Joseph testified that he had not gone near Lakeman then, as he believed that if he had done so, he would have attacked him, but told his wife he would bring the matter before a magistrate on the following day.

Joseph testified at Lakeman's trial that he had been unable to reach to the residence of the magistrate, John Oxley, after this incident. Mary Ann made no complaint to Mrs. Lakeman or in fact to anyone else until after the following Thursday when Mrs. Lakeman had gone to Sydney and Mary Ann was again alone in the house with her employer, and claimed he had raped her again.

---

[39] Arrival date as per his death certificate
[40] "Camden" - Alan Atkinson
[41] Camden Inn was later known as the Royal Hotel; it was demolished in the 1970s and replaced by the Merino Tavern.
[42] "Camden" - Alan Atkinson
[43] "Law – Central Criminal Court Tuesday Before Mr. Justice Dickinson – Rape" SMH 8th August 1855

She at once told her husband. They remained in the house that night, but on the following day had Lakeman charged with both acts of violence.

On 7th August 1855 he was tried in the Supreme Court on the charge of rape. Under cross-examination Mary Ann agreed that she would not have prosecuted for the first rape if a second had not been committed, and that she had virtually intimated as such to the prisoner by threatening that if he touched her again she would *"summons him or take the law of him."*

Lakeman's defence was that Mary Ann had been a consenting party. His defence council, Mr. Holroyd, pointed out to the court the absence of any effort to get Lakeman punished, or even to remove her from his house until after the affair on Thursday. He contended that but for the second affair there would never have been any prosecution for the first, and there were also some slight discrepancies between her evidence at the trial and that at the Police Court.

The Attorney General, in reply, contended that the fact that Mary Ann had made her husband acquainted with the circumstances at once wholly rebutted the assumption of any consent on her part. *"The husband might have acted with unusual coolness, but it was the conduct of his wife, and not that of her husband with which the jury had to do; and she, by placing herself wholly in the hands of her husband - of the man whose honour was affected - had done just what a virtuous woman and a faithful wife, she was bound to do."*[44]

His Honour told the jury, that in order to find Lakeman guilty they must be convinced, not only that Mary Ann had been violated against her will, but that Lakeman was aware of this fact. Lakeman's guilt must be established to the exclusion of all reasonable doubt. The jury, after having deliberated for 45 minutes found Lakeman guilty, but recommended mercy, on account of his long residence in the Colony, and generally good conduct. Lakeman when asked whether he had anything to say why sentence of death should not be passed replied that he had not, if the jury convicted him upon that evidence. As rape was a capital offence the judge sentenced Lakeman to death by hanging. In passing the death sentence the judge said that he wholly concurred with the verdict, and dwelt briefly upon the clearness of the proof. Lakeman appeared perfectly calm while the sentence was being passed.

Fortunately for Lakeman, James Macarthur who had been the presiding magistrate when he was arraigned in Camden became concerned as new evidence began to emerge. Macarthur became convinced the Woods had actually set a trap for Lakeman in order to be freed from their obligation to work for him until their passage had been paid. Once Lakeman had been found guilty they were freed from their bounty obligations.[45]

When this became general knowledge a number of people changed their minds about Lakeman's guilt and signed a petition to the Governor asking for his pardon and release.[46] Due to public pressure Lakeman's sentence was remitted to 10 years hard labour and he was interred on Cockatoo Island in the middle of Sydney Harbour.

Catherine Lakeman continued writing to the authorities asking for a pardon. Luckily, this fell into friendly hands. The Attorney General was a close political friend of James Macarthur. Lakeman's case was quickly referred to the judge who had presided at the trial, but he refused to change his decision. The matter was then referred to Cabinet, and in January 1857 Lakeman received a pardon.

---

[44] Ibid
[45] "Camden" – Alan Atkinson
[46] Ibid

Lakeman returned to Camden and led an uneventful life until May 1869 when Camden was experiencing a flood. In fact it appears, from comments made at the Coroner's Inquest on 11th May 1869, he *"was well known as always ready to help forward any movement for the general good."*[47]

On Saturday 8th May Constable Thomas Byrne and Constable Beck launched the police boat to collect the midday mail, the flood boat having been damaged. On their return their passengers were Mr. Pallier the driver of the mail coach, and his passengers John Lakeman, George Newton, and Patrick Connolly. Connolly and Byrne were rowing and the river was at that time about a ¼ of a mile (0.4 km) wide, with the flood waters extending from Elderslie to Thompson's Mill. The boat had nearly reached the Camden side when it struck a fence, which broke under the strain. The rowers succeeded in freeing the boat and in heading her round, before the current caught them. With the keel facing downstream the boat overturned and all the parties were thrown out.

Constable Thomas Byrne, who was heavily clothed with a cape fastened round his neck, sank at once. Constable Beck swam to a tree, and was rescued by a young man named Anthony Rogers, who passed a rope to him, and then pulled him ashore. Connelly and Pallier managed to use a fence to get to safety. Newton reached a tree, where he stripped, and managed to swim to safety. Lakeman managed to grasp one of the oars and was carried downstream, but was next seen clinging to a tree about 200 yards (182.9 metres) lower down, and about 200 yards (182.9 metres) from land. He appeared to have good footing on a branch, and was about breast-high in the water. Charles Augustus Thompson volunteered to carry a rope out to him, but, just as he reached him the violence of the current wrenched it out of his hand. Thompson managed to get to a tree and rested, but was so weak from exertion and cold that he had to be assisted back by a young man named James Collins who had swum over to help him.

Some attempts were made to launch rafts from a point higher up stream, but the rows of willow trees and fences rendered it impossible to float anything in the right direction. The accident had happened in about the worst possible place. Lakeman had been in the water about an hour and a half, and his rescuers commented that he was behaving with surprising courage, quietly watching the proceedings.

Collins made some noble attempts to reach him by swimming out on horseback, but failed. Thomas Cross, assisted by Thomas Death (pronounced "deeth") then succeeded in swimming over with a rope. By this time Lakeman could scarcely speak, but fastened the rope to his body and urged Death to go back and get the people to haul him across. He afterwards repeatedly nodded his head as a sign for them to pull.

The position between Lakeman and his rescuers made it necessary to pull him upwards at angles against the stream in an endeavour to avoid a clump of trees about half way over. By this time Lakeman was exhausted and unable to assist. When he was near to safety the river swung him round and the rope snagged against one of the trees. The rope parted and Lakeman sank from sight. His body was found the next day, after the flood had subsided, and he is buried in the family plot in Section A102.

Alfred John Bayley
Alfred John Bayley was born in Lancaster England, the youngest son of Thomas Bayley and Elizabeth and his father was for many years the District Manager of the London and North Western Tramway Co. Bayley received his early education in Lancaster and then in London and Cambridge where he obtained first class honours, and first prize for all England in chemical

---

[47] "Camden – From our Correspondent" SMH 12th May 1869

analysis. He was a member of the Pharmaceutical Society of England but for health reasons felt compelled to leave England for Australia, arriving with his brother in March 1889.[48]

Due to his qualifications it was not long before Bayley obtained a position in Sydney. In 1891 he came to Camden and became the local chemist and was known to be always attentive and courteous. He was a popular resident however his health deteriorated, and when more serious chest symptoms ensued he was ordered to take complete rest.

Despite following his doctor's orders, and careful nursing from his brother, Bayley died on Tuesday 5th September 1899 and is buried in Section B085.

Susannah Butler
Susannah Richardson was born in Essex, England in 1826 the daughter of William Richardson. Susannah and her first husband, John Poole, had first settled in Uaitemata County, Eden, New Zealand where a son, George, was born on 30th July 1844. In April 1844 they moved to Sydney where a son John William was born on 14th October 1849 and John Poole died about the same time. On 24th March 1851 in St. John's Camden Susannah married widower James Butler a former convict and now respected farmer.

James Butler first had a clearing lease at *Glendarulen* near Mount Hunter, which he had taken up from Sir George Macleay. He later purchased *Pleasant View Farm*[49] at Spotted Gum Range from William Wheatley.

At the time of James Butler's death on 13th June 1888 Susannah was living in Redfern; afterwards she was living with a relative, John Wheeler, at Waterloo. Susannah died of bronchitis, 76 years of age, on 15th July 1889 and is buried near her husband in Section D003.

Henry Thompson
Another Camden businessman was Henry Thompson born in Shadwell, Middlesex, England 30th April 1820, the son of Joseph Thompson and Mary Brown. The family arrived on the *James Harris* as free settlers on 30th April 1834 and Joseph set up a wholesale drapery business in Pitt Street known as Joseph Thompson & Son. The drapery business soon expanded with a chain of general stores opening in Camden and Yass.[50] In Camden there was not only a general store but also a steam flour mill with his brother Samuel looking after the store, whilst Henry was in charge of the mill.

On 16th April 1845 Henry married Anne Bardwell at the Congregational Church in Sydney. In 1852 he purchased 4 acres (1.6 hectares) of land from his father in Argyle Street Camden which included a dwelling house, steam mill, store and other buildings. He then went on to purchase additional property in Elizabeth Street. He added to his property holdings in April 1855 when he purchased a half acre allotment in John Street from the estate of Sarah Middlehurst (nee Milford and previously Tiffen) who had been the housekeeper at *Camden Park*. Sarah had purchased the property from the Macarthurs with money she had inherited from her father John Milford and then had a building erected that was rented for a short time to the Camden Bench for use as a Court House.

---

[48] "Obituary – Mr. A.J. Bayley" – Camden News 7th September 1899
[49] "Obituary – Mrs. James Butler" – Camden News 28th July 1898
[50] "Camden" Alan Atkinson

Free Settlers – Landowners, Storekeepers and Tradesmen

Henry had the old house demolished and in 1860 started to build an elegant schoolhouse on it which was to be known as *Macaria*.[51] His intention was that the building would be used by the Classical and Commercial School opened by William Gordon in 1857. This intention was thwarted when Gordon moved instead to the new homestead built at Macquarie Grove for the Hassalls.

Macaria, 37 John Street, Camden

Due to the discovery of gold in Victoria and in the west there was a shortage of labour; *Macaria* would not be completed until 1871. Henry was never to live in the new house as on 29th July 1871 he was kicked in the head by his horse and killed instantly. He is buried in Section B020.

His son Charles Augustus Thompson lived in *Macaria* between 1871 and 1874. It was eventually sold in 1880 and became the home of Camden Grammar School. In 1900 the school moved to *Studley Park* after the Principal and most of the students made claims of strange events taking place; the house was believed to be haunted.[52] Despite these rumours the house was used by Dr. West from 1901 to 1932 and today is part of the council chambers for Camden Council. It is thought that Sarah Middlehurst is the ghost; others claim it is "Bill" (William Gordon).

Thomas Dawson

Thomas Dawson was born at Weelsby in Lincolnshire, England in December 1820, the son of John Dawson and Mary Hockney. On 3rd September 1835 he arrived on the *Canton* with his parents and the rest of the family. Another brother William, a botanist, had arrived previously and the family had decided to join him. John had trained as a solicitor in England and practised his profession in Sydney.

An etching of Thomas Dawson's farm circa 1887

Dawson was employed for about 4 years in a shipping office where he became acquainted with William Macarthur. He was appointed manager of the Macarthur estate at Camden[53] and on 1st March 1848 married Elizabeth Scott.

Early in his work at *Camden Park* he surveyed a subdivision of a large portion of land in an area known as the North Cawdor Estate, for clearing leases. In 1860 he purchased from the Macarthurs an area of land known as Westbrook which he named *Brooks Flat* and erected a homestead

---

[51] Macaria is both of Spanish and Greek origin and means "blessed."
[52] "Back Then – Macaria's Century Old Residents" – by Mark Powell – District Reporter 10th March 2000
[53] "Camden News with Records of Dates, Commemorating the 50th Anniversary of the Municipality of Camden" Camden News 9th March 1939

and farm buildings. This was the first individual farm in that locality. Thomas continued to work for the Macarthurs and employed John Monk as caretaker between 1860 and 1887.

Thomas was actively associated with Sydney's first agricultural show serving as a member of the committee of which Sir William Macarthur was president. The first show was held in Prince Alfred Park in 1869. In 1887 Thomas resigned as manager of *Camden Park* and retired to live on his farm at Westbrook. He died, aged 72, on 8th October 1893 and is buried in Section A129.

George Poole
George Poole was born in Uaitemata County of Eden, New Zealand on 30th June 1844, the son of John Poole and Susannah Richardson. He was born "*on the battlefields of New Zealand*"[54] during the Maori war with Great Britain when his father was serving with the 58th Regiment of the British army. After the war ended his parents brought their family to Australia, and as a young man he took up farming on the *Camden Park* estate. In 1870 he obtained a clearing lease of 53 acres (21.4 hectares) and grew wheat and other cereal crops. On 2nd September 1875 he married Esther Thorn at St. Paul's Church Cobbitty and worked a farm at Brownlow Hill. Following the failure of the wheat industry in Camden he took up dairying.

In 1893 George suffered a serious accident whilst trying to stop a horse in the paddock at night. He ran into a stump and severely injured his abdomen and required treatment in Sydney. Whilst the operation greatly relieved his pain he was to suffer from ongoing ill health and died aged 54 years on 23rd November 1899 and is buried in Section D083.

Jessie and Mabel Sidman
Jessie Sidman was born in Hull, England on 29th April 1882, the daughter of William Sidman and Honor Elizabeth Dickinson. In 1888 the family sailed for N.S.W. on the *Coptic* her father bringing with him a small printing press; during the journey he produced a regular tabloid for both passengers and crew.[55] The family arrived on 10th August 1888 and took up residence in Woollahra.

Three years later the family moved to Mount Hunter and settled at *Brockley Vale* and William Sidman acquired the Camden News. In 1906 the family moved to 65 John Street, Camden. Apart from this, little is known of Jessie's life before World War I.

During World War I Jessie became actively involved with the Red Cross and took an active part in the war effort. After the war she continued her community activities as well as working for the Camden News in the shop section of the office. She bound books, was a proof reader, and would wrap the newspapers. Her brother

William Sidman

---

[54] "Mr. George Poole" Camden News 30th November 1899
[55] "Celebrations for Miss Sidman's 100th Birthday" – Camden Council Local Citizens' Guide, May 1982

Free Settlers – Landowners, Storekeepers and Tradesmen

George Sidman became the proprietor of the Camden News after their father died on 21st February 1918.

Jessie also took an active role in the home being *"chief cook and bottle washer for her brothers and sisters for a number of years."*[56] Together with her mother and sister Mabel, Jessie was involved in her local church. Firstly at Mount Hunter where she and Mabel were choir members and after the move to Camden both continued to be choir members at St. John's. Jessie and Mabel also washed, mended, and ironed the church linen for many years. Jessie continued her involvement with the Red Cross during World War II and together with her sister was made a life member of the Red Cross.

Mabel died on 11th September 1961 aged 78 years. Jessie celebrated her 100th birthday in April 1982 with family and friends at Carrington Nursing Home and died on 11th August 1982. The Sidman family grave is in Section F006.

---

[56] Celebrations for Miss Sidman's 100th Birthday" – Camden Council Local Citizens' Guide, May 1982

A New Beginning – Bounty and Assisted Immigrants

In the early 1800s in Britain unemployment was high and those in employment worked long hours for meagre wages. After the end of the Napoleonic Wars there was a great influx of former soldiers released into the workforce increasing the numbers of the unemployed. The situation was exacerbated by two failed harvests and the decrease in demand for Southdown wool. Workhouses rose all over England as a ruthless attempt to solve the problem of poverty, and in 1834 a *Poor Law Amendment Act* was passed ensuring that conditions within workhouses should be made worse than the worst conditions outside of the workhouse. The aim was that workhouses should serve as a deterrent so that only the neediest would consider entering them.

At the same time the British Government[1] was encouraging people to immigrate to places like Canada and Australia. The Governor of N.S.W. was pleading for larger numbers of immigrants, especially mechanics and agricultural labourers to be sent to the Colony. However those most in need i.e. people resident in a workhouse, or in the habitual receipt of Parish relief, were not eligible to immigrate and of those willing to immigrate and take advantage of a new life, many were unable to afford the cost of travel. Two systems were devised to assist as long as those willing to immigrate met the age requirements and had the skills needed.

In the early days of the Colony, most were poor labourers who gained a free passage by the assisted immigration system. Assisted immigrants were free immigrants whose passage was paid by the colonial government. Some immigrants paid a portion of the amount but had no guarantee of employment once they arrived in the Colony. In some instances the shipping records indicate their fare was paid "by the Parish."

Immigrants were generally married couples, up to 40 years of age at their last birthday. For every child above 14, an excess of one year was allowed in the age of the parents. The candidates most acceptable were young married couples without children.

Assisted immigrants were "steerage passengers" and as such were housed in the lower decks. Married couples and children under 14 were housed in the centre of the lower deck. The single women and girls were in the aft berths and single males and boys in the fore births. Steerage quarters were generally cramped with only 6.4 feet (193 cm) of headroom. A table ran the length of the ship, with two levels of bunks on either side.

The regulations also stated that no family would be allowed a free passage to Australia where the family consisted of more than two children under seven, or more than three under ten years of age. In instances where the number of children exceeded the quota, parents were required to pay £7 ($14) for each additional child. Single women, under 18 years, were not permitted to travel without their parents, unless they were under the immediate care of some near married relative, or were under engagement as domestic servants to ladies going out as cabin passengers in the same ship.

The bounty scheme began in October 1835 when Governor Bourke offered settlers in the Colony who had the means, and who would prefer to engage their own mechanics or agricultural labourers, a system of bounties equal or nearly equal to the expenses of the passage.

Under this scheme, an incentive or reward was paid to recruiting agents in Britain to find suitable skilled labour and trades people, then ship them out to the new Colony which urgently needed

---

[1] Authentic Guide to Sydney – Parts 4 & 5 – New Image Magazine – September & October 1977

A New Beginning – Bounty and Assisted Immigrants

the working class people to do the manual labour in the Colony. The scheme was financed by the Government who sold land by auction, and used the money to pay the passages of the labourers.

Under the bounty scheme newly married couples, or single men and women were given preference. Large families were rarely accepted. Selected immigrants were generally shepherds, ploughmen and agricultural labourers, with a lesser number of trades people such as brick makers, carpenters, blacksmiths, tailors and needlewomen. Once the ships arrived in Sydney prospective employers would visit them and engage suitable immigrants as employees on contract, usually for a small wage plus rations. Contracts varied from a few months to one year, and at the end of the contract the immigrant was free to negotiate with the same or another employer.

Bounty immigrants, whilst still travelling steerage, received better accommodation. As can be seen in an extract from "The Saturday Magazine – 11th May 1839 – Emigration to N.S.W." referring to the *Royal George* which departed England on 31st October 1838 and arrived in Sydney on 10th March 1839.

> *"In cases where colonial proprietors themselves have been enabled to superintend the outfit, emigrants are accommodated as shown in the plan of a ship given in the annexed table. It will be seen that every family has a separate cabin; with a sleeping berth or berths. If there are in the family more than one child, a separate berth and bedding are provided; and when there are several children they have separate cabins. Single men, or boys of more than 10 years of age, sleep in hammocks, in the open space between the cabins..."* [2]

The passengers and crew on voyages to the Colony were faced with the hazards of the voyage and the possibility of the ship foundering. There are many examples, including the *Hibernia* which caught fire in the Atlantic Ocean in 1833 with the loss of 153 lives. The convict ship *Waterloo* wrecked at Table Bay, South Africa in August 1842 with the loss of 190 lives and the *Cospatrick* which caught fire off the Cape of Good Hope in 1874 with the loss of 470 lives. Another was the immigrant barque *Julianna* wrecked at Mouille Point, Table Bay, South Africa on 19th January 1839; all passengers and crew landed safely and were eventually taken to Sydney on the *Morayshire* and *Mary Hay*.[3]

Another hazard faced was that of infectious disease with North Head being first used for quarantine purposes when the passengers and crew on the *Bussorah Merchant* were detained in Spring Cove in 1828 when a number were found to be suffering from both smallpox and whooping cough.[4]

Sophia Cox
Despite the known dangers many made the voyage to the Colony including Thomas Cox from Farnham, Dorset. Cox arrived in Sydney on the *Brothers* on 8th April 1837 accompanied by his wife Sophia Gumbleton, the daughter of Samuel Gumbleton and Elizabeth Golding, and 1 year old son John. Cox had been recruited as a bounty immigrant by the Rev. John West, rector of Chettle and Farnham, Dorset to work for James and William Macarthur at *Camden Park* as a butler and Sophia as a house servant. Sarah died on 24th October 1844 and was buried at the new Cemetery at St. John's Camden in Section E082. Her gravestone, believed to be the first in the Cemetery, often causes confusion as it bears the inscription *"In memory of SOPHIA GUMBLETON"* with the comment *"wife of Thomas Cox"* in smaller letters.

---

[2] "Ancestor" – Summer 1987
[3] "Shipwrecks on the UK – Australia Run" - Encyclopaedia of Australian Shipwrecks
[4] "North Head, Sydney, New South Wales" – Australia's National Heritage

A New Beginning – Bounty and Assisted Immigrants

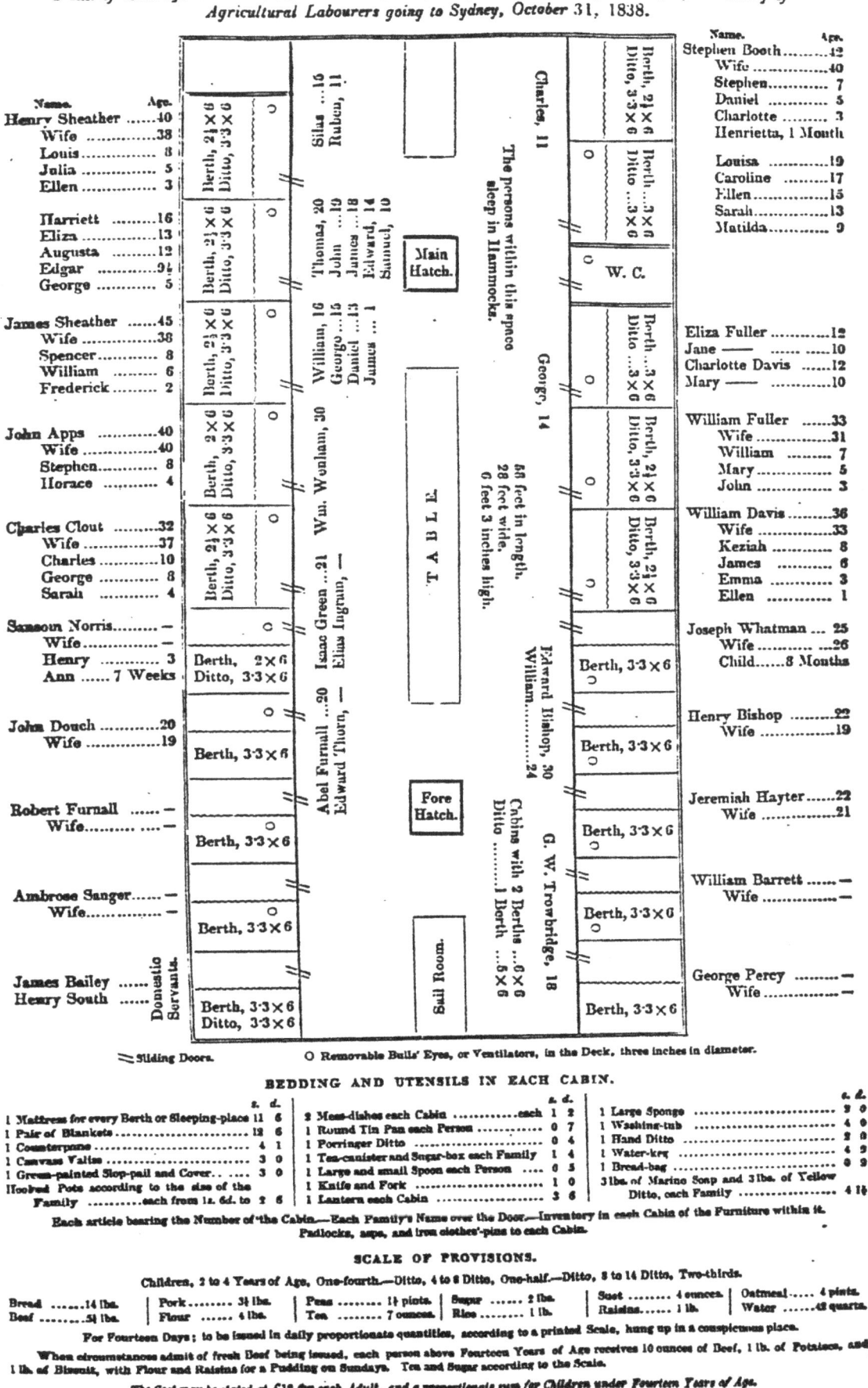

A New Beginning – Bounty and Assisted Immigrants

Thomas Dockery Richardson

Another to arrive in 1837 was Thomas Dockery Richardson.[5] Richardson was born in Sussex, England in 1830, the son of William Richardson and Hannah. In 1837 the family left England on the *Augustus Jersey* and settled on the Kirkham estate as bounty immigrants in the employ of John Oxley. Thomas Richardson originally worked on the *Kirkham* estate as a coachman and later was a boot maker at Elderslie. In later years he relinquished this trade and worked at *Camden Park*, before leasing a farm at Cawdor.

He married Anna Maria Price, the widow of William Platt, and in 1877 left *Camden Park* and purchased a farm and vineyard at Elderslie. He died 14th February 1903 and is buried in Section C020.

William Fairall

William Fairall was born in Icklesham Sussex, England on 26th July 1789 to Edward Fairall and Grace Offin. William, a farm labourer married Hannah Weller a house servant, also from Icklesham, on 24th March 1811. The Fairall family left England, as assisted immigrants, on the barque *Morayshire* and arrived in the Colony on 20th April 1839. This vessel had stopped briefly at the Cape of Good Hope to take on some of the survivors of the *Julianna* which had been wrecked a short time before.

The Fairalls were employed at *Camden Park* and in 1849 William obtained a clearing lease of 62 acres (25.9 hectares) from the Macarthurs; the farm was situated on the eastern side of Cawdor Road. In 1854 this lease was increased to 120 (48.6 hectares) acres and in 1862 to 278 acres (112.5 hectares). Hannah died of pneumonia on 5th June 1864 aged 71 years; William died five months later on 5th November 1864. They are buried in Section A131.

William Rofe

William Rofe the son of William Rofe senior and Frances Marchant, was born c.1823 in Robertsbridge, Sussex and arrived with his family on the *Neptune* on 29th September 1839. After a short stay he left to try his fortune in the newly discovered goldfields in California.[6] He was reasonably successful in this venture and on his return to Sydney joined the police force for a short time. At one time he travelled from Sydney to Adelaide with cattle and next tried his hands at contracting on the roads before taking a clearing lease at Mount Hunter from the Macarthurs. On 9th August 1855 he married Mary Ann Cranfield and settled down to farming. He died 17th January 1896 and is buried in Section A084.

Jesse Dunk

Jesse Dunk was born in Battle, Sussex on 22nd April 1787 the son of John Dunk and Sarah Blunden. Jesse worked as a labourer but employment opportunities were scarce. In 1808 the Peninsular War against Napoleon began, so with the call to arms and the offer of regular pay, 22 year old Jesse enlisted in 1809 in the 39th Foot Regiment of the British Army. Jesse saw service in France and Spain

Jesse Dunk courtesy - Shirley Rorke

---

[5] "Thomas Dockery Richardson" Camden News 19th February 1903
[6] Obituary – "Death of Two Old Residents of Camden" Camden News 23rd January 1896

at the battles of Busaco, Albuhera, Vittoria, Pyrenees and Toulouse. In 1812 he was sent to Canada, taking part in the War of 1812 which was fought between the United States and Great Britain (rising out of a dispute on blockading trade with France). The war began in June 1812 and continued until 1815 although the Peace Treaty ending the Napoleonic war was signed in Europe in December 1814. The main land fighting of the war occurred along the Canadian border and also in the Gulf of Mexico. Jesse took part in the Canadian campaign in the Chesapeake Bay region. However by 1814 he was back in France, taking part in the battle of Montmartre (Paris). Jesse was awarded the Military General Services Medal in 1848. This medal was not authorised until 1847 and then issued only to survivors living at that time who had applied for the medal.[7]

Medal awarded to Jesse Dunk - courtesy Shirley Rorke

On 12th June 1816 Jesse was discharged and returned to Battle. Now that the war was over, there was a large increase in the number of men seeking work so Jesse moved to Mountfield, a short distance away, where there would have been limited work available for labourers. On 6th June 1818 he married Charlotte Sellings at All Saints, Mountfield.

Sadly Charlotte died 24th March 1835 leaving Jesse to raise a young family of 7 children aged 3 years to 16 years. In 1836 he married Susanna Silvers but with the industrial revolution threatening the family with hardship and the workhouse he decided in 1839 to take the opportunity of assisted immigration to Australia. The family sailed from Plymouth on 29th June 1839 on the *Florist* arriving in Sydney on 26th October 1839.[8]

Jesse at first found work with a Mr. Manning of Sydney and later worked at *Vermont*[9] for William Charles Wentworth later settling at *Shankamore*[10] before moving to Cobbitty where he had a clearing lease. In later years he moved to Kenny's Hill, then to Elderslie, then to *Camden Park* before moving back again to Elderslie. The incessant shifting about proved very unfavourable to the education of the children, and they were never sent to school to learn to read and write. Susanna died without issue in 1853.

Five years later on 4th March 1858 Jesse married Sarah Hilder a girl of just 19 years of age. At this time he was 71 years of age, but the marriage records claim that he was 54 years. Sarah, also from Mountfield, had arrived on the *Marquis of Hastings* on 4th February 1841, with her parents Eli Hilder and Mary Playford and grandparents Henry Hilder and Keturah Haines. Sarah was only 3 years old when her mother died and on 10th August 1842 her father married Sarah Piall. By the

---

[7] Some 25,650 application were made for the medal. The reason for the delay in issuing the medal is said to have been due to the Duke of Wellington, who was opposed to the issue of a standard medal to all ranks – Orders Decorations and Medals
[8] The shipping records list the family as Donk
[9] Grant of 1750 acres to William Charles Wentworth, near Greendale, west of Bringelly
[10] Obituary – Thomas Dunk – 23rd April 1896

A New Beginning – Bounty and Assisted Immigrants

time she was 19 years of age, Sarah was desperately unhappy at home and marriage to Jesse gave her a reason to leave. Jesse was kind to her but he died 15th June 1860 less than 2 years after their marriage. Sarah married Robert George Britt on 19th June 1861. Jessie is buried in Section A134.

Francis Ferguson

Francis Ferguson was born c.1824 in East Hampshire, Essex, England the son of James Ferguson and Janet. He had worked at *Chatsworth House*, and other large English gardens[11] where he trained as a nurseryman. In 1848 he married Sophia Camp Shepherd before they departed London for Australia on the *John Bright* arriving on 8th June 1849. It is believed that Sir Thomas Mitchell engaged Francis when he first arrived, utilising his skills and knowledge in laying out his country estate *Park Hall*.[12] He also worked for William Macarthur at *Camden Park* up to 1856.[13]

Francis purchased property on the river opposite Macquarie Grove on what is now known as Ferguson's Lane, and had by 1864 established his Australian Nursery as it is known that John Gould Veitch visited the Nursery in November 1864.[14] He later also purchased one of the Macarthurs tenant farms, known as the Cawdor Farms, which were offered for sale in 1885 and 1887.

Francis was also active in public life being involved in organising the petition for the formation of the Municipality of Camden and was the Returning Officer in 1889 when the first Council was formed.[15] On his death 8th September 1892 the Australian Nursery was run by his son Francis John Ferguson and later by his granddaughter Margaret Elizabeth's husband Alfred Denison Little. Francis Ferguson is buried in Section C002.

Henry Pollock Reeves

Henry Pollock Reeves was born in London c.1831 and received his early education in England becoming a school teacher; teaching in Wales and afterwards at Coxhead near Maidstone in Kent.[16]

After coming to the Colony with his wife Emma Ann Allen on the *Eliza* on 18th September 1855 as a bounty immigrant, he first taught in Paddington and was later the same year appointed by Bishop Frederic Barker as the master of the Church of England Denominational School at St. John's Camden. On 10th May 1861 Emma died, and in 1863 he married Ann Kemp. Reeves held this position at St. John's until 1879 when the school closed and he, together with his pupils, moved to the Public School in Camden.

Reeves was a prime mover in the erection of the Camden School of Arts; designing the front of the building and aiding in schemes to raise the building funds. He was also closely associated

Henry Pollock Reeves

---

[11] Ferguson's Nursery Site, Camden, page 79 – "Colonial Landscapes of the Cumberland Plain and Camden, N.S.W., 2000" – Colleen Morris & Geoffrey Britton for the National Trust of Australia (N.S.W.)
[12] *Park Hall* was later known as *Nepean Towers* and is now known as *St. Mary's Towers* – "Place Names of the Camden Area" – joint publication by the Camden Historical Society and the Camden Area Family History Society.
[13] "They Worked at Camden Park" – Richard Nixon and John Wrigley
[14] "Through English Eyes, Extracts from the journal of John Gould Veitch during a trip to the Australian Colonies" – Colleen Morris, page 11 "Australian Garden History, Vol 5 No 6 May/June 1994.
[15] "Camden Characters" – J D Wrigley (ed) - Camden Historical Society, Camden, 1990
[16] Obituary Camden News 29th November 1900

with the Camden A.H. & I. Society for which he was a Vice-President and also served many years on the Ground Committee. He was one of the Trustees for Onslow Park and served as Mayor of the Municipal District of Camden in 1894. He was also a Freemason, a Past Master and a member of the Royal Arch Chapter, and instigated the setting up of Abbotsford Lodge.[17]

For a quarter of a century he was oratory organist and choirmaster at St. John's and ably conducted its fife and drum band. He had for many years suffered from chronic rheumatism and died aged 69, on 26th November 1900 and is buried in Section F007.

Fanny Wheeler
Fanny Hopson was born in Stroud, Gloucestershire, England in 1832 the daughter of William Hopson and Emma Jackaway. She was just 5 years old when the family left England in 1837 as bounty immigrants to the Macarthurs of *Camden Park*. They arrived on the *Layton* on 19th January 1838. On the same ship was 12 year old John William Wheeler, the son of Jonathan Wheeler and Jane March. Her father later became a butcher at Cawdor.

Fanny and John William Wheeler married at St. John's on 8th August 1849 and shortly after Wheeler obtained a clearing lease at Ellis Lane from the Macarthurs. During her lifetime Fanny witnessed many "*stirring scenes and startling changes*"[18] in the district. She died, aged 81 years, on 4th June 1912 and is buried in Section D197 alongside her husband.

Joan Vaux
Life expectancy in the 19th century was short, although many did live long and fruitful lives. There was no social security, and most widows found it difficult to survive without marrying as soon as possible in order to provide for their needs as well as those of their children. One such was Joan Vaux, wife of William Derriman, who had come to the Colony from South Pertherton, Somerset, England in 19th January 1856 on the *Morayshire*.

William Derriman died in Camden on 21st May 1868 and was buried in Section A023. On 3rd July 1872 Joan married Jacob Butt at St. John's Camden, but this marriage was to be a short one as Jacob died on 15th May 1878. On 20th July 1880 Joan married Rufus White at St. John's Camden and they lived at Cawdor. "*She experienced many trying and stirring scenes incidental of the earlier history of Camden*" and she and her third husband "*were types of the good old pioneers who did so much towards bringing Camden to the fore.*"[19] Jane's third husband died on 20th February 1898 and was buried at Cawdor. Jane went to live with her daughter in Picton where she died aged 96 on 30th April 1913 and was buried in Section A028 not far from her first husband William Derriman.

Eliza Jane Rapley
Eliza Jane Linn was born in Londonderry, Ireland in 1836, the daughter of Robert Linn and Mary Ann Cunningham. The family arrived on the *Wilson* on 31st December 1841 and lived at Brownlow Hill. On 2nd August 1852 Eliza married Thomas Rapley, a farmer, at Brownlow Hill.

Her husband died on 25th November 1890 and she continued to live on the farm with her sons for the next six years.[20] For the last four years of her life she lived in Camden where she was deeply respected. Eliza died on 21st June 1903 and is buried in Section B057

John Leonard Monk
Like many who had arrived from Europe, Johann Leonhard Munck anglicized his name and in Camden was known as John Leonard Monk but was commonly referred to as Leonard. He was born c.1822 in Baden Germany and married Christina Fredrica Worner in 1849 prior to

---

[17] Now known as Camden Lodge
[18] Obituary "Fanny Wheeler" Camden News – 6th June 1912
[19] Obituary "Mrs. R. White" Camden News 22nd May 1913
[20] "Mrs. T. Rapley" – Camden News 25th June 1903

coming to the Colony as a bounty immigrant for the Macarthurs. He was then employed as a caretaker at Thomas Dawson's property *Brooks Flat* at Mount Hunter, and continued to live and work on the property after Dawson retired.

At approximately 10:00 o'clock on Thursday 13th May 1897,[21] after having delivered his milk to the tramway, Monk was getting into his cart alongside the Camden Post Office when his horse became restive. A sudden jerk unbalanced Monk knocking him into the bottom of the cart. The head gear broke and the horse bolted up Argyle Street with Monk jammed between the seat and the floor. Whilst he had the reins in his hands, Monk had no control over the horse and shouted for assistance. The horse and cart turned a number of corners, finally turning into John Street with several men galloping after it on horseback. George Watson was finally able to stop the runaway, and with the help of others unharnessed the horse to prevent further danger. Monk was shocked but fortunately not seriously injured apart from cuts about the hands. He was conveyed to his daughter's residence at Brownlow Hill by Major Mr. W.C. Furner. Monk died a few months later on 29th December 1897 and is buried in Section B003.

Oliver Hinde

Oliver Hinde from Roscommon, Bedfordshire, England and his wife Mary Hamilton Hall arrived on the *Switzerland* on 13th April 1858. The shipping records indicate that he was a brushmaker however it is known that he had worked for the police prior to arriving as an assisted immigrant. Hinde worked as a policeman in the Mounted Constabulary and was deployed to Camden where he quickly became Senior Sergeant. Two of their ten children died in Camden and are buried in the Cemetery; Ethel Augusta Hinde died on 1st April 1876 aged 3⅓ years and Alice Cruise Hinde died aged 9 years on 11th April 1878.

The Hinde family memorial

Hinde died aged 56 years on 24th April 1877 and Mary Hinde was buried next to her husband after her death on 3rd July 1881. The family are buried in Section A012 and a marble plaque in the church commemorates the family. The names of three of the children appear to have been added after the plaque was erected as witnessed by the different type face.

John Thomas McMinn

John Thomas McMinn was born in Armagh, County Down, North Ireland in 1834, the son of Samuel McMinn and Martha. McMinn arrived on the *Annie Wilson* on 14th December 1859 and was appointed manager of *Logan Downs Station*[22] on the Isaac River near Rockhampton in Queensland owned by Messrs. Campbell and McLaren.

McMinn has been described as a "*humane man, he was kind and generous to the natives.*"[23] This was at a time when there was warfare being waged between the settlers of the Moreton Bay Settlement and the local aboriginal tribes. Local aborigines had stolen a few sheep and the settlers pursued

---

[21] "A Marvellous Escape of Mr. Leonard Monk" Camden News 13th May 1897
[22] "An Australian Pioneer" Camden News 1st June 1939
[23] ibid

and killed two or three of the tribe. In retaliation the aborigines took revenge killing shepherds and ravishing the flocks and herds.

It was customary, when raids by the aborigines were taking place, for the shepherds to strike camp and make for the homestead. During one of these raids in December 1863 McMinn was out riding looking for distressed shepherds and flocks. The first indication he received as to the presence of aborigines was when his horse was killed by a spear thrown from dense scrub. McMinn was captured and stripped and the aborigines stuck spears into the ground around him to form a fence.

McMinn was saved from death when an aboriginal woman ran towards him and threw herself at his feet. Apparently she had been in the habit of calling at the main homestead and had received a whole twist of tobacco from McMinn. The aborigines seemingly impressed by her story allowed him to run. As he was some 70 miles (112.65 km) from the homestead with no protection from the harsh sun, McMinn's body was soon blistered and he was attacked by inspect pests. He became delirious as well as helplessly lost in the bush.

Fortunately once those at the homestead realized he was missing a search party was organized and he was found, after a two day search, in a pitiful condition. It took over seventeen weeks for him to recover.

After his recovery McMinn had several other lucky escapes from the aborigines and finally decided it would be safer to leave *Logan Downs Station* and return to N.S.W. Following his return to Sydney he took up a lease on the University paddocks at Sydney and also a lease of *Smidmore's Paddock* at Enmore Hill.

He married Ann McKnight from Mulgoa on 23rd February 1869 and started dairy farming at Cecil Hills near Liverpool before, in 1870, transferring to *Freshfields* at Cobbitty. He became a pioneer of dairy farming in the district and won many blue ribbons at Camden Show with his celebrated "J.T.M." brand. After an eventful life he died aged 79 on 7th July 1913 and is buried in the family vault in Section B008. His funeral procession was reported to have been a mile (1.6km) long.

Richard Hawkey
Richard Hawkey was born on 2nd March 1836 in Lantegles, near Camelford, Cornwall the son of Richard Hawkey and Mary Rundle. From an early age he was employed as a yeoman farmer, and on 30th August 1856 married Mary Anne Burton from St. Breock, Cornwall. Shortly after they departed England on the *Plantagenet* and arrived on 13th February 1857. Two days before their arrival a daughter, Sarah Plantagenet Hawkey was born on 11th February 1857.

He made his home in Camden and was employed by Thomas Hobbs, a farmer and storekeeper, until Hobbs' death in 1862. After which he was employed by John Tickner at *Camberfield* Razorback until Tickner's death in 1875. He was then employed at *Camden Park* as a labourer and then as a stockman before being promoted to Overseer and later Farm Manager, a position he held for fifteen years[24]. During this period the family lived in *Belgenny Cottage*, until during the 1890s he was given the management of a dairy farm on a share basis at Menangle. The farm later became the location for the Rotolactor.

Along with many of his contemporaries Hawkey joined the Camden branch of the Royal Order of Foresters shortly after it was established in March 1874. He suffered a heart attack on 15th

---

[24] "Family's Long Association With District" Camden News 7th March 1957

August 1901 whilst bridling his horse in the farm yard at Menangle and dropped dead at the age of 65 years. He is buried in the family grave in Section C126.

Samuel Ellis

Samuel Ellis was born at Mudford, Somerset England in 1850, the son of Solomon Ellis and Eliza. On 18th September 1855 he arrived with his parents, who were assisted immigrants, on the *Eliza*. Samuel was just 5 years old.

The family settled in Elderslie and at an early age Samuel worked as a teamster and carrier, driving his bullock team between Sydney and Bourke. On 9th June 1874 he married Margaret Miller at St. John's Camden. In 1880 he leased 84 acres (34 hectares) of cleared land from the Macarthurs at the rear of what is now Camden District Hospital and settled down as a farmer and agriculturalist.[25] Samuel later moved to *Fernleigh* Cobbitty Paddocks where he continued to farm until the time of his death.

Richard Hawkey

He identified himself with many local activities, and in particular the Camden A.H. & I. Society. His services, not only at show time but in the preparation of the grounds leading up to the show, resulted in him being unanimously elected a Life Member and an honorary member of the Committee. He was also an active member of the old Royal Order of Foresters which later became known as Camden Lodge. Not the least of his public duties was his involvement in the municipal life of the town. He was elected to the first council at the inauguration of the municipality and served as Alderman for some years. He died on 16th July 1926 aged 76 years and is buried in Section B102.

---

[25] "Obituary – Samuel Ellis" Camden News 16th July 1926

First Fleet Connections

The third window in St. John's, on the southern side, is in memory of the fifth Rector, Rev. Cecil John King, and his twin brother, Rev. Copland King. What many may not know is that the King family goes back to the First Fleet.

Philip Gidley King
Rev. Cecil and Copland King's great grandfather, Philip Gidley King, had served as a 2nd Lieutenant under Captain Arthur Phillip on HMS Sirius on the voyage to set up a convict settlement in N.S.W. After the First Fleet arrived in Botany Bay in January 1788 King was selected to lead a small party of convicts and guards to set up a settlement on Norfolk Island. The Norfolk Island settlement was established in March 1788, after the party had some difficulty in landing due to the lack of a suitable harbour.[1]

Land was cleared, huts built and crops planted, and more convicts sent to the settlement. In March 1790 King returned to England to report on the difficulties of settlement in the new Colony and whilst there married Anna Josepha Coombe in March 1791. Shortly afterwards he returned to Norfolk Island on *HMS Gordon* with King taking up the post of Lieutenant-Governor. His son Philip Parker King was born in December 1791 and four daughters were to follow.

In October 1796 the Kings return to England as Philip Gidley was in ill-health. After he regained his health the family returned to Sydney on 26 November 1799 with King carrying the dispatch recalling Captain John Hunter. On 28 September 1800 King assumed the position of Governor of the Colony.

In early December 1803 accompanied by his wife Anna Josepha, King visited the Cowpastures to inspect the cattle. The Sydney Gazette of 11th December 1803 reported Mrs. King *"we may confidently affirm, is the first and only lady that has every crossed the Nepean."*[2]

Philip Gidley King made great contributions to the early years of the Colony. His regulation for prices, wages, hours of work, financial deals, and the employment of convicts, brought some relief to small land holders. He also encouraged the construction of barracks, wharves, bridges, and homes and under him the government herds and flocks greatly increased. He encouraged experiments with vines, tobacco, cotton, and hemp; whaling became an important source of oil; and coal mining began. He took an interest in education, encouraged smallpox vaccinations, strove to keep peace with the indigenous population and encouraged the first newspaper — the Sydney Gazette.

He came into conflict with the N.S.W. Corps when he attacked the misconduct of officers, particularly their illicit trade in liquor. He faced military arrogance and disobedience from the Corps and failed to receive support from England when he sent an officer, John Macarthur, back to face court martial. The increased animosity he faced from the N.S.W. Corps eventually led to his resignation in 1806 and he returned to England. Philip Gidley King died on 3rd September 1808; but the family's connection with the Colony was to continue.

On 13th February 1812 his daughter, Anna Maria King, married Hannibal Hawkins Macarthur, the son of James Macarthur (the elder brother of John Macarthur) and Catherine Hawkins. Hannibal Macarthur had been persuaded by his uncle John to accompany him on his return

---

[1] "King, Philip Gidley (1758-1808)" – A.G.L. Shaw - Australian Dictionary of Biography
[2] "Camden District, A History to the 1840s" – Peter Mylrea

to N.S.W., but returned to England in 1810. In March 1812 Hannibal returned to Parramatta, at the request of his uncle, to assist his aunt Elizabeth[3] with the running of *Camden Park*.

Philip Parker King

Philip Gidley King's only legitimate son, Philip Parker King, returned with his family to England in 1796 where he was educated prior to enlisting in the Royal Navy in 1807. A friend of the family, Matthew Flinders, interested him in surveying and introduced him to Captain Thomas Hurd, the Admiralty hydrographer. By 1817 he had completed his training and married Harriet Lethbridge, the daughter of Christopher Lethbridge of Launceston, Cornwall an uncle of Rev. Henry Tingcombe the third rector of St. John's. Captain King returned to Sydney in 1817 where he was appointed commander of an expedition to undertake a hydrographical survey of *"the yet undiscovered coast of New Holland"*.[4] This expedition on the 84 ton cutter *Mermaid* included in the crew the aborigine, Bungaree.[5]

In April 1823 Captain King returned to England and due to ill-health considered retiring to his Australian estates, 660 acres (267.1 hectares) on South Creek near Rooty Hill which he had called *Dunheved*. In 1824 he became a shareholder in the Australian Agricultural Co. but in May 1826 was again at sea in command of *HMS Adventure* which together with *HMS Beagle* had been requested to chart the coasts of Peru, Chile and Patagonia. His son Philip Gidley King (the younger) accompanied him on this voyage. The expedition returned to England in 1830 and as Phillip Parker King was again in poor health he returned to Sydney in 1832 on the *Brothers*.

Philip Gidley King (the younger)

The King Grave

Philip Gidley King (the younger) joined *HMS Beagle* as a Midshipman in December 1831. *HMS Beagle* continued to survey the southern coast of South America with Charles Darwin on board and Darwin and the young midshipman were to become lifetime friends. In 1836 he returned to Sydney and re-joined his parents at *Dunheved* near Penrith. In 1842 he entered the service of the Australian Agricultural Co. in charge of its horse and cattle studs at Stroud and on 1st June 1843 married his cousin Elizabeth, the daughter of Hannibal Macarthur and Anna Maria King, at St. John's Church Parramatta.

Robert Lethbridge King

Robert Lethbridge King, the fourth son of Captain Philip Parker King, was born at sea enroute to England in February 1823. He was educated at The King's School, Parramatta, before continuing his education at St. John's College, Cambridge in 1841[6] where he studied for the ministry. On 30th December 1841 he married Honoria Australia Raymond the daughter of James Raymond the Post Master General. After completing his education he returned to Sydney and was made a Deacon on 19th September 1847 and served his curacy at St. Phillip's Church Hill before being ordained Priest on 17th December 1848.

Robert Lethbridge King was active in the movement which led to the inauguration of synodical government, and became Episcopal Chaplain in 1858 and Canon of the Cathedral in 1867.[7] In

---

[3] "Macarthur, Hannibal Hawkins (1788-1861)" – Australian Dictionary of Biography
[4] "King, Phillip Parker (1791-1856)" – Australian Dictionary of Biography
[5] "Bungaree (- 1830)", - F. D. McCarthy -Australian Dictionary of Biography
[6] The Headmaster at the time was Rev. Robert Forrest, later to become the first rector of St. John's Camden
[7] "King, Robert Lethbridge (1823-1897)" – Australian Dictionary of Biography

January 1868 he took office as principal of Moore Theological College until June 1780 when he returned to Parish ministry and in 1881 was appointed Archdeacon of Cumberland.

Three of Archdeacon Robert Lethbridge King's sons entered the ministry and his twin sons are of particular interest to St. John's Camden.

Cecil John King and Copland King were born on 24th June 1863 at Parramatta and were educated at home until aged 15, when they attended Sydney Grammar School and later Sydney University where both obtained their BA's in 1885 and MA's in 1887. Both served as Lay Catechists at Holy Trinity Church, Sydney, from 1885 and were ordained in September 1887.

Rev. Cecil John King

Rev. Cecil John King - courtesy St. John's Camden

In March 1891, the Rev. John Fleming Moran left St. John's on a trip to England and the week after his departure Bishop Frederic Barker of Sydney asked Rev. Cecil John King to take charge of the Camden Parish for Sundays and some of the week days pending Rev. Moran's resignation. At that time Rev. Cecil King was curate at Holy Trinity under his father Archdeacon Robert King, and his brother Rev. Copland King was attending Sydney Hospital preparatory to going to New Guinea as a Missionary. This arrangement held until his brother's departure in late July 1891 and in September 1891 Rev. Cecil King came to live at the rectory as Rector-in-Charge of the Parish. Rev. Moran's resignation was not received until his return to Australia in 1892 and it was not until 18th July 1893 that King was appointed Rector by Bishop Frederic Barker. The cause of the delay was uncertainty with regard to the fulfilment of the original terms of the agreement between Bishop Broughton and the Macarthur family, by which each party had the right to alternate nomination of the rector.[8]

In 1900 Rev. King married Adelaide Maria White, the widow of Roderick Murcheson Mackenzie. He was the first rector to produce monthly bulletins, and in 1919 prepared the first history of St. John's to commemorate the 70th Anniversary of the consecration of the Church. It is due to the bulletins that have survived that we have extra information on Rev. King.

From the "Monthly Notes" we know that in December 1913 the Kings left for a period of approximately 12 months to go to Yarrabah, a Mission Station near Cairns North Queensland leaving the Parish in the charge of Rev. Harold A.C. Rowsell. Rev. King tells us that he had not volunteered to go but *"was most clearly called upon by the Church authorities, to take up this work"*.[9] He returned to Camden at the end of 1914 and remained until he retired 31st October 1927. Rev. King passed away on 18th April 1938 and is buried in Section B152 alongside his brother and later his wife Adelaide King who passed away on 12th October 1945.

---

[8] Rev. King resigned in 1927, and the right of nomination passed to the Parish.
[9] Parish Notes December 1913

Rev. Copland King

Rev. Copland King was a Lay Catechist at Holy Trinity Church, Sydney, from 1885 until 1887 and later served curacies at Castle Hill, Rose Hill and Dural.[10] In 1890 he heard an address by

Rev. Albert MacLaren recently appointed to launch an Anglican mission in New Guinea, and accepted the challenge to join him. They arrived at Wedau on the eastern end of New Guinea on 10th August 1891 establishing their headquarters at nearby Dogura. Having lost many of their Papuan and European workers to sickness and desertion, the two leaders also fell sick. King was sent back to Sydney to recover but unfortunately McLaren died in New Guinea.

Rev. Copland King - courtesy St. John's Camden

Against the advice of family and friends Rev. Copland King insisted on returning to New Guinea in March 1892, and was appointed head of the mission. He continued in this work for 26 years and in 1897 declined an invitation to become the first Bishop of New Guinea, believing his talents were more suited to subordinate positions. With his flair for languages, he soon mastered the Wedauan tongue used around Dogura. He spent his time mainly in missionary journeys and translating the scriptures and educational material.

Rev. Copland King was with Sir William Macgregor when he discovered the mouth of the Mambare River in 1898, and the discovery of gold in the upper reaches resulted in a rush of miners to the Gira and Yodda goldfields. Rev. Copland King took charge of the government post at Tamata Creek (in the goldfields) in 1900 and remained in the North East for the rest of his time in the country. He was the first, and one of the very few Europeans ever, to master the difficult Binandere language.

On his return to Australia he brought with him a clam shell, which was used for many years in the baptism font. In 1914 he was awarded the Diploma of Scholar of Theology by the Australian College of Theology

While in New Guinea Rev. Copland King made valuable anthropological observations, collected plant specimens, and corresponded with botanists abroad. He donated his botanical library and specimens to the Royal Botanic Gardens, Sydney where after his death his photograph was placed in the fern herbarium.

Rev Copland King died of kidney and heart disease in the Coast Hospital[11] Sydney on 5th October 1918 and is buried alongside his brother in Section B152. In 1972 his portrait was published in a series of stamps of Papua New Guinea honouring early missionaries.

---

[10] "King, Copland (1863-1918)" - Australian Dictionary of Biography – Ian Stuart
[11] Later known as Prince Henry Hospital

Australian Born – The First Generation

Unlike their parents the children born to the earlier settlers and convicts had not had to face the hazardous sea voyage to Australia or face the lash like the convicts. Whilst life was still hard, they were able to flourish in the land of their birth and to reap the benefits.

Jessie Carron
Jessie Pearson was born in Sydney 25th July 1834 the daughter of James Pearson and Eliza Doodey. On 19th September 1867 she married William Carron a bounty immigrant who had worked as a gardener for Alexander Macleay on the gardens of *Elizabeth Bay House* and later at *Brownlow Hill*. William Carron, better known as a botanist and explorer, was one of only three survivors of the ill-fated Kennedy expedition to Cape York Peninsular in 1848.

Carron was appointed collector for the Sydney Botanic Gardens on 1st November 1866 and the family lived in the *Domain Lodge* behind St. Mary's Cathedral. In May 1869 Carron visited Lord Howe Island with members of the Survey Department to collect specimens but at the end of 1875 resigned from the Botanic Gardens and became the Inspector of Forests and Forestry Ranger in the Clarence District. Early in February 1876 he went to Grafton, but whilst making arrangements for his family to join him, died on 25th February 1876.[1]

Friends of Carron gave his widow Jessie money to purchase a property at Old Guildford where she set up a shop and post office. Jessie held the position of Postmistress of Old Guildford until shortly before her death on 19th May 1910. Jessie is buried alongside her mother in Section F004.

Henry Thomas Close
Henry Thomas Close was born 18th October 1856 at *Glenmore* the son of Jonathan Close and Sophia Small. His father had been a convict from Bourne, Lincolnshire England who had arrived on 22nd March 1839 on the *John Barry* and was assigned to work at *Camden Park*. On 21st July 1848 after completing his sentence, he married Sophia Small who had arrived in the Colony with her parents on 7th September 1841 on the *China*.

For many years Henry worked at *Camden Park* and married Mary Ann Biffin at St. John's on 16th July 1890. In later years he entered the service of the Camden Council where he served for many years. He was regarded as a faithful employee in whom they reposed every confidence and was the council's oldest employee. Close suffered from a long illness[2] and due to his enfeebled condition was entrusted with lighter duties. A good deal of the gardening in Macarthur Park was done by him and he was held in high esteem by all who knew him. He died on 15th December 1912 and is buried in section A037.

---

[1] "Carron, William (1821-1876) Australian Dictionary of Biography – by L.A. Gilbert
[2] Obituary Notice "Henry Close" – Camden News 19th December 1912

Philip Benjamin Hodge

Philip Benjamin Hodge, known as Ben, was born at Concord on 9th April 1877 the son of John Hodge and Ellen Strongman who had arrived from Cornwall in 1870. Ben was educated at a private school in Croydon and later apprenticed to J. Green of Burwood to learn the trade of watchmaking and jewellery.

After completing his apprenticeship he came to Camden in January 1897. All that he owned was in one carpet bag and he had just £10 ($20) in his pocket when he set up his business in the window of a grocery shop.[3] He later purchased a business at 76 Argyle Street on the corner of Hill Street. He married Maud Huthnance the daughter of Samuel Stevens Huthnance (the Station Master at Menangle) and Emma Beetson at St. James Church, Menangle on 12th April 1889. They lived first in View Street, Camden before moving to *Belvedere* 59 Menangle Road.

Their only children Edna Emma and Eric Victor died in their infancy; Edna Emma aged 7 months and Eric Victor aged 6 months. Despite the sadness of their loss the Hodges lived otherwise peaceful and happy lives and were involved in activities at St. John's with Ben serving as Sunday School Superintendent for a period. He also maintained the Church clock and was the Auditor for St. John's for more than 50 years.

Philip Benjamin Hodge - courtesy of Camden Hospital

Ben didn't restrict his community involvement to the Church. For a number of years he served in an honorary capacity as the Secretary of the Camden Hospital Board of Management to which he was elected in 1901. In 1935 he was offered the position full time and served as the Secretary for 50 years. He was also Auditor for Camden Council and the Financial Scribe to the Sons of Temperance. In 1916 he was appointed the District Registrar for births, deaths and marriages and a Justice of the Peace. He was a member of Camden School of Arts and the official Timekeeper for the Camden Show Society and was a keen sportsman. He enjoyed playing tennis and watching Rugby League.

Maud died aged 80 years on 14th December 1953 and was buried beside her young children in Section D146 and Ben died aged 102 years on 20th May 1953 and is buried beside her. Ben Hodge holds the distinction of being the oldest person buried in the Cemetery.

Charles Hopson

Charles Hopson was born in 1839 at South Creek, the son of William Hopson and Emma Jackaway. For a number of years he was employed by Henry Thompson at the flour mills in charge of the horse teams. During his trips to Campbelltown and the western districts, he came into contact with the bushrangers Hall and Gilbert[4] on several occasions.

---

[3] "Camden's Oldest Citizen Dies Aged 102" Camden News 23rd May 1979
[4] "Charles Hopson" – Camden News 29th October 1914

On 28th December 1864 he married Dorcas Stuckey, and after giving up the horse teams went to work for *Camden Park*, where he worked for many years. Charles Hopson died at Elderslie 18th October 1914 aged 77 years and is buried in the family grave in Section C137.

George Edward Kettley

George Edward Kettley was born at Randwick in 1846, the son of William Kettley and Eliza Coleman. In 1872 he married Maria English at Campbelltown and by 1874 he had begun working at *Camden Park*. George and Maria had eight children prior to her death on 18th February 1886. On 14th March 1887 he married Harriet Ann Brown. Harriet already had two children by her first husband and had two daughters to George.

The family lived in Broughton Street Camden and Kettley continued to work at *Camden Park*, breaking metal on the estate and often camped near his work. On Monday the 7th December 1903, at about 9:30 am he left for work and appeared to be in excellent health. At about 4:00 pm on Tuesday 8th December 1903 he was found dead outside his tent and the Coroner concluded that he had died of natural causes, namely heart failure accelerated by a large dose of alcohol.[5] Kettley is buried in Section B108 together with his second wife and one of the daughters of that marriage. His first wife and two of her children are buried in Section D065.

Ellen Rosetta McMullen

One woman fondly remembered by early Camden residents was Ellen Rosetta Hughes born in *Albion House* Surry Hills on 20th September 1826 the daughter of John Terry Hughes and Esther Marsh. Her father had the first flour mill in Kent Street Sydney and owned a number of other properties beside *Albion House*. At a period when Surry Hills, and a good deal of Paddington, were mostly covered by sand hills, her home was surrounded by a beautiful flower garden. As a girl Ellen had the honour of laying the foundation stone of the Royal Hotel built by her father in George Street, Sydney.

In 1850 Ellen married her cousin, Samuel Terry Hughes in St. Andrew's Cathedral, Sydney. After the death of her father in 1858 she came into possession of *Theresa Park*, *Moreton Park*, and other valuable Sydney properties. Her husband built the *Moreton Park* homestead with Ellen laying the foundation stone. In the kitchen, carved in stone, were the words *"Enough and to spare"*. Ellen took these words to heart; she could not bear to see anyone go hungry. For nearly half a century she provided food and shelter for wayfarers. It is said that she often denied herself in order to give more liberally to others.[6]

In 1868 Samuel Terry Hughes died aged 58 years, but it was not until 1874, six years later, that she married again. Her second husband was Franklin McMullen. During her lifetime pastoral and dairying work were carried out at *Moreton Park*, as well as horse breeding under the management of Edward Keane.

Ellen was known for her vivid recollections of early Camden and was very knowledgeable about *Nepean Towers* built by Sir Thomas Mitchell and later owned by Dr. Jenkins and Mr. Wetherell. She died on 3rd April 1914 aged 87 years and is buried in the family tomb in Section A010.

Edward Lomas Moore

Edward Lomas Moore the son of Edward Moore and Elizabeth Lomas was born in Lower Minto. N.S.W. on 29th October 1822. Both his parents had arrived in Australia as convicts, but after completing their sentence purchased land at Glenmore they called *Hardwick*. Early in his career Moore was often away buying and selling produce and later added to this business by buying stock. After the discovery of gold in Victoria he saw the opportunity to supply meat to the

---

[5] "A Sudden Death – George Kettley Found Dead" Camden News 10th December 1903
[6] "Ellen Rosetta McMullen– Camden News 16th April 1914

goldfields, and gave up the produce business, acquired land at Burragorang, and concentrated on livestock.

On 22nd November 1855 he married Ann Bull, the widow of William Burcher of Liverpool. Together with his brother William he bought *Booligal Station* on the Lachlan. They would move the cattle from Burragorang to *Booligal Station* for fattening and then take them to the Sandhurst and Melbourne markets. The Moore sold the Lachlan property at a considerable profit and after di-

Edward Lomas Moore - courtesy of Janet Moore

Ann Bull - courtesy of Janet Moore

Frances Margaret Harley - courtesy of Janet Moore

viding the money with his brother Edward began acquiring freehold estates in Camden as well as other districts.

Moore's foresight, perseverance and hard work made him wealthy, but he was known to be a generous man, helping the less fortunate and giving freely to religious and charitable institutions. The family lived at *Molles Main* near *Gledswood*, and Ann was to bear him 6 children 2 of whom were to die in infancy. Ann died on 10th September 1868, aged 44 years shortly after the birth of her son John Edward on 27th July 1868. On 2nd February 1871 Moore married Frances Margaret Hartley who would bear him 3 children.

At the time of his death on 9th February 1887 Moore and his family were living at *Badgally*.[7] Frances lived until she was 59 years and was visiting Sydney on 30th May 1901 when she was struck by a *"sudden paralysis"*[8] and conveyed to Windermere Private Hospital in Flinders Street. Despite appearing to be making a good recovery Frances died on 5th June 1901. Edward Lomas Moore, his two wives and 3 of their children are buried in Section C038.

Henry Clarendon Hughes

Henry Clarendon Hughes was born about 1860 at *Moreton Park* to Samuel Terry Hughes and Ellen Rosetta Hughes. He lived all his life on the *Moreton Park* estate and took a great interest in agricultural pursuits and in breeding horses and was highly regarded locally as a fine judge of horses. For the last few years of his life he suffered from a throat infection which did not respond to medical treatment. He died on 12th October 1904 and is buried in the family grave Section A010.[9]

---

[7] Badgally is now St. Gregory's Marist Brothers College near Campbelltown
[8] "Death of Mrs. E.L. Moore" – Campbelltown Herald 12th June 1901
[9] "Obituary" Camden News – 20th October 1904

William Rapley

William Rapley was born at Mulgoa Forest[10] on 5th March 1869, the son of Thomas Rapley and Eliza Jane Linn; his father had arrived on the *Sovereign* on 2nd April 1832 and his mother on the *Wilson* on 31st December 1841. The family lived at Greendale on the Nepean River and on at least two occasions they lost everything due to floods.

Rapley worked on the farm but early in his life joined the West Australian gold rush. On returning to Camden he was employed for a short period by Mrs. McMullen on the *Moreton Park* estate at Douglas Park. After the death of his father on 25th November 1890 he took over the family farm and in 1899 married Mary Jane Small in Sydney. He later went into partnership with James Rideout at Brownlow Hill until Rideout's accidental death on 5th December 1915 when he was employed by of Arthur Rideout at Camden Saw Mills. He remained there until retiring due to ill health. Rapley died on 14th April 1943 aged 74 years and is buried in Section C109.

Joan Stuckey

Joan Stuckey was born in Cawdor on 16th July 1868 the daughter of Elgar Stuckey and Aimy Backs. In 1871 her parents opened a small mixed confectionary business in the lower end of Argyle Street; this shop was to move several times. After the death of Elgar in 1899, her mother continued to run the business, now referred to as "grandma Stuckey's," with the help of her daughter.

Elgar Stuckey

During her life Joan was involved in many local activities including acting as organist at the Camden Methodist Church and being connected with the Sons and Daughters of Temperance. She was described as having a *"friendly disposition and helpful nature,"* which *"endeared her to the community."*[11] After the death of her mother Joan continued to run the fancy goods, stationery, and newspaper business until her own death at age 77 years on 28th April 1946. Her grave is located in Section B061.

William John Taplin

In 1872 two year old William John Taplin arrived in Camden. Taplin was born in Sydney in 1870 the son of Edwin Taplin and Mary Lysaught from Wiltshire, England who had arrived in New South Wales in 1869 and settled at Pyrmont. He was just 8 years of age when he

Stuckey's Store - Joan Stuckey in black apron

---

[10] Now known as Werombi
[11] The Camden Herald, 2nd May 1946

started working for his father as a water carrier, drawing water from the Nepean River.

His father died on 20th May 1881 and 12 year old Taplin became the breadwinner for the family. He met with an accident whilst drawing water for the flour mill for Charles Thompson. He fell off the water wagon which then ran over him resulting in a broken thigh in two places. The treating physician was Dr. Goode who subsequently employed him to look after his ponies. Taplin rode the ponies at the early Camden Shows with great success.

Taplin later returned to being a teamster and became an expert in bush work, particularly in gathering heavy logs from thickly timbered country. He also became interested in athletics having some success in foot races alongside James Stuckey. On 24th June 1889 he married Gertrude Eleanor Rix and they lived at Brownlow Hill until on 11th April 1936 he suffered a heart attack whilst helping his son Will load sleepers at the Camden railway yards and died before medical assistance arrived. He is buried in Section B059 alongside his wife who was for many years midwife to the district.[12]

George Wheeler
One of the early settlers in the Camden District was Jonathan Wheeler who had arrived on the *Layton* on 19th January 1838 and settled near Cawdor. On 7th February 1839 his youngest son, George Wheeler was born. George Wheeler married Anne Fuller at St. John's on 7th October 1858 and they settled at Mount Hunter.

In his early working life he was a teamster but later settled down to dairy farming. For thirty five years he served as Sunday School Superintendent at St. John's, and was also involved with the branch church, St. Paul's Mount Hunter, from the time it was built in 1878.[13]

George Wheeler passed away aged 77 years on 30th September 1914 and is buried in Section D001. The rector at that time was Rev. Cecil King who remembered him fondly *"not only as a Parishioner but as a friend."*[14]

---

[12] "Death of Mr. W.J. Taplin" Camden News 16th April 1936
[13] Obituary – George Wheeler - Camden News – 8th October 1914
[14] Parish Notes for St. John's – 1st October 1914

The Young Ones

In the young and old illnesses which we would not regard as serious today could and did prove fatal at times in the 19th century. As previously mentioned, antibiotics such as penicillin, were not available until the 1940s. Reports by Charles Tompson Jnr. to the Sydney Morning Herald, provide some information on epidemics and illness prevailing 1847-1845.

On 14th September 1849 he reported:

> *"Compared with other parts of the country, ours has been but slightly visited by the prevailing epidemics; there has been, no doubt, a solitary case of scarlatina[1] here and there; but upon the whole, troublesome, though by no means dangerous, catarrhal affections have been the only malady affecting the many."*

And on 23rd February 1850:

> *"Opthalmia[2] is disappearing, but there is a good deal of sickness of a temporary nature, affecting the throat and causing cough and other usual concomitants[3] of catarrh. Wherein due attention is not paid to the state of the system of cleanliness, there is an inordinate disposition in wounds and abrasions to rankle and be troublesome – this may, perhaps, be owing in great measure to the peculiar sultriness of the atmosphere, and the absence of invigorating breezes. Cold plunges and frequent ablutions cannot be too strongly recommended."*

Elias Thorn
Infant mortality was quite high in the early 1800s. The first burials took place in the cemetery in 1844 and it is quite sobering when one realises that of the 5 burials that took place in that year only one was an adult, another an 18 year old youth, and 3 children all under 3 years of age. The first burial was that of 6 day old Elias Thorn, the son of Elias Thorn and Sarah Lane, who died on 28th June 1844 and is buried in an unmarked grave in Section E093.

Of the 8 burials in 1845 only 3 were adults, one a child of 7 years, another 4 years, and the rest were infants under 1 year of age.

Jonathon Spice
The twelve year old son of John Spice and Mary Cooper was killed instantly on 20th April 1849. Jonathon Spice was walking near a burnt tree when it suddenly fell crushing him.[4] He died as the result of massive head injuries and is buried in an unmarked grave in Section E009.

Robert Veness
Robert Veness, the four year old son of John Veness and Ann Britt, died as a result of an injury sustained to the head by a sharp instrument whilst he was playing with other young friends. A fever resulted, and the boy died on 13th March, 1850.[5] He is buried in the family plot in Section A078.

---

[1] The term Scarlatina may be used interchangeably with Scarlet Fever
[2] Opthalmia (also called Opthalmitis) is inflammation of the eye.
[3] (following as a consequence): accompanying, adjoining, attendant, incidental
[4] 'News From a Country Village, Camden 1847-52 – Reports made by Charles Tompson Jnr. to the SMH 27th April 1849
[5] Ibid

The Young Ones

William Gibson
On 6th July 1852 tragedy was to strike the family of Camden's Chief Constable, James Gibson, formerly of the 99th Regiment. Twelve year old William Gibson had ridden his horse down to the river but whilst returning the horse bolted throwing the young boy. His head struck the ground, and although medical treatment was provided, he died the next day[6] and is buried in Section A112.

Alice, Florence and William Boyd
From 1856 a series of tragedies were to strike Robert Boyd and his wife Augusta, resulting in the deaths of the youngest three members of the family.

On 9th December 1856 Alice, their 4½ month old daughter, died of whooping cough.

On 12th December 1864, 3 year old Florence died from Scarlet Fever.

Less than 12 months later, on 17th October 1865 their only son William 7½ years of age, died *"of a sudden paralysis of the heart, and he dropped dead"*[7]. In all probability William had also suffered from scarlet fever which may have resulted in an enlargement of the heart, eventually resulting in a heart attack. The three children are buried together in Section A062.

Grave of the 3 Boyd children

Ethel May Anderson
One cannot imagine the anguish faced by John Anderson and Lily Wright when their 10 week old baby Ethel May Anderson was severely burnt on Thursday, 19th June 1901.[8] A spark from the fire had ignited her clothing despite it having been placed at what was thought a safe distance from the fire. Ethel May died on Friday 20th June 1901 and is buried in the family grave in Section C091.

Maggie Blow
Maggie Blow was born in 1890 to John Blow and Ena Brown of *May Farm* Camden. Maggie was only twelve years of age when she contracted pneumonia[9]. The illness lasted for approximately four weeks, and despite careful nursing by her mother and the best of medical attention she died on Friday 29th August 1902 and is buried in Section B114.

---

[6] Ibid
[7] Burial Register for St. John's Camden
[8] "Baby Burnt in its Cradle" – Camden News 27th June 1901
[9] Obituary – Camden News 4th September 1902

Leonard Ross Cranfield

The death of a child is always hard to understand, but at times when a child has been suffering for some time the sorrow may have been eased for his family. Such may have been the case with Leonard Ross Cranfield. Leonard was born on 10th October 1898 to John Cranfield and Emma Packenham.

He had been a member of St. John's Choir until he contracted an illness which was to cause him much suffering which was to continue for 7 years[10]. At the age of 15 years, Leonard died on 16th April 1914 and is buried in Section A142.

Reginald George Gardner

Reginald George Gardner, known as Reggie and also as Rex, was born in Elderslie c.1893 the son of George Mitchell Gardner and Frances Jean Hubbard. The families were regular worshipers at St. John's where Reggie was a popular member of the choir and was also showing *"very unusual promise in several directions"*. He was described as being 5ft. 9in. tall, *"a strong well-built lad and a great favourite amongst his schoolfellows and companions."*[11]

Leonard Ross Cranfield

On Saturday afternoon, 18th May 1907 14 year old Reggie, in the company of others, was riding his bicycle over to Picton to take part in a football match. At the end of a steep descent, on the Picton side of Razorback near what was known as the Flaggy Crossing, Reggie lost control of his bike and landed on his head. He was taken to Camden Hospital by Charles Derriman and A. Hindes but never regained consciousness and died on Wednesday morning 22nd May 1907. He is buried in the family grave Section A099 and also re-

The Reggie Gardner Memorial Plaque in the Church Vestry

membered by a plaque over the door of the vestry in the church.

Unnamed Infant

The death of a baby is always a tragedy for the family but when the body of an unnamed child, parents unknown is found it touches the hearts of the community. On 15th February 1922 the body of a newborn baby girl was found by fettlers alongside the railway line at Douglas Park.[12] The baby had been wrapped in sheeting and then in newspaper and Dr. West believed she was alive at birth. The mother was never identified and the newborn was buried in an unmarked grave in Section C154.

---

[10] Camden News – 16th April 1914
[11] Camden News 23rd May 1907
[12] Camden News 16th February 1922

William James Barry

William James Barry the son of Allan Barry and Alice May Rowe was born in Camden in 1927. Christmas 1941 was to end in tragedy for the Barry family. Late in the afternoon Jimmy went alone to swim in the Nepean River at Menangle near the diving board, not far from the bridge, near an area known as 50 rock. Witnesses were to testify at the Coroner's inquest as to how the accident occurred.

Ronald Francis Curry, aged 11 years, gave evidence that at about 5:00 pm Jimmy had come up to him carrying his wet shorts and had said *"Someone threw my shorts in the river"*[13] He then left and went towards 50 rock with the intention of collecting the rest of his belongings before going to change in the dressing sheds.

John James, Allan Lind and Basil Mahoney were to testify that they saw a shoe drop from the hand of a person on the bank of the river on 50 rock. The person then appeared to overbalance or dive into the water. The witnesses concluded that Jimmy was diving for his shoe but when he didn't surface they became concerned. A hand was reported to have come briefly out of the water before disappearing. The witnesses ran to the spot, but despite diving in and attempting a rescue the three boys were unable to locate Jimmy.

Constable A. Neal was nearby and noticed the activity on the river bank. He dived in but as water was deep and he could not reach the bottom he went to Camden Police Station to get the grappling irons. The body was located on the first pull of the grappling irons and brought to the surface. The witnesses attempted rescucitation but Dr. Crookston on his arrival at the scene pronounced life was extinct. Jimmy is buried in the family grave in Section F039.

---

[13] "William James Barry – Accidentally Drowned – Coroner's Inquest" Camden News 1st January 1942

Following Generations

Camden has grown and prospered in the years since the formation of the township in 1840 and the lives of many have touched the community. In 1919 Camden, like the rest of Australia, was affected by the most serious epidemic to sweep Australia, probably brought here by soldiers returning from World War I. To prevent the virus from spreading everyone was required to wear a gauze mask in public. Schools, churches, hotels etc. were forced to close and the 70th Anniversary Service planned for July 1919 had to be cancelled. People were forced into quarantine including three houses at *Belgenny Farm* and a number of people succumbed to the epidemic. But Camden continued to grow and its residents continued to have a lasting impact on our lives.

George William Armour

One of Camden's more endearing residents of the early 20th century was George William Armour born at Shooters Hill, near Oberon c.1885, the son of Robert William Armour and Mary Harris. Armour has been described as having

> *"an outstanding knowledge of Australian literature, a writer of entertaining verse, a Commonwealth-wide reputation as an apiarist, the best gun-shot this district has produced, a breeder of champion foxhounds, and the possessor of a rare wit. Add to this: A good father and husband and a staunch friend, and you have a condensed description of a real Australian."*[1]

George Armour

In 1908 he married Isabel Sharman the daughter of James Sharman and Caroline Brailsford in Sydney and they were to have two daughters and one son. For more than thirty-years he was a hairdresser in Camden, but preferring the outdoor life sold his business and concentrated his energy on apiary and raising foxhounds. He exhibited at the Sydney Royal Show, and his successes included championships with foxhounds, and many awards in the honey and queen bee sections.

One story told of Armour is about a time in June 1931when he was fox-hunting at Oakdale. After his two favourite foxhounds, Postman and Relish had chased a fox for several miles they suddenly disappeared. A wombat's burrow was discovered, but, as the tunnel was small, he dismissed the idea that they could have entered so small a space. He spent a week in the bush searching for them without success before deciding to blast the burrow and remove about 100 tons (101.6 tonnes) of rock and earth. After opening it to about 25 feet (7.62 metres), he heard a

---

[1] "Death of Mr. George Armour" – Camden News 27th May 1937

faint whimper. The dogs were rescued, in a pitiable condition because of what they had been through but responded to treatment.[2]

George Armour died on 23rd May 1937 and is buried in Section F031. His grave always causes comment from the curious as a hunting horn has been embedded into the headstone.

William Alfred Ernest Biffin
William Alfred Ernest Biffin was born at Theresa Park on 30th September 1868 the son of John Biffin and Elizabeth Martha Brown. His grandfather Aaron Biffin had a clearing lease on the Brownlow Hill side of Mount Hunter Creek on the Werombi Road. For a number of years he worked for Frederick Arthur Downes at *Brownlow Hill* and on 27th March 1890 married Jane Mills at St. Peter's Church, Theresa Park. In the early 1900s he worked on *Camden Park* as an orchard and garden supervisor; he was to work on the estate for 17 years until he retired. After his retirement he purchased *Woodburn*, a property in the Mount Hunter area and later built a home in Camden.

Biffin took an active interest in community activities. For many years he was a church officer both at St. Paul's, Mount Hunter and St. John's, Camden and served as a sideman and as Church Warden. He joined the committee of the Camden A.H. & I. Society in 1919 and was elected Vice-President in 1933. He took a keen interest in the Junior Farmers' Movement and was a member of the advisory committee.

In 1939 he strained his heart whilst involved in heavy work during the building of an air raid shelter. He died on 31st December 1942 and is buried in Section D162.

James Kinghorne Chisholm

James Kinghorne Chisholm
One long term resident was James Kinghorne Chisholm who was born at *Gledswood* on 30th August 1830, the son of James Chisholm and Elizabeth Margaret Kinghorne. In 1813 he was sent to Sydney College to complete his education, and *"became an accomplished scholar and an effective speaker."*[3] His grandfather James Chisholm Snr. had come to the Colony in 1790 and had commenced business in Sydney as a wine and spirit merchant.

His father took a pastoral lease on the Breadalbane Plains and on 9th June 1829 married Elizabeth Kinghorne and settled at *Gledswood*. In the early 1800s the Government used to give grants to newly married couples who settled on the land and his mother Elizabeth received 1,280 acres (518 hectares) near Goulburn as her marriage portion.

James Kinghorne resided at *Gledswood* with his wife Isabella Macarthur Bowman whom he married on 28th July 1858. He served on the bench of magistrates in the Camden district, and for 30 years was the senior magistrate. He identified himself with the Camden A.H. & I. Society and

---

[2] Camden News 27th June 1931
[3] "Obituary - James Kinghorne Chisholm" - Camden News 6 September 1912

was the president and patron for many years. When James Macarthur made an effort in 1862 to establish a farmers club he was supported by James Kinghorne.

At one time he was encouraged to offer himself for parliament, having the full support of the Camden community but he declined. Chisholm was closely identified with St. John's and is first mentioned in Church Records as having attended the Twelfth Annual Meeting of St. John's Vestry on 2nd April 1861. He also held office as a Church Warden in 1882 and at the Jubilee of Consecration in 1899 gave £50 ($100) towards the repair and enlargement of the organ. He gave generously to the fund to erect the Lych Gate and was a Rural Decanal Representative and Synods man. He died aged 82 on 28th August 1912, and is buried in the family grave in Section F001.

At the funeral service the Rev. Cecil King remarked "I feel I have lost one whom I have known since, when a boy of ten years old, I used to come to this district for my holidays".

Mary Jane Dawson

Mary Jane Cranfield was born at Spring Creek, Camden on 8th October 1864 the daughter of George Henry Cranfield and Elizabeth Rourke. On 16th December 1891 she married John Dawson at St. Paul's Westbrook. Throughout her life she took an active interest in her district; particularly in St. Paul's Church which had in earlier days been known as Westbrook Church. She was a foundation member of the Mothers Union and had also been involved with the Red Cross since its inception in Camden.[4] Up until the time of her death she regularly attended the Red Cross sewing meetings in aid of the war effort. She died aged 79 years on 29th June 1944 and is buried in Section B055.

Emma Dengate

Emma Boardman was born at *Daisy Vale,* between Picton and Razorback, on 8th April 1868 the daughter of John Boardman and Ann Condell. In 1899 she married Edward John Dengate the grandson of Edwin Dengate who had settled in the Liverpool district in 1838. Emma and her husband lived at *Osterleigh* at Mount Hercules on the Cawdor side of the Razorback range. After Edward's death on 8th May 1944, Emma moved to Camden and was a foundation member of the Camden Red Cross Society and St. John's Mothers Union.[5] She continued to work tirelessly for both these organisation until her death on 10th June 1952, and is buried alongside her husband in Section D145.

Richard George Hindes

Richard George Hindes was born on the Euchunga gold fields in South Australia in 1857 the son of Frederick Ayton Hindes and Ann Ruth Riddett. His family returned to England in 1862 and it was there that he spent his early youth. He returned to Australia in 1874 and was offered employment in Fiji where the Sugar Refining Company was about to erect sugar mills.

Two years later he returned to Camden where he set up a carpentry and building business in partnership with H. Farrindon. Several public buildings and business houses were erected by him including Camden Public School and the first silos built at *Camden Park*.

In 1883 he married Margaret Rix the eldest daughter of John Rix and Eleanor Snedsdell Coe at St. John's. He was associated with a number of local activities and took special interest in rifle shooting and was a foundation member of the Camden Rifle Club. He was also a prominent member of the old Royal Order of Foresters.

His wife died in 1930. He was living with his daughter Addie Mooney at Mosman when he died aged 85 years on 28th September 1942 and is buried in the family plot in Section B058.

---

[4] "Obituary – Mrs. Mary Dawson" Camden News 6th July 1944
[5] Campbelltown Camden News 26th June 1952

Following Generations

William Henry Hopson

William Henry Hopson was born in Cawdor on 17th August 1866 the son of Charles Hopson and Dorcas Stuckey. While he was still young the family moved to Boorowa where he was later employed at Scott's Flour Mill. The family then moved to Cootamundra where he worked at the Trade Palace Store.

The family returned to Camden, and lived in Elderslie. William gained employment with Mr. A. Stuckey the boot-maker and later purchased the business.

Hopson has been described as not being *"a robust man"*[6] but he took an interest in outdoor activities such as cricket, cycling, football and shooting. He was for some years Vice-Captain of the Camden Cricket Club and had also been a member of the committee of the Camden Football and Rifle Club and a steward of the Cycling Club. He died aged 41 years on 9th November 1907 and is buried in Section C137.

Agnes Elizabeth Lowe

Agnes Elizabeth Whysall was born in 1862 the daughter of William Whysall and Lucy. Her father was an engineer who under T.S. Mort established the Sydney Ice Works, the first of its kind in N.S.W. As a consulting engineer he was also responsible for the machinery of the first butter factory at Lismore, and the factories at Bega, Bemboka, Nimmitabel and Adaminaby and was also involved in the construction of the Glaciarium in Sydney.

In her early years Agnes was a school teacher at various schools including Fort Street, and St. Andrew's Cathedral School.[7] In 1887 she married Edwin Frederick Lowe of Clarence Town. The Lowes had three sons – Bruce Whysall Lowe who died in infancy, Eric Lyndon Lowe who died of wounds received in World War I and Harold Lowe.

After the death of her husband on 10th January 1917 Agnes resided with her son Harold in Elderslie. Agnes was Honorary Secretary of the Mothers Union, a foundation member of the Camden Red Cross in 1914, and held the position of Vice President up until the time of her death. She was also actively involved with the Camden A.H. & I. Society and acted as stewardess in the indoor section for many years. Agnes died on 18th September 1947 aged 85 years and is buried in Section A110.

Rev. Arthur George Rix

Rev. Arthur George Rix was born c. 1880 the son of John Rix, a butcher in Camden for many years and Eleanor Gertrude Snedsdell Coe. Arthur was rector-in-charge of St. John's Church Balmain North until his retirement. He died in Camden aged 72 years, on 30th December 1953.

---

[6] "Obituary – Wm. Hopson" – Camden News 14th November 1907
[7] "Death of Mrs. Lowe" Camden News 25th September 1947

Ellen Stanner

Many women have played an important role in the development of Camden. Women like Ellen Hourn born at Menangle on 13th September 1857 the daughter of John Hourn and Ruth Freeman. Ellen lived her early life on her parents' farm which was leased from Sir William Macarthur. Her father also made bricks in what they called the "Factory Paddock." Some of these bricks were used to construct St. James' Church, Menangle and Ellen helped her father with this work.[8] Ellen was regarded as an authority on the early history of the neighbourhood.

In 1879 Ellen married Albert Stephen Stanner in the new church at Menangle and continued to live in the area until her death on 20th October, 1942. During her life she was involved in many activities including the Menangle Mothers Union, the Sewing Circle, St. James' Choir, the Red Cross and the Agricultural Bureau Women's Club. She is buried beside her husband in Section F017.

Charles John Sutton

Researching historical records can at times become quite daunting both for genealogical as well as historical researchers. There are some excellent examples of conflicting information in the cemetery at St. John's in Camden as well as other local cemeteries. That is why it is essential that even if you are only researching for historical information you must not ignore the need to check genealogical facts. An excellent example is the headstone for Charles John Sutton which reads -

Charles John Sutton
died 7th July 1922 aged 35 year
"A patient sufferer"
"At rest".

The Camden News published an obituary which gave details of his life including that he had been a miner for 15 years at the Colong Peaks Mine at Yerranderie, and also detailed his involvement with the Masons asnd other organisations. The paper also mentioned that his funeral was held at the St. John's churchyard with Rev. C. J. King presiding. However the church Burial Register makes no mention of a Charles John Sutton and instead refers to Charles John Mellon. The Registry for BDMs record this death as Sutton. Why the inconsistencies?

---

[8] "Death of Mrs. Stanner" – Camden News 5th November, 1942

Charles John Mellon was born in Sydney in 1887 the son of Felix Mellon and Jessie Couch nee Robinson. In 1911 Charles Mellon married Ada May Rideout at St. Marks C/E Picton but when a daughter Adeline was born in Picton in 1913 the birth was registered as Sutton.

The mystery deepens with Henry Sutton who is also buried in the same plot. Henry Turbet Harvey Sutton died September 13, 1965 with both the church Burial Register and BDMs agreeing. However Henry was born in Sydney on August 25, 1882 to William Couch and Jessie Florence Robinson. Henry's WWI records also record him as Sutton as does his marriage to Laura Aird Munro at Randwick in 1913.

What is the reason for these confusing discrepancies? It appears that Jessie Florence Robinson married four times: firstly to William Couch; then to Felix Mellon; then to William Sutton; and finally to John McEachern. After Jessie's third husband William Sutton died at Yass in 1911 her 3 sons by her earlier marriages changed their names to Sutton. Walter Henry Sutton the son of Henry is also buried in the same Section E032.

William George Watson

William George Watson was born at Picton on 3rd October 1878 the son of George Watson and Eliza Ann Fryer. When he was still a child his parents moved to Camden, farming on the Carrington Road. In July 1899 he joined the local Sons of Temperance and was to adhere to its ideals for the rest of his life.

On 14th April 1906 he married Evelyn Maud Sheridan in Gunning and shortly after purchased a bakery business on the corner of Argyle and Hill Streets Camden where the family lived until he acquired a home block on the corner of Elizabeth and Mitchell Streets.

William George Watson's bakery

He was an alderman of Camden from 1908 to 1914 when he resigned "*to procure road metal cheaper by using council's own stone crushing plant.*"[9] The council accepted a tender from another contractor and Watson re-entered council at the next election only to resign over a difference of opinion within a few months.

As a hobby Watson had a team of trotters which he trained and raced himself. He then purchased a property known as *Calf Farm* at Spring Creek where he grew peas and raised stock. He died aged 65 on 23rd March 1944 and is buried in Section D167.

---

[9] "Obituary – William George Watson" Camden News 30th March 1944

John Edward Veness
John Edward Veness was born at Cawdor on 11th December 1879 the son of Edward Veness and Sarah Plantagenet Hawkey. At 14 years of age he entered the employ of Elizabeth Macarthur-Onslow at *Camden Park*. Major Astley John Onslow Thompson trained him in the estate office and he rose from being a clerk to accountant, and maintained this position until the *Camden Park* estate became a proprietary company, at which time he became Secretary.

Prior to marrying Martha Abigail McMinn of *Freshfields* Cobbitty on 17th February 1909 he had been actively involved with St. James' Anglican Church Menangle, serving as Superintendent of the Sunday School. After his marriage he and Martha took up residence in Hill Street Camden and became actively involved with St. John's. Veness served as a representative to Synod and for over thirty years organised the annual flower show conducted by the Parish. In addition he held the positions of Honorary Secretary and Treasurer of the Parish, was Honorary Secretary of the Cemetery Trust for St. John's and also fulfilled a similar role with respect to Camden General Cemetery.

Edward Veness

His other interests included the Sons of Temperance Friendly Society, the Masonic Lodge for which he was a Past Master of Camden Lodge, and Camden A.H. & I. Society on which he served as committeeman and Secretary. Another of his interests was the Boy Scout movement and he held the position of committeeman of the Near Southern District Boy Scouts' Association.

Ill health led to his resignation from his position at *Camden Park* after over 40 years' service, but his services were retained by the Macarthur family for private business. John Edward Veness died aged 62 on 8th March 1941 and is buried in Section B013.

Francis James West
Francis James West was born in England c.1843 the son of Dr. George West and Jane. He arrived in Sydney with his parents c.1855. After studying in Sydney he moved to Queensland and continued his studies, but instead of entering the medical profession as his father hoped, Francis James studied agriculture. He became the owner of *St. Helen's Station* and in 1872 married Kathleen Hussey Greenup the daughter of Dr. Greenup of Parramatta. After 30 years farming sheep and crops he sold *St. Helen's Station* and carried on the management of the *Pilton Estate* on the Darling Downs until that property was sub-divided to allow for "closer settlement" when he retired to Toowoomba, Queensland. In December 1911 he came to Camden to visit his son Dr. Francis William West for a few weeks but unfortunately was in failing health. He died on 4th February 1912 and is buried in the family plot in Section B121.

Dr. Francis William West

Francis William West

Francis William West was born at *Maryland Station* on the Queensland border c.1874 the son of Francis James West and Kathleen Hussey Greenup and educated at Toowoomba Grammar School. He later followed the career path of his grandfather Dr. George West and studied medicine at Sydney University. After some years of experience at Sydney Hospital he came to Camden in 1901. In the same year he married Adeline Lydia Jones the daughter of Dr. Robert Theophlus Jones and Lydia Sophia Hinde and they lived at *Macaria* in John Street.

It was as a medical adviser and physician and Government Medical Officer that he became well known throughout Camden. He was respected for his devotion to the welfare of the district and had an interest in many aspects of community life. At the time of his death he was the President of Camden Parents and Citizens Association. He was held in high regard for his work with Camden District Hospital and could always be relied upon to extend a helping hand to those in need.[10] He died on 20th October 1932 aged 58 years and is buried in Section B121. His funeral procession stretched along Argyle Street and was at the time the largest ever seen.

Funeral procession for Dr. Francis West

Milton Brettel Ray

One of the last grave plots sold is that of Milton Brettel Ray the son of Alfred Ray and Jessie Lottie Ridgeway who was born in Picton on 18th March 1926. He attended Camden Public School and in April 1947 married Elaine Dawn McEwan.

His father was a test pilot for De Havilland at Bankstown Airport so at an early age Milton also developed a lifelong interest in flying, and planes and would recall how, as a young boy, he sat on Charles Kingsford Smith's knee in the Southern Cross. At the age of 16 he would drive out to meet his father at Camden aerodrome for a quick flying lesson.

During World War II he joined the Camden Volunteer Fire Brigade as a reserve fireman and was responsible for driving and servicing the brigade's engines. Milton became the longest serving member for the Macarthur District after 35 years was awarded, in 1971, the Long Service Medal and Bar and Queen's Medal for his *"exemplary fire service."*[11]

Milton Ray

---

[10] "Camden Mourns – Death of Dr. F.W. West" Camden News 27th October 1932
[11] Ibid

As a young man he completed an apprenticeship with Dan Cleary, welding and working on machinery to build airstrips, and then went to Clinton Motors where he assembled tractors.[12]

He was well known for his love of documenting the activities of Camden and in the early 1960s he filmed a documentary on the final days of "Pansy" the Campbelltown to Camden train. The activities of the Camden Historical Society, of which he was a founding and long standing member, were recorded in detail. He was involved in winding the clock in the St. John's tower, and was a member of the Camden Show Society; not missing a show during the 50 years he was a member.

Milton will be "remembered as a gentleman in every respect; he was gentle of nature, kind of word and had a strong sense of duty to his family, his church and his community."[13] He was well known for his involvement in St. John's, Camden Bush Fire Brigade, Camden Probus Club and the Camden Historical Society.

In 2000 he was awarded the Commonwealth Recognition Award for Senior Australians; recognising his significant contribution to the Macarthur Community. Milton died on 16th November 2009 and is buried in Section A092 the plot he had purchased in 1956.

---

[12] Reminiscences by one of his daughters
[13] "Man of Duty, Kind of Word" Camden Advertiser 2nd December 2009

Dr Francis William West, who died in 1932, standing alongside his car

Funeral of Dr Francis William West at St John's cemetery - courtesy Roy Dowle

Tragedy at the Home Farm

One tragedy that occurred in Camden was to shock not only the town but Sydney as well. The gravestone on the grave of James Stewart points us to the story.

James Stewart had recently been employed at *Camden Park* as a Clerk/Storekeeper. He was the son of a squatter, James Stewart Snr. and Ann, from Rolland's Plains near Port Macquarie and was born about 1847. Apart from the story of his violent and tragic death, history does not have much to relate about this young gentleman, and the weathered gravestone located in Section B017 is now difficult to read, but the words *"struck down by the hand of a maniac"* are a tantalizing clue to the story.

As is often the case, more is known about the murderer than the victim, particularly when the murderer was a well-known local.

The other person involved in the tragedy was Robert Boyd, the second son of Richard Boyd and Sarah Higgins born at *Camden Park* on 4th February 1826. At an early age he went to work with his father in the stables at the *Home Farm*[1] and earned the respect of William and James Macarthur for his treatment of the horses. On 24th February 1848 he married Augusta Maria Sheather who was with child at the time of the marriage. Their daughter Emily was born 14 days later.

Augusta Maria Sheather, the daughter of James Sheather and Mary Milham, was born in Beckley, Sussex, England on 30th March 1827. The Sheather family arrived in Sydney 10th March 1839 on the *Royal George* as bounty immigrants under contract to James and William Macarthur.

Shortly after their marriage Boyd and Augusta went to *Nangus Station*, the Macarthurs' property located on the Murrumbidgee River near Gundagai, where he was in charge of the Macarthurs' horses. The family stayed at *Nangus Station* until 1854 when the property was sold, and then returned to *Camden Park* where Boyd continued to work as a groom, and above his wages earned money for horse breaking.

For many years he was held in great respect and regarded as an honest man. He played cricket for a local team and was reported as having saved a child from drowning in the river. During the floods of August 1857 he crossed the river in order to get the Sydney mail – *"We are greatly indebted to Mr. Robert Boyd for the skilful and brave manner in which he crossed the river on a sheet of bark, formed in the shape of a canoe, to get the Sydney mails, etc. Had it not been for him we should have waited till late on Sunday evening before getting Friday's mail."*[2]

By 1860 Boyd was known to be suffering from violent bouts of temper and irritations and was attending a doctor for treatment. The behaviour was put down to Boyd having suffered a few kicks to the head over the years whilst breaking in horses.

Soon after the death of their daughter Florence from Scarlet Fever, Augusta suffered a stroke and was bedridden and unable to speak. Boyd continued to work at the *Home Farm* and took care of his sick wife with the help of his deceased brother John's widow, Sarah Sharpe who acted as housekeeper. By now there were reports that Robert had started to drink which, due to his worsening brain condition, was unadvisable.

---

[1] The Home Farm, the working farm of the Camden Park estate, is better known as Belgenny Farm
[2] SMH 26th August 1857

Tragedy at the Home Farm

On the morning of Friday, 5th January 1872, Robert Boyd and William Avery went to Camden in a small farm cart. Boyd had some business to attend to, but on the way home the pair stopped at Arnold's Public House[3] for *"some drink."*[4] Avery told the Coroner, Edward Palmer, they left for home but turned back and had a second drink before calling at McEwen's for bread, and returning to *Camden Park*. According to Avery, Boyd *"did not appear to me to be drunk or excited, nor did he in any way mention the name of the deceased to me; he did not take home any spirits that I know of."* Avery does not appear to have told the Coroner what, or whom, they were discussing during the ride back to the *Home Farm*.

George Mills, the sawyer, told the Coroner he saw Robert Boyd returning from the village and though he appeared *"to be very much excited; he was mad rather than drunk"*. However according to Sarah Sharpe, Boyd *"came home drunk from Camden, and after he came home he drank more brandy"* and then rushed into his wife's room for his guns. He failed to get the guns as Augusta had directed Sarah to keep them from him. She handed the guns through the window to her niece Sarah Johnson who ran off, with Boyd calling after her to come back.

Sarah Johnson gave the guns to the sawyer, George Mills, who hid them at the corner of the store and then went to James Stewart telling him that *"the girl's uncle was going to shoot himself."* Stewart apparently replied *"There is little fear of that; he has more sense."*

Mills then heard Boyd call out *"Sarah, come here I will not hurt a hair of your head."* Sarah stopped for about a second but then noticed Boyd was carrying a knife, so she again fled and went into the Wrights house. George Mills reported that it was at this time that he observed Boyd having *"cross-words"* with the Superintendent, his brother-in-law James Wright, and making two or three passes with the knife at him. Wright, with Robert following him brandishing the knife, managed to escape when Boyd stumbled.

Boyd then came across James Stewart who was about to mount his horse, and ride to the main house to get assistance from Sir William Macarthur. Boyd pulled Stewart from his horse and said *"Mr. Stewart you are a nice young fellow"* and stabbed him on the left side of his chest penetrating the heart.

George Mills and James Wright were horrified, and Mills offered Boyd's guns to the overseer so that he might protect himself. Wright refused the guns and ran to his house to protect his wife in the fear that Boyd may go there. Boyd first went in the direction of Stony Range[5] changed his mind, and then turned towards Wright's house and went in the front door. He was prevented from entering the room where the Wrights and Sarah Johnson were, as Wright had barricaded the door whilst his wife and Sarah escaped through the window.

Boyd left the Wrights house by the back door and went first to where Stewart lay, and then went into his own home. It was here that Boyd cut his own throat in the presence of his wife. Augusta's clothes were covered in blood. He then staggered back to Stewart's body and dropped the knife before going to Avery's house. Sir William Macarthur arrived together with John McMahon[6] and told George Mills and his brother to secure him. Boyd offered considerable resistance, but the Mills were able to subdue him and brought him out and placed him on the verandah.

---

[3] Arnold was the Innkeeper at the Plough and Harrow Inn in Argyle Street
[4] Evidence at the inquest – reported SMH, Monday 15th January 1872 and Sydney Gazette 12th January 1872
[5] *Stony Range* or Stony Hill is the ridge on the south side of the private road of *Camden Park* estate, where there were a number of cottages.
[6] John McMahon had arrived as a convict on the *Blenheim* in 1834 and worked for William Macarthur at *Camden Park*. William Macarthur referred to him as "my own trusty right hand." In 1850 he set up his own nursery at Elderslie and was a frequent visitor to Camden Park.

Dr. Edwin[7] Chisholm had been sent for, and arrived about 40 minutes later, and first checked on James Stewart before examining Boyd's wound, and stitching it. Boyd was left on the verandah and died approximately 15 minutes after having the wound stitched. At the inquest, Dr. Chisholm deposed *"the deceased had been labouring for some considerable time from disease of the brain, which rendered him liable to violent exhibitions of temper under the least excitement, so that he would not be conscious of what he was doing."*

As Robert Boyd had committed suicide Church law forbade his burial in consecrated ground. Captain Arthur Onslow M.L.A[8] prevailed on the rector Rev. Henry Tingcombe to let him be buried alongside his three infant children and thereby allow the family to rest together. Boyd was buried without ceremony, and without his burial being recorded in the Church's Burial Register, alongside his young son and daughters.

Augusta went to live with her daughter Mary Ann and son-in-law John Edward Thornton in Redfern. On her death on 16th October 1884 Augusta was buried alongside her husband. The unmarked graves are located in Section A063 alongside the marked graves of their young children A062.

---

[7] Dr. Edwin Chisholm had his practice on the corner of Argyle and John Streets on the site for the present Commonwealth Bank
[8] SMH, Wednesday, 10th January 1872

James Stewart - courtesy Wikitree

Grave of James Stewart - courtesy John Wrigley

Lives Lost Too Soon

Many that lie within the Cemetery had their lives cut short due to accidents, their stories gleaned from newspaper reports of the time. The newspaper reports in some instances give a full account of the Coroner's enquiry thus giving us a greater understanding of how the incident unfolded. These are particularly valuable as Coroner's reports for the mid 1800s are not available.

When we look at some of the accidents that occurred and the resulting deaths, it seems inconceivable to us today that lives could not have been saved. We need to understand progresses that have occurred in medicine. Before 1846 anaesthesia as we know it today was unknown. Doctors operated using alcohol, morphine and other sedatives to dull the pain of surgery but most patients were held or strapped down, some fainted from the agony and many died. Additionally, many were to die of infection, as penicillin was not available until the 1940s when Howard Florey and Ernst Chain isolated the active ingredient and developed a powdery form of the medicine. With no effective treatment for infection, many died from a simple cut.

Many were also to die as a result of traumatic blood loss as a result of an accident or problems resulting from childbirth. Why couldn't they have been saved with a blood transfusion we may ask? Whilst blood transfusion had first been attempted in 1492 it resulted in the death of the patient and the donors. It was not until 1818 that Dr. James Blundell, a British obstetrician, performed the first successful blood transfusion of human blood. But many patients died and it was not until 1901, when an Austrian, Karl Landsteiner, discovered human blood groups that blood transfusions became safer. It was not until the 1910s doctors discovered that by adding anticoagulant and refrigerating the blood it was possible to store it for some days, thus opening the way for blood banks. The first non-direct transfusion was performed on 27th March, 1914 by the Belgian doctor Albert Hustin, using sodium citrate as an anticoagulant. The first blood transfusion using blood that had been stored and cooled was performed on 1st January, 1916.[1]

Jeremiah Martin
Many accidents occurred on the road such as the one suffered by Jeremiah Martin[2] from Gundagai. On Friday 28th December 1849 a carrier, Jeremiah Martin, was travelling from Sydney to the Murrumbidgee via Camden with a load of goods *"belonging to several persons."* He was passing through Camden when he attempted to leap on to the pole of his bullock dray and fell. One of the wheels of the dray passed over him *"fracturing one leg and contusing the trunk of the body."* Martin was killed instantly and is buried in an unmarked grave in Section C029.

William Boyd
William Boyd, the eldest son of Richard Boyd and Sarah Higgins was born at *Camden Park* 13th May 1824 and at an early age went to work with his father in the stables of the *Home Farm*[3] becoming a groom and horse breaker.

On 13th January 1849 the James Macarthur had William charged with misconduct and neglect of work, and he was brought before the Police Court. A valuable mare had been injured whilst being broken in, and although William claimed in court *"it was an accident"* James Macarthur stated he had repeatedly cautioned William about his neglect of work, and his drinking habits, to no effect.

---

[1] "A Short History of Blood Transfusion" – Phil Learoyd - Scientific & Technical Training Manager, Lead DDR, Leeds Blood Centre

[2] News from a Country Village, Camden 1847-52 – Reports made by Charles Tompson Jnr. to the SMH 5th January 1850

[3] Home Farm was also known as Camden Park Farm and as Belgenny Farm.

William was sentenced to 6 weeks in Parramatta Gaol and discharged from his position at *Camden Park*. After he had completed his sentence William returned to the *Home Farm* and continued to live with his parents.

On 9th October 1849 he married Jane Wright, the 15 year old daughter of Samuel Wright and Ann Dimmer. There were 2 children of this marriage, Alice born on 10th February 1848 and Sarah Ann, born on 22nd September 1850 but died on 8th November 1850. Tragically William and Jane's marriage was short-lived.

William received serious injuries on Friday, 7th June 1850 after he was thrown from his horse. The Sydney Morning Herald reporting[4] Boyd

> *"...was lately thrown from his horse, which reared and fell on the top of him—concussion of the brain was produced by the fall, and the poor fellow never recovered, although all was done for him which circumstances rendered possible; he died in about forty-eight hours, having remained in the interval in a state of rigidity."*

William died Sunday, 9th June 1850 and was buried in Section E067. His infant daughter Sarah Ann was later buried beside him. His wife, so tragically widowed soon after her marriage, went to live with her parents at Cobbitty Paddocks. On 4th April 1855 Jane married James Hawes and left the Camden district.

Elias Casson and his family

Elias Casson was born on 28th January 1826 in Broughton-in-Furness, Lancashire, England and had worked as a farm labourer prior to departing Plymouth on the 18th June 1851 on the *Earl Grey* and arriving on 15th October 1851. On 10th December 1851 he married Catherine Gillespie, whom he had met on the voyage at St. James Sydney.

He was employed by the Macarthurs and worked as a Dairy Supervisor at *Camden Park* where their first daughter Margaret was born on 27th September 1852. Two years later on the 26th January 1854 a second daughter, Catherine Gillespie Casson, was born. Just 8 days later the mother Catherine died on the 3rd February 1854 as a result of complications following the birth, and 2 months later on 24th March 1854, baby Catherine also died.

Tragedy had not yet finished with this family. On 20th May 1854 Casson was killed in an accident at *Camden Park*. Elias, his wife, and baby daughter are buried in an unmarked grave in Section E120. The surviving daughter, Margaret, was raised by the Macarthur family and in 1875 married Francis John Coker at Waterloo.

Thomas Watson

Thomas Watson, who was born on 2nd February 1824 in Brede, Sussex, the son of William Watson and Jane Hicks, had arrived in Sydney with his parents and siblings on the *Florist* on 26th October 1839. On 4th April 1848 he married Mary Ann Eleanor Watkins at Narellan.

Watson worked as a carrier for Mr. Thompson of Camden. About 4:00 pm on 3rd April 1865 Thompson and Watson were driving bullock wagons laden with hay through Liverpool with Watson in charge of the second team. Watson, who had been working the previous night, was feeling fatigued and rather than walk beside the wagon chose to ride on the shaft. He fell from the shaft landing in such a position that both wheels of the wagon passed over his legs just above the knees inflicting serious crushing injuries and severing the artery.[5] Doctors Nind and Smith were quickly on the scene but were unable to save his life; he is buried in Section D028.

---

[4] SMH 5th July 1850
[5] "Liverpool" SMH 5th April 1865

His wife Mary Ann Eleanor known as Ellen and her 9 children moved to Rockhampton, Queensland where she married William Langworthy Wilton on 11th September 1875. Ellen was to suffer another tragic loss when her husband William fell into a saw at the saw mill on 25th May 1883 and bled to death on the way to hospital. She returned to Sydney with her son Henry and his family and died at Petersham on 25th August 1886 and is buried next to Thomas Watson in Section D029.

John Tickner

One of the more unusual deaths was that of John Tickner born in East Guildford, Surrey c.1819 the son of Edward Tickner and Sarah Towner and baptized at East Guildford on 21st March 1819. Twenty years later he married Mary Ann Morris on 21st March 1836. Tickner and his wife sailed from Plymouth on the *Florist* on 29th June 1839 together with his parents and six of his brothers and sisters, and arrived on 26th October 1839. During the voyage their daughter Eliza Florist was born on 24th September 1839.

Edward Tickner

The Tickner family were employed by the Macarthurs as shepherds and shearers. John Tickner later obtained a clearing lease at Cawdor originally known as *Richfield* and by 1854 had leased additional land. By the 1st July 1866 Tickner's land holdings included *Richfield* 320 acres (129.5 hectares), *Funnell's Farm* 375 acres (151.8 hectares), and another farm west of *Funnell's Farm* 492 acres (199.1 hectares). He also leased additional land to the south on the Razorback Range known as *Camberfield*;[6] portion of this property had originally been reserved as Church and school land.

On 9th March 1875 Tickner came to an untimely end after drinking carbolic acid which he had mistaken for gin. He had put carbolic acid in an old gin bottle and been using it to clean his cattle[7] sheds. He came into the house carrying the bottle with his hands still smelling of the carbolic acid and placed it on the table. Feeling thirsty and wishing to rid his mouth of the taste, he decided to take a swig of gin but inadvertently picked up the bottle of carbolic acid. He took just one mouthful before he realised his mistake and died within 15 minutes and is buried in Section D088. His son in law, Frederick Dengate, later purchased the property and named it *Mount Hercules*.

Benjamin Weeks

Another unusual accident involved Benjamin Weeks who was born in March 1812 in Sixpenny, Handley Dorset the son of John Weeks and Diana Hayter. On 17th October 1836 he married Frances Jeans before arriving in Sydney on 8th April 1837 with his extended family on the *Brothers*. Weeks and other members of the family worked at *Camden Park* before moving to a farm at Cawdor and later to Kimber near Hovell's Creek in the Burrowa Shire.

At the time of his death Weeks was visiting family whom he hadn't seen for about 20 years in the Camden area and was staying with his niece Esther and her husband Robert Johnson at Cobbitty Paddocks.[8] On Friday, 27th February 1885 they were visiting his nephew George, a carter in Camden and Weeks went out for a walk quite late in the evening. When he hadn't

---

[6] A plateau at the top of old Razorback, the name "*Camberfield*" was presumably chosen because of a Tickner connection with the town of Camber in Surrey
[7] Campbelltown Camden Times March 1875
[8] "Bounty Immigrants from Dorset – Weeks" by John W. Weeks

Benjamin Weeks

returned by 10:30 pm, his niece and her husband enquired for him at the hotels, without success and then went home.

Not long afterwards Weeks returned to his nephew's home. George told the Coroner's Inquest that his uncle appeared sober and had told him he had been to the Wesleyan Chapel and on hearing that his niece and her husband had left for home in their cart said he would walk back.

Weeks however then decided to stay in town and went to the Plough and Harrow[9] and asked for lodging. The proprietor, John Arnold, told the Court that he had looked in on Weeks at 11:30 pm and he was in bed and appeared to be asleep. The next morning, the 28th February 1885, 14 year old William Taplin was on his way to take care of George Weeks' horses when he found Benjamin Weeks dead on the footpath.

The inquest returned a verdict of accidental death and concluded that at some time during the evening he had woken and decided to sit on the windowsill of his room to get some air, had gone to sleep and fallen from the window of the Plough and Harrow Inn and died instantly.[10] He is buried in Section E078.

Jennings Starr

One cause of death common to a number in the cemetery is *"killed by a falling tree."* One such incident took the life of Jennings Starr the son of William Starr and Elizabeth Arnold, who had emigrated from Mountfield Sussex and arrived on the *Orient* on 4th April 1839. He was born at Cooks River 13th March 1843 and on 1st November 1871 married Sarah Elizabeth Young at Menangle. Jennings worked as a labourer, farmer and sleeper cutter, and on 1st May 1889 he was killed at Mt. Gilead, Menangle whilst felling a tree, supposedly to obtain some honey high in the tree. He is buried in an unmarked grave in Section C049.

William Hall

Another killed by a falling tree was William Hall born c.1828 the son of David Hall and Mary. In 1852 he married Margaret McCulloch at Kincumber near Gosford. Not much more is known about him other than he died 7th May 1868 and is buried in Section D158. His headstone contains a touching tribute from his wife *"The hue of his cheek and lips decayed, aroud his mouth a sweet smile played, they looked and he was dead."*

Thomas Cranfield

Thomas Cranfield the son of William Cranfield and Mary Ann Gittoes was born at Spring Creek on 30th March 1846 and on 21st May 1879 married Mary Dawson. Cranfield, a dairy farmer, lived at Mount Hunter and was a keen follower of the local hunt.

---

[9] The Plough and Harrow was later renamed the Argyle Inn
[10] SMH — 2nd March 1855 and Burrowa News 6th March 1855

On Thursday 27th August 1897 Cranfield had ridden into Camden accompanied by his son Arthur and Walter McLeod, leading one of his hunters which he intended to use the horse in the hunt on Saturday. The group were returning home at about 10 pm along The Oaks Road with Cranfield cantering about 30 yards (27.4 metres) ahead of the others. The snaffle bit on Cranfield's horse broke causing him to lose control of the horse.

Cranfield was thrown onto a stony portion of the road and was unconscious when his companions reached him. Walter McLeod rode to obtain medical help. Dr. John Morton reached the injured man after midnight. He was conveyed to Carrington Hospital and despite surgical intervention Thomas died on Friday 28th August 1897 from a fractured skull and bleeding and pressure on the brain.[11] He is buried in Section C097.

Thomas Cranfield

Robert Henry Druitt
Robert Henry Druitt was born in Sydney on 21st January 1850 the son of Venerable Archdeacon Thomas Druitt and Helena Clementina Shaw. He spent his early life in the Monaro and was schooled at home. He was interested in farming and for many years he managed Mr. Bennett's estates at *May Farm,* Oaklands where he was responsible for the construction of The Oaklands Creamery. On 6th May 1885 he married Emma Wallworth Goldsmith at *Kameruka* Bega. After he left *May Farm* he was employed by *Camden Park* as Farm Manager.

He was involved in the Anglican Churches in Camden and at The Oaks and was instrumental in the building of a new church at The Oaks. At St. John's Camden he held the positions of Sidesman, Parochial Nominator, and Synod Representative and worked on various sub-committees. He took a keen interest in the Westbrook[12] Church, part of the Camden Anglican Parish, and was one of the chief movers in adding the chancel and vestry and together with his wife purchased the organ.[13]

Druitt was also involved with many activities in the community including serving as Treasurer of the Camden Progress Association, on the committee for the Camden A.H. & I. Society, a member of Abbotsford Lodge and early in 1899 elected as an Alderman on Camden Council.

On Saturday the 30th September 1899 he was gored by a Guernsey bull known as Rose Prince.[14] The accident happened in a small paddock adjoining the Farm Manager's residence at *Camden Park*. The bull had been leased by the estate from the Agricultural Department for stud purposes and Druitt and two farmhands, James Wheeler and John Gillespie, led the bull from the stalls to the paddock and released him from the two nose rings. As Druitt turned to leave the paddock the bull gored him in the back, with a horn penetrating the right shoulder blade and extending to the lungs. The bull continued in its attack turning Druitt over and over until the fence was reached and James Wheeler was able to reach under and drag Druitt clear.

---

[11] "Fatal Riding Accident in Camden" Camden News 3rd September 1896
[12] Now known as Mt. Hunter
[13] "Obituary – Alderman Robert Henry Druitt, J.P. ÆAT 49" – Camden News 6th October 1899
[14] "Death of Alderman R.H. Druitt, J.P. of Camden – Gored By a Bull – Great Public Sympathy" – Camden News 6th October 1899

Druitt told those assisting him that he was bleeding internally so they carried him into his house on a sheet of corrugated iron where his wife telephoned Dr. Morton. After seeing his condition Dr. Morton administered a restorative and then called Dr. Bell to seek assistance. Together they administered an anaesthetic and attended to the wound but the injury was fatal and Druitt died about midday. He is buried in Section B112. Emma Wallworth Druitt died aged 87 years on 17th July 1938 and is buried beside her husband.

Dorothea Campbell

Not all the accidents happened to men. Dorothea Earl was born at sea in 1823, the daughter of John Earl and Annie Moonsey. The family arrived on the *Thalia* on 18th June 1823 and first settled in the Maitland district.[15] Dorothea married Captain Henry Augustus Lyle Richards in Maitland and after his death in 1850 came to Camden with her young family.

On 19th August 1852 she married James Campbell then farming at Mount Hunter. The family later moved to Elderslie and in 1900 she was visiting her daughter Annie Wheeler the wife of Samuel Wheeler, at Mount Hunter when she fell down the steps and sustained a fracture of the hip bone. From that time Dorothea was bedridden and never fully recovered from the accident. She died 30th September 1901 and is buried in Section A056.

Richard Mitchell

Accidents on the road were common. Richard Mitchell was born at Bargo on 5th March 1856, the son of Richard Mitchell and Jane Roffe, and on 15th September 1886 married Mary Ann Tomkins.

Mitchell, a wood carter, was described as a man of sober habits, and his horses were quiet and easily managed. On Friday 24th March 1903 he left home with his team of three horses and two drays to bring wood from Spring Creek but was brought home about 2:30 pm after having been kicked by the lead horse when he had struck it on the rump with the handle of his whip.

Mitchell had received the full force of both hind feet so Dr. West was called and found that Mitchell was suffering from shock and a state of partial collapse. The doctor applied the usual remedies, and returned at 8:00 pm and found Mitchell practically free from pain, but ever cautious warned his wife of the possible seriousness of her husband's condition.

Dr. West called again at 10:00 am on Saturday 25th March 1903 and finding Mitchell's condition had deteriorated had him taken to Camden Hospital where he died within 10 minutes of his admission. He is buried in Section C153. A post mortem examination established the cause of death as *"shock following peritonitis from the rupture of the gut."* [16]

Thomas Bryant

Thomas Bryant was born in Bodmin, Cornwall in 1832 the son of Walter Bryant and Mary and was just 9 years old when the family arrived on the *Earl Grey* on 24th June 1841 as assisted immigrants. By the time he married Sarah Elizabeth Drury in Sydney in 1857 Bryant had a dairy farm at Brownlow Hill.

On 11th February 1906 he went on horseback to put some cattle into a paddock whilst his sons were in the milking yard. Shortly after, the sons witnessed the horse returning home without its rider and went to the paddock and found him lying face down near a wire fence.[17] Bryant had head injuries indicating he had either fallen or been thrown from his horse and died as a result.

---

[15] "Obituary – Mrs. Dorothea" - Camden News 3rd October 1901
[16] "Fatal Kick by a Horse" – Camden News 2nd April 1903
[17] "Death of an Old Farmer" Camden Times 15th February 1906

Investigation indicated the horse had run into the wire fence and either fallen or thrown the rider. The Coroner delivered a verdict of accidental death. Bryant is buried in Section B143.

James Small

James Small was born at Cawdor on 16th September 1858 the son of James Small and Mary Ann Haddon. In 1897 James, who held the rank of Quarter-master Sergeant in the Camden Mounted Rifles, went to Queen Victoria's Diamond Jubilee in London with several other members including Astley John Onslow Thompson, Arthur John Onslow, John Hawkey and Henry Taplin.

On Tuesday, 14th August 1906[18] Small was bringing a wagon load of hay from Camden to Theresa Park and was going down an incline when he attempted to apply the brakes on the wagon. He lost his foothold and fell and the wheels of the laden wagon passed over the lower portion of his body. Severely injured he was taken to Camden Hospital for surgery but died at 8:00 pm the same day. Small was accorded a military funeral and is buried in Section D142.

George Frederick Heighington

George Frederick Heighington was born in County Sligo, Ireland about 1855 and arrived as an assisted immigrant on the *Northbrook* on 10th March 1878. He lived with his wife Jane at *Camden Park* where he worked as a labourer.

He was normally in good health but was described as being stout and suffering from asthma.[19] On the night of 9th August 1909 he and his wife had gone to bed early and his wife "*heard him make a peculiar gurgling noise.*" Thinking he was snoring she told him not to, but when he did not answer became concerned. Unable to waken him, and thinking he may be having a fit, she called her son Edward and Dr. West. The doctor proclaimed his death at 3:00 am on 10th August 1909 as a result of cerebral haemorrhage. He is buried in Section D164.

Keith Angelo Tornaghi

Gun accidents were also common and such an accident took the life of 22 year old Keith Angelo Tornaghi, the son of Leoni Angelo Tornaghi and Gladys Muriel Hughes grandson of Edward Hughes and great grandson of Ellen Rosetta McMullen.

On the evening of 6th January 1936 he went out to shoot rabbits with a shotgun borrowed from his neighbour Thomas Farrell of Douglas Park. Farrell had heard shooting until shortly after 8:00 pm when it appears Tornaghi decided to return home and whilst getting through a fence held the gun in his left hand near the end of the barrel. The gun accidently discharged, shooting him in the region of his heart.

He was found the next morning not far from the farm buildings lying face down with one leg on each side of the fence and his body on the bottom rail. The District Coroner A. E. Baldock returned a verdict of accidental death due to the careless use of a firearm[20] and Tornaghi was buried in the Hughes Vault in Section A010.

William Leslie Critchley

Not all those who are buried in the cemetery lived in the district or had known connections with Camden. William Leslie Critchley was born in Sydney in 1893 the son of George Critchley and Mary Emily. He lived with his mother at Summer Hill and worked as a labourer at Toohey's Brewery in Sydney.

---

[18] Camden News 16th August 1906
[19] "Inquest" – Camden News 12th August 1909
[20] "Accidental Death – Inquest on Death of K.A. Tornaghi" – Camden News, 23rd January, 1936.

Lives Lost Too Soon

At 2:30 pm on Saturday 22nd June 1912 he left home to go rabbit shooting at Menangle in company with Charles Prior, Norman Hartridge, Clarence Jones and Percy Allen. They arrived at Menangle at about 4:35 pm and he decided to put a couple of cartridges in the double breech loading shotgun he was carrying, thinking he might get a shot in before sundown. He swung a tucker bag and the group had only gone about 600 yards (5486 metres) when Critchley stopped and placed the gun on his left foot, intending to transfer the tucker bag to the other shoulder.[21]

His friends heard the dull report of a gun and saw him lying on the ground, on his back, with his shirt front on fire and a large wound in the right side of the neck. One of his friends ran to Henry (known as Dusty)[22] English's place, about 50 yards (45.7 metres) to ask for assistance. English rang the Police and the Dr. West before going to the accident scene.

Samuel Hughes from Douglas Park came along in his car and it was decided that rather than wait he should take Critchley to Camden Hospital Shortly after Hughes came across Dr. West and Sergeant Schwarer near Menangle where the doctor examined the victim and decided that Hughes should continue to the hospital and he would follow with the police sergeant. Critchley died about 8:00 pm the same day and is buried in Section C068. His funeral was a large one, and his coffin was the first to pass through the new Lych Gate.[23]

Thomas James Rossitter
Sometimes even a simple accident could have fatal results. Thomas James Rossitter was born in 1857 the son of Thomas Rossitter and Mary, and married Cecilia Boland at Cobar in 1899. He lived at The Oaks where he had an auctioneering and commission agency dealing principally with livestock. He also held the important position as Valuator and Sanitary Inspector for the Wollondilly Shire Council.[24]

On 22nd April 1914 Rossitter fell over a bit of metal in Argyle Street, Camden injuring one of his ankles and as the injury involved a deep laceration was conveyed to Camden Hospital. At the time of his accident there was no effective treatment for tetanus as tetanus vaccinations were not available until about 1924. He died of tetanus on 25th April 1914 and is buried in Section D138.

---

[21] "Shooting Fatality" – Camden News 27th June 1912
[22] Len English a nephew of Henry English and a member of Camden Historical Society
[23] Lych gate, (from Old English *lic*, corpse) is a gateway covered with a roof found at the traditional entrance to a (British) churchyard.
[24] Camden News 23rd April 1914 and 30th April 1914

Frederick Nixon

Frederick Nixon was born in Goulburn in 1852, the son of William Nixon and Eliza Smith and came to Camden in 1899 with his wife Elizabeth Batty. He worked on the *Kirkham* estate and

Frederick Nixon and his team in Argyle Street circa 1910 – from the Dick Nixon collection

was highly respected throughout the Camden and Yerranderie districts.[25] On Monday 8th March 1920 at 8:00 pm he was driving one of three wagons heavily laden with provisions and goods[26] along the Oaks Road towards Yerranderie in company with Frederick John Sheldrick and Frederick George Sheldrick. Nixon was with the rear wagon drawn by 11 horses with a load of about two tons (1.8 tonnes).[27]

There was no provision for seating on the wagons so teamsters would walk or ride beside, but Nixon was known on occasions to ride on the shaft, a dangerous practice. Near the camping ground at The Oaks Nixon slipped and fell from the shaft of the wagon and the wheels passed over his arm and feet. He called for help and fortunately Frederick John Sheldrick was only about 400 yards (363.8 metres) ahead and sent Walter Smith, who was travelling with him to find out what was wrong.

On hearing of the accident Sheldrick went to Nixon's aid and sent Smith to The Oaks where after phoning Dr. West to advise him of the accident a car was obtained from Hennessy's Hotel driven by Arthur Seymour. Accompanied by Constable Campbell from The Oaks, Seymour drove Nixon to Camden Hospital.

Dr. West advised the Coroner that Nixon was suffering from a severely lacerated and crushed right hand and arm and despite treatment gangrene developed. The next day the doctor was obliged to amputate just below the shoulder but the gangrene spread and septicaemia set in. Nixon died, aged 68 years on 11th March 1920 and is buried in Section E094.

The Coroner concluded that despite being sober Nixon had fallen from the shaft of his wagon and noted that Nixon had fallen from his wagon only a few months prior to this accident but had escaped injury. The Sheldricks told the Coroner they had on several occasions warned him that it was dangerous to sit on the shafts whilst travelling but he had not heeded the warning.

---

[25] Report on Coroner's Inquest into the death of Frederick Nixon – Camden News 18th March 1920
[26] Camden News 11th March 1920
[27] Coroner's Inquest, Camden News 18th March 1920

Gladys May Shoobridge

Another tragedy was to unfold in Camden on 26th May 1920. Gladys May Tritton was born in Camden in 1899 the daughter of Albert Robert Tritton and Mary Elizabeth Tarman. On 3rd December 1919 Gladys married Robert Shoobridge and they lived in Mitchell Street Camden with her parents. On the evening of 26th May at about 7:30 pm Gladys was sitting in the dining room singing her baby son to sleep when her husband came into the room and an argument developed.

According to evidence given at the Coroner's Inquest, the day before Gladys told her husband she had taken a bad turn and had been to see Dr. West who had recommended a special diet. Shoobridge purchased the special food for her, but subsequently visited Dr. West enquiring about his wife's health. The doctor denied having seen Gladys recently, stating that he had *"only seen his wife once, and that was some weeks before, when I told her of her condition."* What condition Gladys was in was not made clear but her mother stated that her daughter *"often imagined she could see things that were never there."* [28]

Shoobridge confronted his wife and an argument developed. Her mother heard something break before the light went out followed by *"a dull thud and a gurgling sound."* Mrs. Tritton went into the dining room holding a light and found her daughter sitting at a chair at the table with her head back and her throat cut. She saw the husband looking for something under the table before he jumped up and ran out the backdoor and then cut his own throat.

Mrs. Tritton ran to the front door and called to her son Thomas who slept next door to get the police. Thomas ran towards the police station and met his sister Florence on the way and sent her to get the police while he fetched their father. He found Albert Tritton at the stables feeding his horses and told him the horrifying news.

Dr. West advised the Coroner that Gladys had died instantly but Shoobridge was still alive when he arrived at the house. He treated Shoobridge and tried to stem the blood loss before having him taken to Camden Hospital where he died the same evening. Gladys May Shoobridge is buried in Section C148 in an unmarked grave and her husband is buried in Camden General Cemetery.

Bertie Stewart Gunn

Bertie Stewart Gunn was born in Camden in 1906 the son of William George Gunn and Agnes Jane Thom. On Wednesday 10th February 1926 19 year old Gunn, an employee of the Metropolitan Water Board, and his mate John Donohue, were engaged in laying the new water main along the Main Southern Road[29] between Narellan and Camden.[30] In the mid-afternoon the men had stopped for a break and while Donohue had the billy on the boil Gunn began skylarking around tossing small pebbles at him. Donohue remarked *"If you shoot one in the billy, I will throw this tea over you."*[31]

A stone did fall into the billy and Gunn realizing Donohue would make good his threat took off out of the way of the mug of tea. He was watching Donohue not the road and his companions had no opportunity to warn him. The bus travelling between Sydney and Goulburn was passing at the time and whilst it was only travelling at 25 miles an hour (40.2 kms) the driver, Horace Gray, had no time to avoid him and he was struck heavily and died shortly after in Camden Hospital. He is buried in Section D069.

---

[28] "Tragedy at Camden - Murder and Suicide" Camden News 3rd June 1920
[29] Now Camden Valley Way
[30] "Fatal Accident – Mr. Bert Gunn Killed by Motor Bus" Camden News 11th February 1926
[31] Campbelltown News 26th February 1926

William Arthur Channell
One of the more unusual accidents occurred in 1935.

William Arthur Channell was born on 22nd May 1880 on the farm opposite the *Camden Park* lodge gates the son of John Channell and Winifred Elizabeth Humphries. William was the third generation of the Channell family to be connected with *Camden Park*, where his father was a tenant farmer, and he worked as a labourer. On 29th May 1901 William married Alice Matilda Veness the daughter of William Veness and Eliza Smart.

The knock-off bell at Belgenny Farm today

For years it had been the custom to ring a large bell weighing 165 pounds (74.8 kgs), which was on a 20ft 6in (6.3 metre) high post, to call employees to and from work. On Friday, 15th February 1935 William was ringing the signal for knock-off time at noon when the heavy bell fell to the ground striking him, inflicting such serious injuries to his head and body that he died in the Camden District Hospital the following day.

Robert William Murdoch, a general farm hand, told the inquest that as he turned the corner he saw William ringing the bell; "he rang it twice and then the bell collapsed; he never made any move to get away; there was absolutely no warning; the bell seemed to hit his head, and as he hit the ground the bell somersaulted off."

Sergeant Porteus of Camden Police made an inspection of the bell and advised the Coroner that although the post had been repaired on 7th July 1934 in his opinion the post was not strong enough for the bell and in addition the post was quite weather worn. It appeared that the bolt holding the shackle to the post had been hanging loose in the socket.

The Coroner, A. E. Baldock, J.P. returned a verdict of misadventure and commented on the state of the post and said "*Had precaution been taken in this regard this unfortunate man may not have lost his life.*"[32] William Arthur Channell is buried in Section C168. The knock off bell is now atop a brick pillar in the farm square as a memorial to William Arthur Channell.

---

[32] Camden News 21st February 1935

Rev Thomas Henry Druitt and family, 1856 - photographer William Hetzer
L to R: Charles b.1848, Georgiana b.1853, Mrs Helena Druitt, Thomas b.1846, Robert b.1850, Rev Thomas Druitt, and Helena b.1851

Dr Crookston's House, 75 John Street
Said to have been built for Mr Robert Druitt, Overseer, of Camden Park in 1880s

Lest We Forget

The men and women of Camden have served their country in many conflicts, including the Boer War, World War I, World War II, Vietnam, and more recently the Middle East. Many lost their lives and are buried on foreign shores, others returned home to Camden. The memorial in Macarthur Park lists those who lost their lives, but in some cases family members have placed memorial plaques on family graves to honour them. A small Roll of Honour inside St. John's Church also acknowledges those who were members of the church and lost their lives during World War I and World War II.

Memorial Plaque to Brigadier General George Macleay Macarthur Onslow

In a number of cases the involvement of those who served their country but have died since the War are also acknowledged on their gravestones. It is not possible to recognize the military service of all those who have served this country in times of war and are buried in the churchyard. This has only been possible where military service is acknowledged on a memorial or gravestone within the church or churchyard.

As well as the Roll of Honour, the following memorials can be found within the church. The fourth window on the southern side in St. John's is a memorial to those who lost their lives during World War I whilst the third window on the north side is dedicated to the memory of Brigadier General George Macleay Macarthur-Onslow

On the northern side, near the electric organ, can be found a plaque dedicated to Brigadier General George Macleay Macarthur-Onslow by the 7th Light Horse. In conjunction with the memorial plaque the 7th Light Horse also donated the floodlighting for the front of the church.

The Roll of Honour contains the following names and inscription –

    Capt. A.W. Macarthur-Onslow
    Lieut Col. A.J. Onslow-Thompson
    Lce. Sgt. F.H. Paul
    Ser. Rex Smith
    Corp. Hector Small
    L.Corp. Eric Lowe
    James Clarke
    John Poole
    Sydney Brain
    Richard Hawkey
    Vivian Gardner
    William Liversey
    Hilton Chesham
    Cecil Wheeler
    Father in Thy gracious keeping
    Leave we now Thy servants sleeping

Roll of Honour

Lest We Forget

Boer War

The Boer War has been called "the forgotten war." It took place between 1899 and 1902 and during this period six waves of small contingents were despatched from Australia to take part in the conflict, including a number from the Macarthur area. Of those with memorials within St. John's Church or buried in the churchyard or the private Cemetery at *Camden Park* are:-

> Arthur William Macarthur-Onslow
> Francis Arthur Macarthur-Onslow
> James William Macarthur-Onslow
> Reginald (Rex) Smith
> Carlton Smith

Apart from Francis Arthur Macarthur-Onslow, James William Macarthur-Onslow and Carlton Smith the service of these men are acknowledged under World War I.

Francis Arthur Macarthur-Onslow

Francis Arthur Macarthur-Onslow, known as Arthur,[1] was born at *Camden Park* on 7th June 1879 the youngest surviving son of Captain Arthur Alexander Walton Onslow R.N. and Elizabeth Macarthur. Following the death of Captain Onslow in 1882 Elizabeth took her surviving children to Europe for their education whilst she studied dairy farming. Arthur was educated at Rugby and Exeter College, Oxford.

On 29th April 1897 he was commissioned in the N.S.W. Mounted Rifles and was promoted to Lieutenant in July 1899. During the Boer War he was attached to the 7th Dragoon Guards and saw active service in Cape Colony, the Orange Free State and the Transvaal including the actions at Johannesburg, Diamond Hill and Belfast. He was awarded the Queen's Medal with 5 clasps.[2]

He returned to Australia in 1902 after recuperating in London from rheumatic fever and on 16th May 1903 married Sylvia Seton Raymond (nee Chisholm) in Goulburn. In 1907 he transferred to the officers' reserve and was placed on the retired list in 1919 with the rank of Lieutenant.

From 1916 he was a grazier at Macquarie Grove and was already a Director of *Camden Park* Estate Pty. Ltd., Camden Vale Milk Co., which became amalgamated with the Dairy Farmers' Co-operative Milk Co. He was a progressive farmer and in 1924 his herd was the only one in the State tested for tuberculosis.

Arthur was a keen racing man and had his own track and stud in Camden. He was a member of the Australian Jockey and Australian Clubs and a keen freemason; he also served as Mayor of Camden for three terms.

Lt. Francis Arthur Macarthur-Onslow in Camden Mounted Rifles uniform

---

[1] "Macarthur-Onslow, Francis Arthur (1879-1938) – G.P. Walsh – Australian Dictionary of Biography - Volume 10, Melbourne University Press, 1986, pp 196-198.
[2] "Macarthur-Onslow, James William (1867-1946)" – G. P. Walsh - Australian Dictionary of Biography - Volume 10, Melbourne University Press, 1986, pp 196-198.

After retiring as Managing Director of *Camden Park* Estate Pty. Ltd. he moved to the city and became involved in real estate. He died suddenly of a cerebral haemorrhage on 3rd March 1938 and is buried in the private cemetery at *Camden Park*.

James William Macarthur-Onslow

James William Macarthur-Onslow was born at *Camden Park* on 7th November 1867 the eldest son of Captain Arthur Alexander Walton Onslow R.N. and Elizabeth Macarthur and received his early education at Sydney Grammar School. After the death of his father in 1882 his mother took her surviving children to Europe for their education and he completed his studies at Trinity College, Cambridge and graduated in 1890 B.A. L.L.B.[3] He returned to Australia in 1891 and in February 1892 was commissioned Captain in the Camden Squadron of the N.S.W. Mounted Rifles.

In 1894 Major General (Sir) Edward Hutton selected him for special training in India with the 11th Hussars, the Royal Artillery, and the 1st Battalion King's Royal Rifle Corps, with which he served during the relief of Chitral. Following a coup d'état in Chitral which had cost the life of the ruling chief, there had been an attempt to drive out the British representative.[4] He saw active service in the Chitral campaign, and took part in the storming of Malakand Pass and also at Khar and received the Chitral Medal with the Malakand clasp for this action.

General James William Macarthur-Onslow

He returned to Camden in 1896, was promoted to Major, and in 1897 accompanied a detachment of Mounted Rifles to England for Queen Victoria's Diamond Jubilee celebrations. On 15th December 1897 he married his cousin, Enid Emma Macarthur, the daughter of Arthur Hannibal Macarthur.[5]

In 1898 he was promoted to Lieutenant-Colonel and during the Boer War went, at his own expense, as a Special Services Officer to Cape Town, arriving on 11th April 1900. After a period on the staff of the 7th Division he served as Aide-de-Camp to Major General (Sir) Edward Hutton from June until October 1900; then went to England before returning to Australia in March 1901. In July 1902 he returned to South Africa as Commanding Officer of the 5th Battalion of the Australian Commonwealth Horse. On his arrival he found the war had ended so he returned to Australia in August 1902 and was awarded the Queen's Medal with four clasps and was Mentioned in Dispatches.

He was appointed Aide-de-Camp to the Governor-General, and commanded the 2nd Light Horse Regiment from July 1903 until December 1907 when he was promoted Colonel in command of the 1st Light Horse Brigade. In 1907 he entered State Parliament as member for Waverley until 1913, and represented Bondi from 1913-1917 and Eastern Suburbs from 1920-1922.

---

[3] "Gen. Macarthur-Onslow Dead" Camden News Nov 1946
[4] "British Chitral Campaign 1895" Wars of the World
[5] "Macarthur-Onslow, James William (1867-1946) – G.P. Walsh - Australian Dictionary of Biography –Volume 10, Melbourne University Press, 1986, pp 196-198.

Between January 1910 and August 1915 he was on the unattached list, however after the outbreak of World War I obtained leave-of-absence as Member for Bondi and made several voyages in the Sea Transport Service of the A.I.F. between Australia, the Middle East and Britain as Officer-in-Command of Transports. After two years' service abroad he resumed his political duties. In 1917 he was again Aide-de-Camp to the Governor-General, and held this post until 1920.

In 1922 he was appointed to the Legislative Council and remained a member until the reconstitution of the chamber in 1922 when he retired from politics. On 7th November 1925 he was placed on the retired list with the honorary rank of Major-General.

He returned to his pastoral life living at *Camden Park*, after exchanging houses with his sister Sibella in 1931, and continued to promote the dairy industry. Sibella who had inherited *Camden Park* for life moved to *Gilbulla* which James had built at the turn of the 20th century. He inherited *Elizabeth Bay House*, Sydney from his great-uncle Sir William Macleay (this house would prove to be an enormous burden) and died at *Camden Park* on 17th November 1946. He is buried in the private cemetery at *Camden Park*.

Carlton Smith

Carlton Smith was born at Windsor in 1876 the son of John Julian Smith and Sophia Jane Gambrill. When he was still a child his family moved to Picton where he trained to be a landscape gardener.[6] He served with the 2nd N.S.W. Mounted Rifles in South Africa during the Boer War from 15th March 1901 to 4th June 1902. Following his return to Australia he married Alice Masters in 1903 and tried many avenues of employment including farming at Wyee, storekeeping on the North Shore, and dairy farming in Camden. When his sister, after her marriage, retired from her position as Postmistress at Thirlmere, he became Postmaster. He built a new Post Office at his own expense as the old one was inadequate, and did shoe repairs on the side to help make ends meet. In 1919 he became seriously ill as a result of an old spinal injury and died on 24th April 1919 and is buried in an unmarked grave in Section D020.

Carlton Smith - photo courtesy Camden Remembers

World War I

John George Adams the son of George John Adams and Jane Cuthel was born at Werombi on 29th October 1888 and is described as being "*5 foot 9 inches (1.8 metres) tall, of rosy complexion with blue eyes and brown hair*".[7] He enlisted in the 1st Light Horse Regiment on 30th August 1915 and departed for the front on *RMS Osterley* on 15th January 1916. On 5th August 1918 he was gassed whilst serving on the western front. He returned home on 20th October 1919 and married Ann Butler in 1922. He worked in the coal mines until 1927 when ill health, miner's disease,[8] forced him out of the mines. Miner's disease occurs when miners breathe in large amounts of coal dust in relatively enclosed spaces placing them at risk of developing respiratory diseases which can lead to serious disability. The fact that Adams had been gassed during the war would have exacerbated the condition. Coal dust can irritate the sensitive tissues of the lung and lead to the development of diseases such as pneumoconiosis, emphysema and chronic bronchitis.

---

[6] "The Forgotten Men of a Forgotten War" Colin Sproule
[7] "Service No. 2122 National Archives of Australia"
[8] "Obituary John George Adams" Camden News 10th March 1932

John George Adams

Adams then worked as a gardener at *Camelot* during the last 4 years of his life living in Kirkham Lane until his death as a result of pneumonia on 7th March 1932 aged 43 years. He is buried in Section D022.

Percy Sidney Raymond Brain

Percy Sidney Raymond Brain known as Sidney[9] was born in Menangle in 1894 the son of Thomas Charles Brain and Ellen Reynolds. He is described as being *"fair and 5 foot 8.5 inches (1.7 metres) high with brown hair and eyes"*.[10] He lived with his grandparents, William Brain and Sarah Foster in *Elderslie House* in Macarthur Road, Elderslie and worked as a general blacksmith in Camden. He enlisted in the 3rd Battalion A.I.F. and departed Sydney on *HMAT Euripides* on 2nd November 1915.

On 24th July 1915 he was with members of his battalion in a trench at Pozieres when a shell burst over them and they were buried. Whilst some members managed to dig themselves out Brain wasn't among them. He was buried at Villers-Bretonneux, France and is also remembered on the Roll of Honour.

Alexander Brien

Alexander Brien was born in 1888 the son of Henry William Brien and Martha Davis. He worked as telephone linesman prior to enlisting in the Army on 8th September 1915 as a Gunner in the 5th Field Artillery Brigade. Brien returned to Camden after the War and died aged 64 on 16th June 1952. He is buried in Section D108.

Cecil Clarence Butler

Cecil Clarence Butler was born at The Oaks on 16th March 1897 the son of Charles Butler and Lucy McLennon. He enlisted in the Army on 6th September 1915 and served in the 1st Light Horse Regiment. After the War he joined the family cycle shop business and died aged 90 on 18th March 1987. He is buried in Section C196.

Hilton John Chesham

Hilton John Chesham known as Gilly[11] was born in Camden in 1891 the son of John Chesham and Sarah Hoffmann. He enlisted on 18th July 1915 and sailed from Sydney on *HMAT Themistocles* as a Private in the 18th Battalion A.I.F. on 5th October 1915.

Together with Private Aubrey Payne he was recommended in 1917 for a Military Medal by Lieutenant Colonel G.F. Murphy and Brigadier General R. Smith, the recommendation stating -

These men showed great valour and devotion to duty in carrying a line forward and maintaining it through heavy shell and M.G. fire during the advance of Butte, Gird, Le Barque Switch and Halt Trenches – 24th to 27th February (sic, 1917). Although continually sniped at close range during the afternoon of the 25th February they maintained communication with the advancing companies. During the night 25/26th February when communication was most

The photo of the grave of Lance Corp. Hilton Chesham sent to his parents

---

[9] The Roll of Honour in St. John's lists him as "Sydney Brain"
[10] "Service No. 2580 National Archives of Australia"
[11] Camden News 6th June 1918

essential these men on their own initiative connected their phones to the wire in the barrage area so that they would be nearby when a break occurred. The barrage falling at the time consisted mainly of gas shells.[12]

Chesham was promoted to Lance Corporal but was killed in action in France on 14th May 1918 and was buried in Heilly Station Cemetery Mericourt-L'Abbe France. He is also remembered on the Roll of Honour.

James Coleman Clarke
James Coleman Clarke was born in Preston, Lancashire, England c.1886 the son of James C. Clarke and Annie, and educated at the Higher Walton Church of England School in Preston Lancashire England. He arrived in Australia about 1912 and worked for Butler's Coaches in Camden as a motor driver. Clarke enlisted in the 49th Battalion A.I.F. in December 1915 and departed Sydney on the *HMAT Star of Victoria* on 30th March 1916. He died of wounds in France on 12th August 1916 and was buried in the Eastern Cemetery, Boulogne, France. He is also remembered on the Roll of Honour

Lance Corp. James Coleman Clarke

Edward John Dengate
Edward John Dengate was born at Razorback on 5th January 1866, the son of Frederick James Dengate and Eliza Florist Tickner. He was raised on his father's farm *Mount Hercules* Razorback, and had some early dairying experience in Queensland. In 1888 he purchased property and built his own dairy *Oatenleigh* on the Cawdor side of *Mount Hercules*.[13] On 10th December 1889 he married Emma Boardman.

He joined the A.I.F. in 1914 and served in the 2nd Remount Unit, departing for the front on 10th November 1915 on *RMS Orontes*. After the war he continued to take a keen interest in local matters, particularly the Camden A.H. & I. Society and was Ring Steward for many years. Dengate died aged 78 on 8th May 1944. He is buried in Section D146.

Vivian Charles Gardner
Vivian Charles Gardner was born in Scone in 1896 the son of George Mitchell Gardner and Frances Jean. His family moved to Elderslie Camden in the early 1900s. Gardner is described as *"clean-minded a young fellow as ever went out of our district."*[14] He worked as a Music Teacher and for 4 years prior to enlisting was the organist for the Camden Methodist Church. He was one of the principal promoters of the Boy Scout movement and had been a Lieutenant in the local Cadets.

Prior to enlisting in the Army on 2nd July 1917 he had suffered a serious accident and was still recovering. Whilst the accident would have furnished him with an excuse for not enlisting he was not to be deterred and left Sydney on 31st October 1917 as part of the 54th Battalion A.I.F. He died at Villers-Bretonneux, France 19th April 1918 as a result of a gas attack and he was buried at

---

[12] "Service No 2342 National Archives of Australia"
[13] "Obituary – Mr. E.J. Dengate" Camden News 18th May 1944
[14] "The Late Cpl. V.C. Gardner – An Appreciation" Camden News 16th May 1918

St. Sever Cemetery Extension, Rouen. His memorial is on the family grave in Section A099 and he is also remembered on the Roll of Honour.

Victor Louis Bosker Haigh
Victor Louis Bosker Haigh was born in Kensington, London July 1883 whilst his mother Rosa nee Bosker was on a visit to England. His father Louis Haigh had remained in Australia to manage the family's business interests as well as fulfill his duties as Mayor of Liverpool, a position he held from 1880 to 1890. Having been born with a cleft pallet Victor did not thrive in his first few weeks, and was a sickly baby when he arrived in Australia in October 1883.

The family lived in "*Rosebank*" a stately home in Speed Street, Liverpool originally designed and built by Varney Parkes for his wife Mary Cameron Murray. Victor was schooled at home and in 1889 travelled to England with his mother and two sisters, where his mother gave birth to another daughter in July 1889. In February 1890 Rosa received the news that her husband had committed suicide, hanging himself in the stable at "*Rosebank*". It was thought he may have been suffering monetary difficulties but he left an estate worth £90,000, a sizeable amount. The bereaved wife and children returned to Australia in April 1890.

Victor completed his education at Scots College, Sydney before studying at Sydney University where he obtained a law degree. In 1910 he was admitted to the bar as a barrister and then on December 27, 1910 married Leila Marion Rouse the granddaughter of John Benson Martin of Camden. The couple obviously spent a good deal of time in Camden as Victor was a member of Union Tennis Club, a fairly select group with courts in Elizabeth Street, Camden. It is known that he took part in competitions in 1910 and 1914 and was pictured as a member of the team. To hide his hair lip he had grown a smart moustache.

While he continued with his law career, Victor also took control of Henry Haigh & Son, a company started by his grandfather in Holdsworthy. He quickly turned it into a limited company with himself as the first director. In 1911 the business changed its name to Wool Scour By-Products Ltd. with a capital of £5,000 in shares of £1 each. The first directors were Messrs. George H. Gerber, Victor Haigh, and George Christie. In May 1915 the business was forced to close when the Commonwealth resumed the Holdsworthy property for military purposes for £5,500 despite the plaintiffs claiming £14,818.

Australia was at war in 1915. Along with many of his friends Victor enlisted in the Australian Army but on October 20, 1915 learned that he had been rejected as medically unfit due to an eye defect and his cleft pallet. Not to be deterred he left Sydney in January 1916 and joined the Artillery School, British Army and was accepted as a Lieutenant in the Royal Garrison Artillery Special Reserve.

The recruit rejected by the Australian Army served with distinction in the British Forces. On July 26, 1918 the Supplement to the London Gazette announced the awarding of a Military Cross to –

> *"Lt. Victor Louis. Bosker Haigh, R.G.A., Spec. Res. For conspicuous gallantry and devotion to duty. He kept close touch with the field batteries and placed his section in positions of extreme danger, in order to protect the batteries. On one occasion he stopped a panic, collecting stragglers and leading them to high ground, where they were most urgently needed. He has crashed one enemy aeroplane and has many times kept his guns firing until forced by heavy, fire to withdraw."*

Following the war Victor returned to Australia and took an interest in politics, standing as a candidate for the Progressive Party in the Cumberland Electorate in the State elections in 1919. He was unsuccessful in the elections but continued his political involvement as a member of the executive committee of the Sydney Electorate League.

Lest We Forget

As with many other World War I veterans Victor suffered bouts of ill-health and depression. Camden was a peaceful haven away from the stresses of Sydney. Victor spent long periods recuperating at "Alpha Cottage" in John Street, Camden with Leila's sister Nora Beatrice Rouse and her aunts, Eleanor Gertrude Martin and Henrietta Maria Martin. It was during one of his stays in Camden Victor took his own life. On August 19, 1924 sadly he cut his own throat in his room in Alpha Cottage and was buried in Section B022.

Richard John Hawkey
Richard John Hawkey was born at *Camden Park* 6th March 1894 the son of Arthur Burton Hawkey and Lucy Veness. For a period he worked alongside his father as a gardener at *Camden Park* and then as a blacksmith.

He enlisted in the Army on 6th July 1915 and departed Sydney on *HMAT Suffolk* on 28th July 1915 as a trooper in the 6th Australian Light Horse A.I.F. He was killed in action in Amman, Jordan on 27th March 1918 and was buried in the Damascus British War Memorial Cemetery in Syria. His memorial is on the family grave in Section C076 and he is also remembered on the Roll of Honour.

Wallace Conrad Rofe Jenkins
Wallace Conrad Rofe Jenkins was born at Mt. Hunter on 16th May 1898 the son of Arthur Daniel Jenkins and Lucy Ann Rofe. He worked as a dairyman prior to enlisting in the Army on 20th March 1916 and was part of the 1st Infantry Battalion.

He returned to Camden after the War and died aged 40 on 12th October 1938. He is buried in Section F053.

William Calbraith Livesey
William Calbraith Livesey was born in Higher Walton, Lancashire, England c. 1892 the son of Joseph Livesey and Hannah. He was educated at All Saints School, Higher Walton Lancashire England. Liversay arrived in Australia c.1912 with his wife Elizabeth and they lived in Broughton Street Camden.

He worked as a shop assistant in Camden and was a keen sportsman and a member of St. John's Choir. He enlisted in the A.I.F. in November 1915 and departed on *HMAT Ceramic* on 14th April 1816. He served in the 2nd Brigade HQ Australian Field Artillery as a Gunner and was killed in action in France on 29th April 1918. He was buried in the Caestre Military Cemetery, France and is remembered on the Roll of Honour.

Eric Lyndon Lowe
Eric Lyndon Lowe was born in Clarence Town in 1896 the son of Edwin Frederick Lowe and Agnes Elizabeth Whysall. The family moved to *Erringhi* Camden in the early 1900s. During his school days he received two Military Medals in the Cleveland Street Champion Squad for Battalion competitions.[15] Lowe was a member of the Camden Boy Scouts Colour Sergeant in the Camden Cadet Force, and a member of the Camden Rifle Club and Cycle Club.

Lance Corp. Eric Lyndon Lowe

---

[15] Camden News September 1915

During a stay in Armidale he was O.R. Sergeant in the Armidale Light Horse.

Lowe worked as a clerk and was a popular chorister at St. John's prior to enlisting in the Army 1st March 1915. He served in the 18th Battalion A.I.F as a Signaller and rose to the rank of Lance Corporal. In August 1915 he was wounded whilst taking part in the landing at Suvla Bay, the final British attempt to break the deadlock of the battle of Gallipoli. He was repatriated to London where he died of his wounds in King George Hospital on 10th September 1915, and was buried at Nunhead (All Saints) Cemetery London. His memorial is on the family grave in Section A111 and he is also commemorated on a plaque in the Chancel of St. John's as well as on the Roll of Honour

Memorial Plaque to Lance Corporal Eric Lyndon Lowe

George Griffin Roy Mills

George Griffin Roy Mills was born in Werombi 14th March 1897 the son of William Mills and Sarah Ann Brookes. He worked on his parent's farm at Brownlow Hill and was described as *"a brave, plucky, hard-working boy"*[16] and *"tall, about 5 feet 6 inches (1.7 metres) high, well built (nuggetty) with dark hair"*. He enlisted in the Army on 22nd October 1916 and served in the 17th Battalion A.I.F. On 14th April 1918 the battalion was at Cachy, near Villers-Bretonneux, France and he received permission to go to the village to get timber to build a dug-out. On the return journey he was wounded in the back and thigh when a shell landed nearby. He died at the 41st Casualty Clearing Station on 16th April 1918 and was buried at Namps-au-Val British Cemetery Rouen (Somme). His memorial is on the family grave in Section B027.

Essington Moore

Essington Moore was born at *Oran Park* Narellan on 14th March 1881 the youngest son of Edward Lomas Moore and Frances Margaret Hartley. He was educated at Campbelltown and later at Barker College Sydney. He was studying medicine at Edinburgh University when war was declared in 1914 and enlisted in the British Army, joining the 13th London Regiment (Princess Louise's Kensington Battalion.[17] He served as a Lieutenant on the front line in charge of a Lewis gun detachment. He sustained a shrapnel injury in the spine. After the war he returned to Camden.

Lt. Essington Moore - courtesy Janet Moore

On 6th October 1937 he was driving home from Sydney along Liverpool Road near Cabramatta when he failed to negotiate a bend and collided head on with a lorry[18] and was seriously injured. The lorry driver later told the Coroner he had attempted unsuccessfully to avoid the collision. Moore spent 7 weeks in the Masonic Hospital at Ashfield before dying as a result of his injuries on 26th November 1837, aged 56 years. He is buried in the family grave in Section C038.

---

[16] "Gunner G.R. Mills" Camden News 23rd May 1918
[17] "Obituary" – Camden News 2nd December 1937
[18] Picton Post – 4th December 1937

Lest We Forget

Arthur William Macarthur-Onslow

Arthur William Macarthur-Onslow, the son of Captain Arthur Alexander Walton Onslow and Elizabeth Macarthur, was born at Camden on 25th May 1877. He was in England during the Boer War and enlisted in the British Army sailed for South Africa on the *Montrose* on 11th February 1900.

After the Boer War[19] he returned to Camden and in 1911 married Cristabel Emily Sarah Beech. When World War I broke out he again sailed to England and was a Captain in the British Army and served in the 16th Queen's Lancers. He was killed in action near Ypres, Belgium, in early November 1914 and is remembered on the Roll of Honour.

George Macleay Macarthur-Onslow

George Macleay Macarthur-Onslow[20] CMG, DSO, VD,[21] the son of Arthur Alexander Walton Onslow and Elizabeth Macarthur, was born in Camden on 2nd May 1875. After his father's death in 1882 his mother took the family to England in 1887 where he was educated at Rugby School, England whilst his mother studied dairy farming. The family returned to Camden briefly in 1890 and made further visits to England for longer periods until his education was completed.

Capt. Arthur William Macarthur-Onslow

George Macleay Macarthur-Onslow

He was commissioned in the N.S.W. Mounted Rifles on 5th April 1895 and promoted to Lieutenant the following year. In July 1903 he became a Lieutenant in the reorganized 2nd Light Horse. On 16th October 1909 he married Violet Marguerite Gordon at *Manar* near Braidwood and made his home at *Murrandah* Camden. In 1911 he was promoted to Captain, and on 16th February 1914 to Major commanding the 9th Light Horse Regiment. In December he joined the A.I.F. and was appointed Second-in-Command of the 7th Light Horse Regiment under Lieutenant-Colonel J. M. Arnott. The 7th Light Horse Regiment reached Egypt in February 1915 and completed its training at Maadi. In May 1915 the regiment was ordered to Gallipoli for dismount service, arriving on 19th May 1915.

---

[19] A street in Canterbury was initially named Deutchland Street, but as a result of anti-German feeling soon after the World War I began in 1914, local residents asked for the street name to be changed to either Glossop or Onslow Street (Captain J.C.T. Glossop was the Commanding Officer of HMAS Sydney when it sank the German cruiser Emden off the Cocos Islands in the Indian Ocean on 9 November 1914). Canterbury Council chose Onslow "*as a memorial to* a brave officer who had fallen in the Empire's cause". - www.canterbury.nsw.gov.au

[20] "Macarthur-Onslow, George Macleay (1875-1931)" – G.P. Walsh - Australian Dictionary of Biography - Volume 10, Melbourne University Press, 1986, pp 196-198

[21] VD - Volunteer Officers' Decoration

Macarthur-Onslow took command of the 7th Light Horse in October and on 17th December, two days before the final evacuation of Anzac Cove, organized the famous cricket match at Shell Green.[22] The cricket match, played whilst shells passed overhead, was part of the Allied preparations for the secret evacuation of the Anzac and Suvla Bay sectors.

On 5th August 1916 he was severely wounded in the counter-attack against the Turks at Katia, in what is known as the Battle of Romani,[23] an Egyptian town 23 miles (37 kms) east of the Suez Canal, near the Mediterranean shore of the Sinai Peninsula. He was evacuated and out of action for 3 months, was Mentioned in Dispatches and awarded the DSO.[24] On returning to duty with his regiment he took part in operations at Gaza Beersheba, the pursuit up the Philistine Plain,[25] and operations across the Jordan into Amman and Es Salt.

From May to August 1918 he was appointed Acting Commander of the 2nd Light Horse Brigade and on 3rd September 1918 was appointed Temporary Brigadier General commanding the 5th Light Horse Brigade for the advance on and capture of Damascus.

In January 1919 he contracted typhoid fever and 4 months later was invalided back to Australia. He was twice more Mentioned in Dispatches, awarded the Order of the Nile (3rd class) and appointed CMG.[26]

After the war he held appointments in various light horse militia units and in 1920-23 was an honorary Aide de Camp to the Governor-General, Lord Stonehaven, and in 1927-31 appointed temporary Colonel-Commandant of the 1st Cavalry Division. In addition he was General Manager and a Director of *Camden Park* Estate Pty. Ltd., a Councillor of Wollondilly Shire Council, Alderman of Camden Council and four times Mayor of Camden. He died of pneumonia on 12th September 1931 and is buried in the family Cemetery. He is remembered in a memorial plaque and window in the church.

Astley John Onslow Thompson

Astley John Onslow Thompson VD was born 3rd January 1865 at Ynys House, Eglwysilan, Pontypridd, and Glamorganshire, Wales, the son of Astley John Thompson and Udea Marianne Moriarty Onslow and educated at Rugby in England. He came to Australia in 1883 when 18 years of age and worked in the Harbour and River Branch of the Public Service until he resigned.

---

[22] Situated on a sloping cotton field close to the Turkish Lines, Shell Green was subject to frequent enemy shelling throughout the Gallipoli campaign.
[23] In the summer of 1916, Friedrich Freiherr Kress von Kressenstein began pushing Turkish troops across the Sinai with the goal of attacking the Suez Canal. Aware of Turkish intentions, British forces led by Sir Archibald Murray began preparing defensive positions in the area. As water in the southern Sinai desert was scarce, Murray's line blocked only the northern route across the peninsula and ran from the Mediterranean coast south to Romani. Anticipating that the main Turkish attack would come on his right flank, Murray ordered Romani strengthened.
[24] DSO - Distinguished Service Order
[25] The Philistine Plain is the area in Israel located south of the Nahal Yarkon and north of the Nahal Besor—located south of Gaza.
[26] CMG– Companion of the Order of St. Michael and St. George.

He returned to England and studied dairying before returning to Camden to take up pastoral work at the *Camden Park* Estate Pty. Ltd.

He was a lay reader at St. John's and the way he lead the services was greatly appreciated by the congregation. He was also well known in commercial life and was a Director of several companies including Commercial Banking Company of Sydney and Colonial Sugar Refining Coy. Ltd and was President of the Camden A.H. & I. Society from 1908 to 1915.

He was one of the founders of the Camden Squadron of the N.S.W. Mounted Rifles in 1892 and was appointed 2nd Lieutenant, and later that year became Lieutenant. Three years later he rose to the rank of Captain and then in 1903 was gazetted Major and was in command of the 2nd Australian Light Horse. He had retired from the military but when called to go to the War responded immediately. He served as a Lieutenant Colonel in the 4th Battalion A.I.F. and

Lieut Col. Astley John Onslow Thompson

saw action at Gallipoli. On 26th April 1915 he led the battalion's advance across the 400 Plateau (Lone Pine) and was killed at Johnston's Jolly, Central Anzac. He is buried in the Parade Ground Cemetery at Gallipoli and remembered on the Roll of Honour.

Frank Henderson Paul

Frank Henderson Paul

Frank Henderson Paul was born c.1881 the son of William Henry Paul and Frances Spencer and educated at Milsons Point Public School. He served a 3 year apprenticeship as a stereo electro-typer in Sydney before coming to Camden and taking up farming. He joined the 9th Light Horse in Camden and enlisted in the 1st Battalion Australian Light Horse on 22nd August 1914 at Rosebery Park in Sydney. He departed for Gallipoli on the *HMAT Star of Victoria* on 20th October 1914. He was killed in action on 22nd May 1915 and was buried in Shrapnel Valley Cemetery Anzac. He is remembered on the Roll of Honour.

Rev. Thomas Giles Paul

Rev. Thomas Giles Paul MC became Rector of Camden in 1927 and remained until he retired due to ill health in 1943. Rev. Paul was the first rector to be appointed by the Archbishop on the advice of the Diocesan Presentation Board, who had accepted the recommendation of the Parish Nominators. He has been described as a man of deep human understanding, and a widely beloved personality in the district.

Rev. Paul was born in June 1883 in Chelsea, England, the son of Giles Hodges Paul and Alice Lindsay. The family lived in Lingfield, Surrey where his father was a farmer. He was educated first at Reading College where

Rev. Thomas Giles Paul - courtesy St. John's records

he studied agriculture, and went on to study at Merton College, Oxford University. He arrived in Australia on 14th October 1913 on the *Indrapura* and commenced theological studies at St. John's College, Melbourne.

World War I started on 24th June 1914 and Rev. Paul answered the call to arms enlisting on 21st August 1914. He was assigned to the 6th Battalion, Headquarters (Australian Army Medical Corps) as a private. His unit embarked from Melbourne on *HMAT Hororata* on 19th October 1914 and he was at Gallipoli, and then in France until the 1918 armistice. By the end of 1915 Rev. Paul had been promoted to 2nd Lieutenant and on 28th January 1916 was promoted to Lieutenant, with the citation reading:-

> *"Has acted as Battalion Transport Officer since May 1916, and has also had the whole of Brigade Transport under his charge in the February to September operations. He did especially good work during the August and September advances, when the Brigade was continually attacking and the transport on the move. Lieut. Paul was responsible for all transport arrangements and carried out all duties in a highly satisfactory manner.*
> *Brigade-General*
> *Commanding 2nd Australian Division*
> *28th January 1916"* [27]

He was recommended for the DSO on 4th March 1917 "for consistently fine bearing under hostile fire and in all adverse conditions, having skilfully commanded his Battery at all times," but this honour was to be denied him, as was the recommendation on 25th September 1918 for an OBE[28] with that recommendations reading:-

> *"For his excellent services both as Transport Officer 6th Battalion, A.I.F., and Brigade Transport Officer from 25th February to the 16th September 1918. He did especially good work during the fighting in the Somme locality from the 9th August to the present date and invariably was successful in keeping the men in the front line adequately supplied with ammunition, rations and water, notwithstanding heavy hostile shelling and machine gun fire Lieut. Paul never failed to deliver his stores. His administration ability and personal disregard of danger at all times have been very marked.*
> *Major-General*
> *Commanding 1st Australian Division*
> *25th September 1918"*[29]

By the end of the war he had risen to the rank of Captain and was awarded an MC[30] on 1st January 1919 for his distinguished service. Rev. Paul would never speak of his war service or how he had earned the MC; his only comment was *"my men made it possible"*.[31]

After the war he completed his theology studies, and was priested in 1921 at Newcastle Cathedral by Bishop Crotty. Rev. Paul served at Newcastle Cathedral for 4 years, and in 1924 married Edna Ann Marriott. In 1925 he became the Foundation Padre for Toc H[32] N.S.W. a position he held

---

[27] "Service No 121 National Archives of Australia"
[28] OBE - Order of the British empire
[29] "Service No 121 National Archives of Australia"
[30] MC - Military Cross
[31] The Camden Advertiser 2 June 1949
[32] During WWI there was one place in which those returning from the front line could find some relief from the traumas of war, and this was "Talbot House" in the small Belgian town of Poperinghe just 11 kilometres west of Ypres. In December 1915 Queensland born Army Chaplain, the Reverend P.B. (Tubby) Clayton opened a Soldiers Club there and named it "Talbot House" in memory of a friend, Lieutenant Gilbert W. L. Talbot. So amidst the

Lest We Forget

until 1927. In July 1927 Rev. Paul visited St. John's and on 31st October 1927 ended his ministry with Toc H and moved to Camden.

When the Pauls came to the Parish it was the first time in almost 40 years that there were children in the rectory.[33] Rev. Paul's experience as Padre for Toc H served him well as the late 1920s and the 1930s were a time of great social stress. In October 1929 the Great Depression officially began resulting in massive unemployment and this was followed by a lengthy drought causing great hardship in the area. During the drought the Nepean River, for the first time in 100 years, completely dried up but no one seeking food was ever turned away from the Rectory empty handed.

In 1939, World War II began and army and air force training establishments were set up in the district adding to Rev. Paul's work. The rectory became a hospitality centre open to the servicemen in the district.

Rev. Paul remained at St. John's until ill health, as a result of his war service, caused his retirement in 1943. He died later that year at Windsor District Hospital on 24th December 1943, aged 60. Mrs. Edna Paul became a teacher at Richmond Infants School until her retirement in September 1962. She passed away in Sydney on 12th May 1989, but is remembered in Camden for her tireless work and the way she had supported her husband's ministry. She had been a foundation member of the Hospital Women's Auxiliary, the Red Cross and many other church and community organisations.

The following anecdote was told to John Wrigley (former Past President and now Vice President of the Camden Historical Society) by the well-known Camden character Miss Llewella Davies OAM.

The Paul family remained friends with Miss Davies even after they left Camden. The widow Mrs. Edna Paul and her son John used to come back to Camden occasionally to visit and to tend Rev. Paul's grave.

On one occasion, Miss Davies decided to check the condition of the grave before their visit and walked up to St. John's churchyard from her home in Exeter Street in the late afternoon. She was generally resisting the idea that age was catching up with her but had taken to using a walking stick to keep her balance. As she was tidying up the grave and pulling out some weeds, she lost her balance and fell. At the same time, some of the grave concrete gave away and she slid into the hole in front of the stone. To her embarrassment she found that she could not get back on her feet.

Miss Davies looked around for assistance and spotted an elderly couple in the evening light coming along the path towards her. "Help!" she cried "I'm coming out! Give me a hand!" According to Miss Davies, the couple took one horrified look at her and hurried off in the opposite direction and she never saw them again!

---

horrors of war an ideal was born, a lofty ideal and it found expression in a worldwide movement called simply Toc H, the Army signaller's code word for Talbot House.

After the war ended all of those who had known Tubby Clayton and "Talbot House" decided that the ideals for which the House stood should never be lost and in 1922 the Toc H Movement received its Royal Charter. The Governor General of Australia, Lord (Walter) Forster, wrote to Tubby Clayton in 1923 saying that he and Lady (Rachel) Forster would like to give a Toc H Lamp in memory of their two sons who had died in the Great War. The Lamp reached Australia in 1925 and has since then been enshrined in Christ Church Cathedral, Newcastle. It is the parent lamp of Toc H Australia From 1925 to the outbreak of World War 2 Toc H spread rapidly to all Australian States and its members built a fine tradition of 'Caring for People' carrying on the ideals for which Talbot House stood. They pioneered the Blood Transfusion Service, the Junior Farmers Movement, the Royal Queensland Bush Children's Health Scheme and the Camping Program for children in need or with disabilities.

[33] The last children in the rectory prior to the Paul's were those of Rev. Henry Tingcombe.

John Lambert Richardson Poole

John Lambert Richardson Poole was born at Cobbitty Paddocks[34] 2nd May 1886 the son of George Poole and Esther Thorn. He was a coach driver prior to enlisting in the Army on 22nd August 1914 serving as a Sergeant in the 2nd Battalion A.I.F He died in London as a result of wounds and was buried at Shorncliffe Military Cemetery Kent, England. His memorial is on the family grave in Section D083.

George Quigley

George Quigley was born 1886 but little is known of him other than a comment in the Burial Register that he served in the British Army during World War I and took part in action at Mons France. George died 12th December 1959 and is buried in Section E058.

Robert Alfred Sidman

Robert Alfred Sidman was born in Sydney 3rd July 1889 the son of William Sidman and Honor Elizabeth Dickinson. On 3rd July 1889 he married Jean Tyson. On 31st December 1915 Sidman enlisted in the army and embarked on the *SS Makarini* on 1st April 1916, serving as a Sapper in the 3rd Field Company Engineers. During World War I he was high jump champion of the A.I.F. and in 1920 he competed in the Australian Athletics Championships, coming fourth.

Sidman is best remembered as being a former owner of the Campbelltown-Ingleburn News which was first published on 20th November 1919. He continued to publish the paper at his printing works in Patrick Street Campbelltown until 1953 when he moved to the Camden News office of his late brother George Victor Sidman.

He was active with the Campbelltown Show Society and served as Secretary for a long period. He was involved with the R.S.L. and was President of the Campbelltown Bowling Club for five years.

Ill-health forced him to hand over proprietorship of the Camden News to his brother Charles Warrane Sidman who later sold the paper. Robert Sidman died on 10th October 1964, after a long illness and his ashes are interred in the family grave Section F006.

Hector Small

Hector Small was born in Theresa Park on 9th June 1893 the son of Albert Small and Sarah Ann Percival. He attended school at Theresa Park and later worked as a farmer on the family property *Passchendaele* at Brownlow Hill. He later joined the Camden Mounted Rifles before on 29th April 1914 marrying Alice Mildred Stafford. On 26th August 1914 he enlisted with the 1st Light Horse and embarked for Gallipoli on *HMAT Star of Victoria* 20th October 1914.

Small wrote letters home which were published in the Camden News on Thursday 24th June 1915 entitled "From the Front." The letters were published a few days before he was to die in Heliopolis, Egypt on 4th July 1915. While at

Lance Corporal Hector Small

---

[34] Now known as Ellis Lane

Gallipoli he contracted enteric fever[35] and was evacuated to Egypt where he died in and is buried in the Cairo War Memorial Cemetery. He is remembered on the Honour Roll and in a memorial grave in the churchyard of St. Paul's Cobbitty.

His widow placed her own touching tribute to her husband in the Camden News – *"In loving memory of Corporal Hector Small, 1st Light Horse Regiment who died at Heliopolis, Egypt, July 4th 1915, from illness contracted at Gallipoli 'Love is stronger than death'."*[36] Alice Small was later awarded the honour of officially opening the cenotaph at Macarthur Park.

Reginald (Rex) Sydney Smith

Reginald (Rex) Sydney Smith, the son of Luke and Theresa, was born on the family farm at Wilton in 1879. His father worked for Dr. R.L. Jenkins of *Nepean Towers*[37] at Douglas Park as a gardener and botanist. After finishing school Rex worked as a farm labourer and joined the Picton Half Company of Mounted Rifles. When the Boer War commenced he, along with other members, enlisted and sailed with "A" Squadron of the Mounted Rifles on 3rd November 1899.[38] As Captain John Macquarie Antill's orderly, Rex saw action on numerous occasions and was promoted to Corporal prior to his return to Sydney on 8th January 1901. He had been home for little more than a month when he again volunteered and departed Sydney on 15th March 1901 as a Sergeant in the 2nd Mounted Rifles.

Rex was transferred to the 3rd N.S.W. Imperial Bushmen and promoted to Lieutenant.

Whilst in South Africa he met Amelia Volkmann the daughter of Colonel Christian Volkmann of Kaiser Franz Joseph's Royal Guard and Cristiana Finger. Rex returned home 11th August 1902. Amelia followed him to Wilton where they were married on 18th March 1903.[39] After the birth

Reginald (Rex) Sydney Smith in Boer War uniform

Rex Smith with wife Amelia and daughter Ida Edith

---

[35] Typhoid (enteric fever) is a septicaemic infection of humans caused by Salmonella typhi. A similar but generally milder enteric fever, paratyphoid, is caused by Salmonella paratyphi
[36] "I Remain the Kid, as Ever, Cobbitty Public School" – Cobbitty Child Anzac Committee
[37] "Nepean Towers" was originally known as "Park Hall" and more recently as "St. Mary's Towers
[38] "The Forgotten men, of a Forgotten War"- Colin Sproule
[39] Apparently members of Amelia's family moved to Queensland around the time of her marriage, as the Camden News of 22nd August 1912 noted that she previously lived in Queensland and her direct relatives now resided in Melbourne. It is known that her mother died in Queensland in 1929.

of their daughter Ida Edith in 1905 the family moved to Mount Hunter and Rex purchased his own horse team and carried ore between the Yerranderie Silver Mines and Camden. Later he went on to drive coaches for Butlers between Camden and Burragorang Valley.

Early in 1912 their son Rex junior was born but tragically Amelia died shortly after. Rex was left to tend for two young children.[40]

At the outbreak of World War I Rex enlisted as a Sergeant in the 1st Australian Light Horse and served at Gallipoli and was badly wounded. He was evacuated to Egypt where he died on 19th June 1915 and was buried at Chatby War Memorial Cemetery in Egypt. A memorial stone is included on his wife's grave in Section C108 and he is on the Roll of Honour. His son Rex was raised by the Dowle family and daughter Ida by the Bartlett family.

Cecil Claude Wheeler
Cecil Claude Wheeler was born at The Oaks, 17th September 1894 the son of Walter Wheeler and Hannah Willis. He enlisted on 4th July 1915 and embarked for Egypt on *HMAT Warilda* as a member of the 4th Infantry Battalion A.I.F. He saw action in France, and was severely injured at the battle of Polygon Wood on 20th September 1917 when a burst of shrapnel injured his spine. Cecil was invalided home on the Hospital Ship *Kanowna* on 16th December 1917 and spent years in hospital at Randwick where surgeons did everything possible for him.[41] In 1919 he married Jessie Amelia Maloney and returned to Camden, but never regained full health. He died aged 32 years on 29th March 1927 and is buried in Section C200. His headstone was erected by the people of Camden.

John Edward Williams
John Edward Williams was born in Camden in 1894 the son of Edward Williams and Mary Evelina Fyfe. He worked as a gardener prior to enlisting in the A.I.F. on 23rd August 1915 and served as a Lance Corporal in the 56th Battalion A.I.F. He died in France 2nd April 1917 and was buried at Villers-Bretonneux, France. His memorial is on the family grave in Section B077.

World War II
Astley Arthur Cranfield
Astley Arthur Cranfield was born at Mt. Hunter on 17th August 1919 the son of Frederick Laurie Cranfield and Vera May Dengate. He enlisted in the R.A.A.F. 460 Squadron on 11th October 1941 as a Flight Sergeant and died over Germany on 22nd September 1943. He was buried in Becklington British Military Cemetery, Soltau, Germany. His memorial is on the family grave in Section D062.

Robert Bruce Ferguson
Robert Bruce Ferguson OAM was born in Mosman on 11th May 1916, the only son of Stanley Nigel Ferguson and Claire Ophele Cochin and great grandson of Francis Ferguson. His mother died in childbirth in 1918 and he was sent to live with his grandfather Campbell Ferguson at Rose Bay. Robert Bruce, always known as Bruce, went to Cranbrook School but left before finishing his Leaving Certificate and worked as a messenger boy for a stockbroker. In the late 1930s he met Lillian Mary Sanders, Secretary to the Manager of David Jones in Sydney[42] and married her in 1950.

---

[40] Report of the Coroners Court, Camden News 22nd August 1912
[41] Camden News 31st March 1927
[42] SMH 31 May 2008 – Distinguished in War and Peace

On 24th September 1941 he enlisted in the A.I.F. and joined the 55th Battalion. This battalion was posted to Port Moresby and joined the 39th and 53rd battalions on the Kokoda Trail. When the 53rd and 55th battalions combined in 1942 they were deployed to take part in the battle for Sanananda on the north coast of New Guinea. In January 1943 he was promoted to Lieutenant and was discharged from the army in November 1945.

Robert Bruce Ferguson

After the war he inherited a half share in his great grandfather's property in Camden and built a house in Fergusons Lane. He concentrated on farming, growing vegetables, lucerne and clover as well as rearing cattle. He then began raising pigs and astounded experts at the Department of Agriculture with how quickly he could bring them to market weight. Bruce realised that his talent lay in finance and investing and went on to amass a small fortune.

Bruce took an active interest in public life and was an Alderman on Camden Council from 1950 until 1987, and Mayor from 1964 to 1977. He was the first Civil Defence Co-ordinator for Camden and introduced the Flood Warning Scheme, and was an executive member of the Local Government Association from 1973 to 1986 and Chairman of the Local Government Investment Board until 1987. Often called "Mr. Camden" for his work in the area he was awarded the Camden Citizen's Award in 1981 and the OAM[43] in 1984. Bruce died on 25th April 2008 and his ashes and memorial are in his great grandfather's grave in Section C002.

Ernest Henry McGrath

Ernst Henry McGrath was born in Orange on 18th June 1909, the son of Ernest Millington McGrath and Hannah Frances Barnes. Shortly after 1909 the family moved to Broughton Street Camden, where he worked as a blacksmith. He was keenly interested in local sport, in particular tennis, cricket, football and athletics, was the Honorary Secretary of the Camden District Tennis Association and played on the Camden Cricket Team.

On 15th July 1940 he enlisted in the 7th Recovery Section, 2/3 AFD W/shops AAOC before marrying Heather Irene Maudsley in September. He sailed from Sydney on 28th December 1940 for the Middle East. On 25th May 1941 he was injured as his unit was travelling from Egypt to Palestine through the Sinai Desert and died as a result on 26th May 1941.

His memorial is on the family grave in Section E020. His baby daughter was born after his death and a touching tribute was paid to his memory by

Private Ernest H. McGrath

---

[43] OAM - Medal of the Order of Australia

his unit who cabled £15 ($30) from the Middle East as a gift with the message *"We would like to be associated in some way with the birth of Ernie's child."*[44]

Norman Thomas McLeod
Norman Thomas McLeod was born in Westbrook[45] on 24th October 1887 the son of Norman McLeod and Elizabeth Dawson. He attended school at Westbrook and competed in the district sports days, excelling in cricket. In 1902 he played for the Camden Cricket Club but in 1903 and 1904 he played for the Westbrook Cricket Club and by 1908 was on the committee.

In 1906 he enlisted in the Australian Light Horse and served as a Trooper with the local half-company which was sponsored by the Macarthurs. When World War I broke out he joined the permanent armed forces and in 1915 married Marthe Mabel Gouvernet in Burwood.[46]

He was promoted through the ranks to Warrant Officer and later Sergeant-Major. By the 1930s he was Regimental Sergeant-Major at the Middle Head Barracks in Sydney. McLeod was transferred to Swan Military Barracks in Western Australia as a Captain, and during World War II was District Officer in charge of all ammunition supplies for the state. His wife Marthe died of a heart attack at Granville on 5th February 1962 aged 73 and he married Ethel May Turner. He was living with his son Colonel Norman Ronald McLeod, a career soldier, in Gosford when he died aged 82 on 7th October 1969. He is buried in Section F022 alongside his first wife.

Ivo Garnett Perry
Ivo Garnett Perry was born at West Wyalong on 29th March 1907 the son of Stanley Edward Perry and Daisy May Blunden. He enlisted in the R.A.A.F. on 29th April 1940 as a Flight Sergeant. After he was discharged on 5th November 1945 he returned to Camden. He died aged 41 years on 8th February 1949. He is buried in Section A059.

Edwin Morton Rapley
Edwin Morton Rapley was born in Camden on 1st October 1910, the son of William Rapley and Mary Jane Small. He enlisted in the Army on 18th June 1940 serving as a Gunner in the 2/15 Field Regiment A.I.F. and was in Singapore when the Japanese invaded the Island. He was interred in various Japanese Prisoner of War Camps for 3½ years[47] and after his release he was discharged on 18th January 1946 and returned to Camden. After recuperating he re-joined the staff of Clifton Bros. Store and held a position in the grocery department up to the time of his death.

On Saturday 27th September 1947 he was driving his sports model car from Camden to Picton, and had gone about 2 miles (3.2 km) along the Hume Highway[48] when he collided with a motor lorry conveying four trotting horses returning from a race meeting at Mittagong. His car only struck a glancing blow on the lorry and the cross-member of the truck[49] but it was sufficient to cause the car to overturn and he was thrown to the roadway. Sergeants Bowerman and Dawson, of Camden Police, and the Camden Ambulance were quickly on the scene. He was conveyed to Camden District Hospital and found to be suffering from a compound fracture of the skull, and other injuries to the upper part of the right chest and right hand. He died on Monday morning 29th September 1947 aged 36 and is buried in Section E118.

---

[44] Obituary in Camden News
[45] Westbrook was later known as Mount Hunter
[46] "From the Hebrides to the Colonies" – H. Macleod
[47] Camden News 2nd October 1947
[48] Now known as Remembrance Drive
[49] Camden News 2nd October 1947

Roy Sawyers
Roy Sawyers was born at Armidale on 1st November 1912 the son of George Sawyers and Elizabeth Saggus. He enlisted in the A.I.F. on 12th February 1942 and was assigned to the 130th Brigade Workshop and rose to the rank of Staff Sergeant. In 1844 he married Patricia Hannah McGrath, the sister of Ernest Henry McGrath. He received his discharge on 25th March 1946 and was Mentioned in Dispatches on 6th March 1947. He lived in Camden until his death at age 90 years on 10th December 2002. His grave is in Section E020.

Colin Tate
Colin Tate was born at Randwick 21st February 1917 the son of Cecil Tate and Theresa Little. He was educated at Kings School Parramatta and at Sydney Grammar School. For some years he was a partner with his mother in the Camden Newsagency. In April 1942 he married Gwyneth Taplin.

He first joined the A.I.F. as a gunner with an army anti-aircraft battery. Taplin transferred to the R.A.A.F. on 10th October 1942 and was attached to the 460 Squadron as a Flight Sergeant in a Halifax Bomber Squadron. He died on 30th January 1944 over England as he was returning from an attack on Berlin. One of his engines cut out and he crashed in Catfoss Lane in Yorkshire. He is remembered by a plaque on the family grave Section A064.

Flt. Sgt. Colin Tate

Ernest Leon Wade
Ernest Leon Wade was born in Auburn on 12th November 1916 the son of Percy Wade and Lucy Elizabeth Scott Tuckerman. His service record indicates he enlisted in the A.I.F. in Port Moresby, New Guinea on 26th April 1943 and was a Staff Sergeant in 14th Field Company. In 1944 he married Thelma Muriel New at Granville. He died on 4th July 2005 and his ashes are interred in the "New" family grave section A073.

Last Flight of the Dragon

Not far from the front of the church lies a memorial commemorating a 1943 war time mystery.

Just before 10:00 am on 17th April 1943 a De Havilland Dragon A34-47, a wood and fabric two-bay biplane with folding wings, took off from Sydney's Mascot Airport bound for Wagga enroute to Essington (Melbourne). On board the plane, from No. 34 Squadron R.A.A.F. were five men. The pilot Sergeant Douglas Brian Doyle,[1] from Murrurundi. His co-pilot was Sergeant Francis Joseph Doyle,[2] known as Frank, from Wagga. Passenger, Flying Officer Geoffrey Hugh Lester,[3] known as Tim, was headed home to Mansfield, Victoria on leave. Two United States Marines on their way to report to their Melbourne Headquarters were, Flight Lieutenant Cecil Joseph Umstead[4] and First Lieutenant Horace Albert Teague.[5] The weather forecast was for a fine and cloudless day with light winds from the south west. The usual flight path was to follow the road to Goulburn and then to Wagga. However the aircraft took off in the north-west lane which would allow it to take the more direct, scenic route via the Burragorang Valley.

A De-Havilland Dragon similar to the missing plane - courtesy Geoff Hoskin

One of the Volunteer Air Observer Corp recorded it passing over Chester Hill at 10:07 am. At 10:25 am Catherine Jane Adams, known as Katie, the telephonist at the manual exchange at Werombi, and a member of the Volunteer Air Observer Corp, reported it flying about 1½ miles (2.4 km) from her home heading south and notified her Control Room by telephone. This was the last official sighting.

The plane and occupants were reported as overdue by the aerodrome control officer at Wagga when they hadn't arrived at their destination by 1:55 pm but no search was initiated until 11:00 am the following day. The search was concentrated around the Goulburn area after a report the plane had last been seen in that vicinity. It was not until 11:00 pm on 18th April that the R.A.A.F. realised the Volunteer Air Observer who had reported the Goulburn sighting had referred to the flight log for the 16th April in error.

Three intensive aerial searches on 19th, 20th and 21st April of an area between Camden and Goulburn, including the Burragorang Valley, failed to find anything as the search was hampered by poor weather conditions of storms and strong winds. The aerial search was eventually abandoned, the police notified, and appeals made

Catherine Jane Adams of the Volunteer Air Observers Corp who reported the last confirmed sighting of the plane - courtesy Julie Adams

---

[1] Douglas Brian Doyle- 412236 R.A.A.F.
[2] Francis Joseph Doyle - 420615 R.A.A.F.
[3] Geoffrey Hugh Lester - 0409154 R.A.A.F.
[4] Cecil Joseph Umstead – 0-013899
[5] Horace Albert Teague – 0-014229

Pilot – Sergeant Douglas Brian Doyle

Co-pilot – Sergeant Francis Joseph Doyle

Flying Officer - Geoffrey Hugh Lester

to the public for information as to the plane's flight path. It is doubtful that they would have been unable to locate the plane from the air because *"if an aircraft crashed into the side of one of the steep hills there it might roll down a gorge and become hidden in the thick undergrowth."*[6]

It was not until the 27th April 1943, ten days after the plane was reported missing, that Nattai resident, Hilda Donahue, reported to an enquiring Police Constable that she had heard the noise of a passing aircraft followed by the sound of a crash at about 1:00 pm on the day the plane went missing. She ran outside and saw a cloud of dust rising from behind a hill about 12 miles (19.3 km) to the south-east of Nattai Post office[7] in the vicinity of Mount Wanganderry. She advised that the engine noise had been irregular which would indicate the aircraft may have had engine problems.

Some concerns have been raised as to whether Mrs. Donohue was mistaken as to the time she sighted the aircraft. If this was the De Havilland Dragon, where had it been between 10:25 am and 1:00 pm? The distance between the Burragorang and Werombi would not have taken 2½ hours flying time. The Flight Plan submitted by the pilot had indicated an anticipated arrival time at Wagga of 12:30 pm. It was believed that Mrs. Donohue had mistaken the time due to the delay in her reporting, or it was possible that the clock she had noted the time from had not been reset to eastern standard time when daylight saving had ended on 28th March. Other theories as to the time discrepancy are that she may have sighted one of the low flying search planes on 19th April and that the cloud of dust may well have come from blasting operations from the nearby mines. What is known is that the aircraft was not seen by the watching posts at Mittagong or the southern end of Burragorang Valley near the Wombeyan Caves clearly suggesting that it had crashed somewhere between Werombi and Mittagong.[8]

A ground search was not undertaken until the 28th April 1943, eleven days after the aircraft went missing. Despite an exhausting ground search along the upper reaches of the Burragorang, concentrated on the Wanganderry Tableland no sign was found of the missing aircraft and its crew. It was thought that it was unlikely the aircraft had crashed in the valley as at that time local farmers and graziers were using the grasslands for farming and grazing and they would have found it. More than likely the remains of the plane and its crew lie on one of the mountain tops or in the

---

[6] "Hunt for Lost Flyers – Woman's Story Gives New Clue" – SMH 28th April 1943
[7] "Ibid
[8] "Mystery of the Missing Dragon" – Illawarra Mercury Weekender 12th June 1999

one of the canyons or gorges of the Burragorang. The search was eventually called off much to the distress of the relatives of the crew.

A Court of Inquiry was held some weeks after the disappearance and evidence tendered to the Court noted that the pilot Sergeant Douglas Doyle had noticed engine vibrations the day prior to the flight. He requested that both magnetos, the propeller bolts and control wires be checked, but no problems were found and the plane was cleared to fly. If the aircraft had lost one of its engines it would not have been able to maintain altitude while fully loaded, on the one remaining engine.

In summing up the Court mentioned *"that there had been many instances of aircraft bolt failure of this type on this type of aircraft."*[9] If the airscrews had been over tightened the day before the flight whilst the engine was still warm then they could have cracked under the colder atmospheric conditions on the fateful day.

The remains of the wooden plane have still not been found. All that would remain would be the engines, flight instruments, wheels and some wiring. It is unlikely that the wreckage has been covered by the waters of Warragamba Dam as only the grass valleys and cleared areas were inundated after the dam was completed in 1960.

On Remembrance Day, 11th November 2000 a plaque commemorating the three missing Australian airmen and the two members of the US Marine Corps was unveiled in the Churchyard. The memorial can be found on the grassed area left of the path that goes from the front of the church towards John Street.

---

[9] Ibid

Memorial to the missing plane, its crew and passenger

Radiant Light

The window design is typical of gothic design and has the curvilinear or undulating tracery often seen in 14th century architecture.[1] The original stained glass windows for the Church were installed in 1847 after 12 cases of glass were shipped from England to William Macarthur on the *Sultana* in 1846 with a copy of the Bill of Lading forwarded on the *Angelina*.[2] The windows were commissioned for the Church by James and William Macarthur and the windows made in Castlereagh Street, Sydney by John LeFevre.[3]

One of the original stained glass windows from 1847

---

[1] "Stained Glass" – Michael Archer
[2] Macarthur Papers – letter from Captain Markard dated London 9th November 1846 and stamped "ship letter March 19 1847 Sydney"
[3] "Windows Restored" Camden Advertiser 13th April 1988

The term stained glass is used to refer to coloured glass or the craft of working with it. Glass is coloured during its manufacture by adding metallic salts and then crafted into stained glass windows in which small pieces of glass, held together by strips of lead and supported by a rigid frame, are arranged to form patterns or pictures. The term is also applied to windows in which the colours have been painted onto the glass and then fused to the glass in a kiln. It is an art and also a craft, requiring artistic skill to conceive an appropriate and workable design, and engineering skill to assemble the pieces.

The window must fit snugly into the space for which it is made, be able to resist wind and rain, and be capable of supporting its own weight. The design of a window may be non-figurative or figurative. It may incorporate narratives drawn from the Bible, history, or literature and may represent saints or use symbolic motifs. The detailed designs, known as cartoons, are drawn at full scale with the areas of different colours clearly defined, and laid out on a flat white surface, usually a wooden table.

The Stained Glass Designers
A number of different stained glass workshops prepared the windows for St. John's. All but four of the windows were made in England with the glass and a copy of the full size "cartoon" forwarded to Sydney where the windows were assembled with copper wire used to fuse the lead edged pieces together.

Frederick Pellatt – Pellatt & Co
The original windows came from Pellatt & Co, Apsley, Southwark, London. We know from a letter to William Macarthur from an agent, Captain Makard, that Frederick Pellatt was personally involved in the shipment – *"Mr. Fred K. Pellatt having given his personal attention to it both in the making and packing."*[4]

Clayton & Bell
Clayton & Bell were possibly the most prolific and proficient workshop for stained glass in England during the latter half of the century and made the first of the detailed design windows for St. John's. The company was founded in 1855 and continued until 1993 and in 1883 were awarded a Royal Warrant by Queen Victoria. Characteristics of a Clayton & Bell window are the way rays of light are depicted, and the sweeping robes of strong bright colours. Many of their windows have almond trees and small flowers as a recognition feature and/or the heraldic rose. A feature of their east windows is brightly-coloured 14th century style canopies[5] depicting heaven.

Alfred Charles Handel
Alfred Charles Handel was responsible for two windows on the southern side. He was born in Sydney in 1886 the son of Henry James Handel and Cealey Bourne and died in Croydon on 14th October, 1948. Handel was the principal painter and artist at the premier Sydney firm Lyon, Cottier & Co. until shortly before Lyon's death in 1916 when he set up his own business. Handel signed his windows in the bottom right hand corner. His son Philip Handel, born 1931 followed in his father's footsteps and was responsible for the restoration work on his father's windows using the original cartoons. Philip Handel died on 29th July 2009.

Powell & Sons (Whitefriars) Ltd.
In 1875 Harry James Powell, grandson of the founder, James Powell, joined the family business set up by his grandfather in 1834 when he purchased the Whitefriars Glass Company in London and in 1919 the firm's name was changed to Powell & Sons (Whitefriars) Ltd. The firm's trademark, a friar or monk, can be found in the bottom right hand corner of their windows. Harry

---

[4] Stamped Ship Letter March 1847 per "Angelina" Sydney – Macarthur Papers
[5] "Stained Glass" – Michael Archer

James Powell was responsible for the design the Brigadier General George Macleay Macarthur-Onslow window.

Stephen Moor
Stephen Moor[6] was born in Budapest in 1915 and studied art and stained glass painting at the Academy of the Arts in Budapest. During the 1940s he worked as an art teacher until in 1941 he was conscripted to the Russian Army where he served until 1945 when together with his parents he fled to Vienna. From 1945 until 1950 he lived in Stuttgart, Germany and worked as a stained glass artist and in 1947 married Edith Hoffmann. He migrated to Australia in 1950 and founded his own studio, Ars Sacra, in South Strathfield and was considered one of the foremost practitioners of his time.

Kevin Little
Kevin Little studied art at East Sydney Technical College before succeeding his father as proprietor of the family's Arncliffe business in 1956. He specialized in the restoration of ecclesiastical stained glass doing work all over Australia, New Zealand and Canada and is regarded as one of the most pre-eminent Australian stained glass artists.

The Original Windows
Only five of the original windows made by Frederick Pellatt remain. Two of these are on the southern side of the church nearest the entry; the other three are in the lower tower. Though simple in design the windows are possibly the only remaining examples of this type of stained glass work remaining in Australia. It is possible monetary considerations were the reason more ornate pictorial designs weren't selected, or a decision was made to allow for memorial windows to be installed when required. The original windows are basically of octagonal shaped translucent opal glass with diamonds of red, blue, green and gold coloured glass set at regular intervals within. These colours, including the translucent opal glass, are full of symbolism and represent the seasons of the church but also have additional symbolism i.e.

Windows Colour[7]	**Church Season**	**Symbolism**
White	Christmas/Epiphany Easter Weddings/Funerals/Saint's Days	Purity and Joy
Red	Holy Week Pentecost Ordinations Commemoration of Martyrs	Blood Fire Blood
Blue (or violet)	Advent Lent	Spiritual preparation Mourning and Penitence Heaven and heavenly love
Green	Trinity Sunday When no feast is being observed	God's goodness to us in creation

---

[6] Stephen Moor interviewed by Barbara Blackman [sound recording] – National Library of Australia
[7] Anglican Church of Australia students page

Radiant Light

Rev. Cecil John and Copland King Memorial [8]

The third window on the southern side, was designed c.1930 by Alfred Charles Handel of Sydney is in memory of the fifth Rector, Rev. Cecil John King, and his twin brother, Rev. Copland King. It was installed in 1940 and dedicated by Archbishop Howard West Kilvinton Mowll of Sydney on 1st December 1940. The left window depicts Jesus and the disciples "*Go ye into all the world and preach the Gospel*" and the right window Jesus with children of all nations "*He took them up in His arms and blessed them.*"

The inscription under the window reads

> "*A.M.D.G.*[9] *this window is in memory of Reverend Cecil John King M.A. rector of this Parish 1891-1927 and his twin brother Reverend Copeland King M.A. a pioneer missionary of New Guinea.*"

The inscription incorrectly spells Rev. Copland King's name (i.e. Copeland).

---

[8] See chapter "First Fleet Connections"
[9] A.M.D.G. stands for "Ad maiorem Dei gloriam" which translates to "For the greater glory of God" or "All My Duties to God"

Radiant Light

Rev. Cecil John King and Rev. Copland King Memorial Window

War Memorial

The fourth window on the southern side in St. John's was designed by Alfred Charles Handel as a War Memorial. The window was ready for unveiling in September 1932 but it was decided to delay the unveiling until Armistice Sunday, 13th November 1932, with the ceremony being conducted by a Rev. Cecil John King and Rev. Thomas Giles Paul.

The window on the left depicts St. Mark with a quill and scroll, symbolising the writing of his gospel and at his feet his heraldic symbol, the winged lion. Above is a waratah, the floral symbol for Australia, symbolising the participation of the Australian forces. Below is a shield with the words *"Greater love hath no man than this"*. A scroll refers to *"St. Mark's Day 1915"*. St. Mark's Day falls on 25th April, the day the Australian troops landed at Gallipoli.

The right window depicts St. George with helmet, lance and flying pendant of a red cross on a white background. His right hand rests on his blazing pointed shield, a Christian symbol first used in the 12th century, and at his feet the slain dragon, Satan. Above is a rose, the floral symbol of England, symbolising the participation of the English forces. Below a shield with the words *"Hallowed in Christ be the memory of those who died the death of honour for the freedom of the world"* and *"They died without hate that love might live."*

On a scroll at the bottom are the immortal words of "The Ode" from Laurence Binyon's poem "For the Fallen"

> *"They shall grow not old as we that are left grow old, age shall not weary them nor the years condemn, at the going down of the sun and in the morning we will remember them."*

Underneath the windows is the inscription

> *"A.M.D.G.[10] this memorial window is given by the Parishioners of Camden in proud thanksgiving for those who gave their lives in the Great War."*

---

[10] A.M.D.G. stands for "Ad maiorem Dei gloriam" which translates to "For the greater glory of God" or "All My Duties to God"

Radiant Light

World War I Memorial Window

Rev. Henry Tingcombe Memorial

The fifth window on the southern side, near the pulpit, was given by public subscription as a memorial to the third rector, Rev. Henry Tingcombe. The window was made by Clayton & Bell of England at a cost of £26.13.10 ($53.39) with the funds raised by public subscription. On the left is St. James the Apostle attired in the clothing of a pilgrim. He is wearing a black hat on the front of which is a shell, the badge of a pilgrim or traveller. In his right hand a staff with a wine bottle attached at the top and in his left the scriptures that he is taking to the world. The right-hand window depicts St. John the healer with goblet and his heraldic symbol, the golden eagle.

Underneath the windows is the inscription

Rev. Henry Tingcombe - courtesy of St. John's Camden

"In memory of Rev^d. Henry Tingcombe 14 years incumbent of this Parish who entered into rest 23rd July MDCCCLXXIV"

Rev. Henry Tingcombe was born in Devonshire in 1810 the son of a banker, John Tingcombe and Sarah Arscott Lethbridge. His uncle, Christopher Lethbridge's daughter Harriet, married Captain Philip Parker King the grandfather of our fifth rector. He arrived in Port Jackson in 1834 and was appointed a Commissioner of the Supreme Court. He was ordained in Armidale in 1846 by Bishop Broughton and on 5th December 1850 married Jane Lydia Clements. In 1854 he received a temporary licence for Bathurst. The family moved to Camden on 1st August 1858, and he was the last of the rectors appointed through the direct intervention of the Macarthurs.

In 1859 James and William Macarthur built the Rectory and Coach House at a cost of £1,000 ($2,000) and Rev. Tingcombe and his family were the first to live in it. This would have been greatly welcomed as there were already two children. A third was born shortly after they moved in, and a fourth was born in 1862. Tingcombe resigned in 1872 after 14 years in the Parish and died at North Sydney on 23rd July 1874 at the age of 65 years.

Radiant Light

Rev. Henry Tingcombe memorial window

Radiant Light

Lancet Windows

A lancet window is a tall narrow window with a pointed arch at its top and acquired the "lancet" name from its resemblance to a lance. Instances of this type of architectural motif are most often found in Gothic structures. In the Chancel there are four stained glass lancet windows given in 1874 by Sir George Macleay of *Brownlow Hill* and attributed to the work of Clayton & Bell, England.

Sir George Macleay - courtesy of Camden Park

The Old Testament prophet Ezekiel had a vision where he saw four winged creatures (Ezekiel 1:10) with human faces. In the New Testament book of Revelation, St. John sees about the throne four winged creatures: a lion, an ox, a man, and an eagle representing the four evangelists/gospel writers.

The first window on the southern side depicts St. Luke holding a writing quill and a book and below is his symbol the winged ox. The ox, recognized as the animal of sacrifice, was applied to Luke because his Gospel emphasizes the atonement made by Christ's sacrifice of himself on the Cross.

The second window depicts St. John holding a goblet containing a salamander (mythical winged lizard-like creature said to be resistant to fire) and a book; below is his symbol, the golden eagle. Because it soars upward, the eagle is a symbol of the resurrection or ascension of Christ. The eagle represents John because of his lofty and "soaring" gospel which is much more theological in nature than the other three. The eagle is frequently used in stained glass windows, and often depicted in the form of a lectern for holding the Holy Bible; it is the symbol for far sightedness and the spread of the gospel. The eagle theme is repeated in the shapes of the timber detailing of the internal roof arches of the building.

The first window on the north side depicts St. Mark with quill and book with his symbol, a winged lion below. This symbol comes from Mark's description of John the Baptist's voice "crying out in the wilderness" upon hearing the Word of God (Mark 1:3). His voice is said to have sounded like that of a roaring lion.

The second window on the north side with the plaque to Sir George Macleay below depicts St. Matthew with quill and money box or casket and his symbol a winged man below. Matthew's gospel starts with Jesus' genealogy from Abraham; it represents Jesus' Incarnation, and therefore Christ's human nature.

George Macleay was born in London in 1809 and was educated at Westminster School before coming to Australia on the *Eliza* in 1828. He settled near Camden on the *Brownlow Hill* estate owned by his father Alexander Macleay who was Colonial Secretary of New South Wales.

He accompanied Charles Sturt on his expedition to the Murrumbidgee and Murray in November 1829 more as a companion rather than as an assistant. Because of his services to Sturt he received a grant of 2,560 acres (1,036 hectares) on the Fish River between Goulburn and Yass and later went on to establish a station on the south side of the Murrumbidgee known as *Toganmain*. In 1859 he decided to live abroad before returning to Sydney briefly in 1873 to wind up his affairs. He died in Mentone, France on 24th June 1891.

Radiant Light

St. Luke and the Winged Ox

St. John and the golden eagle

St Mark and the Winged Lion

St. Matthew and the winged man with the Macleay plaque below

East Window – James Macarthur Memorial

The large stained glass East Window above the Communion Table in the Chancel was installed in 1874 after the Chancel and Vestry were added. The window, designed and installed by Clayton & Bell of England, depicts the Transfiguration of Christ and was given by Parishioners and friends as a memorial to James Macarthur who had died on 21st April 1867.

The window is full of symbolism. The central window depicts the transfigured Christ in the tabernacle suggested by Peter, attended by angels with Moses and Elijah on his left (Matthew 7:1-3; Mark 1: Luke 9:8-3). Christ is framed by a Latin inscription which translates

"This is my Son – My Chosen –Listen to Him."

The left-hand window depicts Moses, in his tabernacle, holding tablets of stone, the Ten Commandments (Exodus 20:1). The right-hand window shows Elijah in his tabernacle with the ravens (1 Kings 17:1). Peter, James and John on their knees are at the bottom of the window.

At the top is the sacrificial lamb on a Latin cross holding a banner symbolising Christ and the resurrection (Christ above all). Below, are the four gospel writers – Luke with a winged ox, Matthew with a winged man, Mark with a winged lion, and John with the golden eagle. Beneath are the symbols for "Alpha" and "Omega" (the beginning and the end), the same symbols can also be seen on the Communion Table.

At the top of each of the windows is the "canopy," a magnificent depiction of heaven, a design used by Clayton & Bell in many of their east windows.

Underneath the window is the inscription

"Erected by his many friends and admirers. In memory of James Macarthur Esq of Camden who fell asleep on Easter Day April 21, 1867 in the 69th year of his age."

James Macarthur was born at *Elizabeth Farm*, Parramatta on 15th December 1798 the fourth son of John Macarthur and Elizabeth Veale. He was educated at home until March 1809 when he left for England with his father and younger brother William. He went to school at Hackney, London and in 1813 was apprenticed to a broker in a London counting house.[11] In 1815 and 1816 he travelled in France and Europe with his father and brother William before returning to Camden in 1817.

He returned to England on a number of occasions and married Amelia Stone (known as Emily) in London on 14th June 1838. He was actively involved in politics for most of his life and was elected a member of the N.S.W. Legislative Assembly for the seat of West Division of Camden from 1856 to1857 and a member of the Legislative Council from 1866 to1867. As an agriculturalist and pastoralist he set an exacting standard in obtaining the best results from the land. Together with his brother William he was instrumental in establishing the township of Camden and the building of St. John's Church. He died on 21st April 1867 at *Camden Park* and is buried in the private Cemetery.

In 1937 the large east window was showing signs of bulging outward and expert advice was sought to preserve it. Experts advocated that the window should be taken down, re-leaded and over glazed and this work was carried out at a cost of £128[12] ($256) by O.C. Blanchard of Sydney. Further restoration work was carried out during 1988[13] funded through a grant made by the N.S.W. Bicentennial Authority. This included the installation of internal reinforcing rods and

---

[11] "Macarthur, James (1798-1867)" Australian Dictionary of Biography - J.D. Heydon
[12] "St. John's Church Camden" Camden News 14th November 1940
[13] "Service of Dedication" The Crier, 26th April 1988

external safety/security glass to protect the window from vandalism. Unfortunately this glass has a slight greenish cast which has somewhat diminished the brilliance of the original colours.

Despite the measures taken to prevent vandalism, worshippers were shocked when they arrived for the morning service on the last Sunday in June in 1988. Someone had either climbed a ladder or used the back of a truck to attack the windows with a heavy object. The safety glass was badly damaged and reinforcing rods bent, but the vandals had failed to destroy the windows.[14]

---

[14] "Desecration at St. Johns" The Crier, 5th July 1988

Radiant Light

East Window – James Macarthur Memorial Window

146

Captain Arthur Alexander Walton Onslow
The fifth window on the northern side is in memory of Captain Arthur Alexander Walton Onslow and shows Jesus with his disciples in the boat on the Sea of Galilee. The theme is appropriate in light of Captain Onslow's naval background. It bears the inscription *"He maketh the storm a calm so that the waves thereof are still"* (Matthew 8: 22).

Underneath the window is the inscription

> *"In memory of the Honourable Captain Arthur Onslow of Camden Park R.N. M.L.C. who entered another life on 31ˢᵗ January 1882 aged 49 years. Erected by his many sympathising friends."*

What is unclear is who made the window, where it was made, and who paid for it. It would seem more than likely that his widow Elizabeth commissioned the window whilst she was in England

Arthur Alexander Walton Onslow - courtesy of Camden Park

and that it was probably designed by Clayton & Bell as were other memorial windows for the family. The canopy at the top is clearly similar to other designs of this period.

Captain Arthur Alexander Walton Onslow was born on 2ⁿᵈ August 1833 in Trichinopoly, India the son of Arthur Pooley Onslow and Rosa Roberta Macleay. He was 5 years old when he came to Sydney in 1838 to stay with his grandfather Alexander Macleay. He returned to England in 1841 with the widow of Colonel Henry Dumaresq and re-joined his family.[15]

He was educated in Surrey and Nottingham before joining the Royal Navy in May 1847 as a Midshipman on *HMS Howe*; serving in the Channel and Mediterranean Squadrons and in the suppression of the slave trade on the West African coast. He was promoted to Lieutenant in 1852 and served in the Baltic Squadron during the Crimea War and was present at the bombardment of Sveaborg.

Between 1857 and 1861 he served on the *Herald* during the survey of north eastern Australia, namely Shark Bay, Torres Strait and the Great Barrier Reef before again returning to England where he studied steam navigation, and served in the Gulf of Mexico and the Mediterranean before being appointed Commander in 1863.

In 1864 he took sick leave and went to Sydney with the rank of Post Captain and on 31ˢᵗ January 1867 married Elizabeth Macarthur, the daughter of James Macarthur and Emily Stone and they lived at *Camden Park*. He retired from the Navy in 1871 and in 1874 he went with his cousin William Macleay on the *Chevert* to explore the New Guinea coast.

He won the seat of Camden in the Legislative Assembly in 1869 and in successive governments before resigning in 1880. Onslow served as a Lay Reader at St. John's, was a noted photographer, and a competent landscape sketcher.[16] He died of paralysis at *Camden Park* aged 44 years on 31ˢᵗ January 1882 and is buried in the private Cemetery at *Camden Park*.

---

[15] "Onslow, Arthur Alexander Walton (1833-1882)" Australian Dictionary of Biography – Bede Nairn
[16] "Arthur Alexander Walton Onslow" Dictionary of Australian Artists

Radiant Light

Captain Arthur Alexander Walton Onslow Memorial Window

Elizabeth Macarthur-Onslow Memorial

The fourth window on the northern side, made by Clayton & Bell was given in 1912 by the family of Elizabeth Macarthur-Onslow and depicts Jesus with his disciples, and mothers with their children, and bears the inscription *"Our father which art in heaven – For Thine is the Kingdom, the Power and the Glory"*.

At the top of the window we see the hand of God reaching down, a symbol of God the Father; and God's ownership and providence for all creation. Just below are 2 groups of angels holding scrolls *"In heaven the angels do always behold the face of my father."*

On the right we have Christ seated with or holding a group of children one of whom is giving him some flowers; behind stand Peter and John. On the left mothers are bringing their children to be blessed by Christ against a background of pomegranate trees. Pomegranates symbolise the hope of immortality and resurrection, holiness, love and hope. Below is the message *"Suffer little children to come unto me"* (Matthew 19:13, 15) and children kneeling in prayer. *"Our father which art in heaven" "For Thine is the kingdom the power and the glory"*.

On the right we have Christ seated with or holding a group of children one of whom is giving him some flowers; behind stand Peter and John. On the left mothers are bringing their children to be blessed by Christ against a background of pomegranate trees. Pomegranates symbolise the hope of immortality and resurrection, holiness, love and hope. Below is the message *"Suffer little children to come unto me"* (Matthew 19:13, 15) and children kneeling in prayer. *"Our father which art in heaven" "For Thine is the kingdom the power and the glory"*.

Underneath the window is the inscription

> *"In memory of our mother Elizabeth Macarthur-Onslow of Camden Park wife of Captain Arthur Onslow, daughter of James and Emily Macarthur born 8 May 1840 died England 2 Aug 1911 rests at Send, Surrey."*

Elizabeth Macarthur-Onslow was born on 8th May 1840 at *Camden Park* the daughter of James Macarthur and Elizabeth Veale. Elizabeth was educated at home and had extensive formal training in painting and drawing; at 16 years was tutored by Conrad Martens.[17]

The family left for England in 1860 and in 1862 they did the Grand Tour. Elizabeth also attended the Normal Central School of Art (South Kensington Museum)[18] and also had private tuition from William Collingwood Smith.[19] The family returned to Australia in 1864 influenced by Elizabeth's wish to live in Australia. On 31st January 1867 Elizabeth married Captain Arthur Alexander Walton Onslow.

James Macarthur died on 21st April 1867 and her mother Emily on 27th November 1880. On 31st January 1882 her husband Arthur Onslow died and she inherited *Camden Park* in 1882.[20] In 1887 she took her children to England and studied developments in the dairy industry. Elizabeth returned to Camden in 1890 and on 12th March 1892 was granted by Royal Licence, the right for her and her issue to use the surname Macarthur-Onslow.[21]

She died on 2nd August 1911 at Campden Hill, London whilst on a visit to England and is buried at Sendgrove, Surrey, England.

---

[17] "Elizabeth Macarthur" Dictionary of Australian Artists
[18] Now the Victoria & Albert Museum
[19] William Collingwood Smith was a founder member of the Royal Watercolour Society and at one time had the largest teaching practice in London.
[20] "Elizabeth Macarthur" – Annette Macarthur-Onslow – www.daao.org.au
[21] "Elizabeth Macarthur-Onslow 1840-1911 property owner" 200 Australian Women – Heather Radi

Radiant Light

Elizabeth Macarthur-Onslow Memorial Window

Brigadier General George Macleay Macarthur-Onslow Window[22]

The third window on the north side dedicated to the memory of Brigadier General George Macleay Macarthur Onslow was the gift of his widow Violet and daughter Faith and made by Powell & Sons (Whitefriars) Ltd.

At the top can be seen a Cross passing through a Crown, a traditional Christian symbol, symbolizing the death and victory of Christ as He reconciles the world.

To the left is the Angel Michael, the angel of the Last Judgement, shown with his symbols of the sword of judgement and scales of justice for the weighing of souls, above him is a banner depicting a serpent or dragon. To the right is the Angel Gabriel (the angel of the Annunciation) wearing a sash depicting the Garden of Eden, Noah's Ark, the Ram and the Goat, and the Cross (Genesis 159). Gabriel as the messenger of salvation holds a lily. Angels support a scroll - *"Be thou faithful unto death, and I will give thee a crown of life."*

Below on the left is a soldier dedicating his life before the cross, whilst to the right the soldier receives the crown of life. In the bottom right hand corner of the window is a friar or monk the trademark of Whitefriars Glass Company.

The inscription underneath reads

> *"To the beloved memory of Brig. Gen. George Macleay Macarthur Onslow CMG; DSO; VD, 2nd May 1875, died 12th September, 1931. This window is placed here by his wife and daughter. I thank my God upon every remembrance of you."*

The window was dedicated on 11th April 1937 by the Bishop of Tanganyika.[23]

---

[22] See chapter "Lest We Forget"
[23] Camden News, 14th November 1940

Radiant Light

Brigadier General George Macleay Macarthur-Onslow Memorial Window

152

John William Clinton and Alice Wilson Clinton

The second window on the north side, designed by Stephen Moor of South Strathfield, is a memorial to John William Clinton and his wife Alice Wilson Macdonald.

At the top can be seen the symbol of a Cross passing through a Crown and the symbols of alpha and omega. The symbols of "the Ten Commandments" and "the Book of Life" are also depicted.

The windows show the miracle of Jesus feeding the five thousand. Below to the left is a wheat sheaf and bread the symbol of the Bread of Life, Jesus Christ, who gave himself for us through his broken body in death. To the right the chalice and grapes: symbols of the cup of forgiveness and the new covenant we have in His blood.

The inscriptions underneath read

John William Clinton

"In loving memory of John William Clinton 1885 to 1967 the gift of his family."

And

"In loving memory of Alice Wilson Clinton our mother 1885 to 1975."

John William Clinton, known as Jack, was born on 25th September 1885 in Hinton, N.S.W. the son of Richard Henry Clinton and Elizabeth Ann Cullip. He was not quite 2 years of age when his father passed away on 6th May 1887; his mother remarried in 1891. Clinton worked as a carter and married Alice Wilson Macdonald at St. Andrew's Presbyterian Church, Newcastle on 21st February 1906 and the couple lived in Abermain.

In 1907 they moved to 90 Ruthven Street, Waverley where Clinton worked as a ticket collector on the tram network but by October 1911 they had returned to Abermain, and later moved to Merewether, Newcastle. Clinton's father-in-law, an Underground Manager in the mines, found him work in the mines where he worked until 1930 when he moved to the Burragorang and commenced mining operations in partnership with Charles Kemp and John Bertram Morton Knutsen. The family soon followed but they lived in fairly primitive conditions at Nattai River until they moved to Broughton Street, Camden in 1939; they later moved to Elizabeth Street.

The Clintons quickly became involved in activities around Camden. In the late 1940s Clinton joined the Camden Bowling Club and sponsored the annual J.W. Clinton Trophy competition; he was nominated a Life Member in 1954. He also became involved in horse breeding and racing and owned trotters and gallopers.

He was a generous supporter of various organisations including the Mater-Dei Special School in Camden; the Beverley Park Orthopaedic Hospital at Campbelltown; he also financially supported Camden and Liverpool Hospitals.

John William Clinton died on 31st May 1967 aged 81 years; Alice died on 10th March 1975 at the age of 90 years and is buried alongside her husband in Section D113.

Radiant Light

John William Clinton and Alice Wilson Clinton Memorial

Bertha Victoria Brien

The Bertha Victoria Brien memorial window, the first on the north side, was made by Kevin Little of Arncliffe.

The left window depicts St. Cecilia at the top holding a lute, and below playing an organ. To the right at the top is St. Mary B.V.[24] holding the baby Jesus and below a nativity scene.

The inscription underneath reads

> *"In loving memory of Bertha Victoria Brien who fell asleep April 15th 1961. Organist of this church 1926-1956. Devoted Sunday School Teacher kindergarten 1928-1954. These windows given and installed by her loving husband Michael."*
> *"I know my redeemer liveth. Suffer the little children to come to me."*

Bertha Victoria Cranfield on her graduation in June 1915

Bertha Victoria Cranfield was born in Camden on 25th August 1884 the daughter of John Cranfield and Emma Packenham. As a young girl she was a contralto member of St. John's choir and studied organ and piano under the then organist Leicester Johnson. In June 1915 she secured a Professional Teacher's Diploma and went on to teach the piano, organ, violin and singing for over 50 years.

Prior to *Studley Park* becoming an Army training school and golf course it was the Camden Grammar School, and Bertha taught music there twice weekly. As the organist for the Methodist Church had enlisted in the army during World War I, Bertha assumed the position and held this for the next seven years. She then went on to be the organist in St. Peter's Church Campbelltown following the installation of the Memorial Organ; she was the first organist for St. Peter's and held his position for two years.

Bertha Brien with her husband Michael

Bertha was then offered the position as organist for St. John's, and on 19th April 1924 Bertha married Michael Charles Louis Brien. Bertha continued as organist at St. John's for 30 years, and in addition was superintendent of the Sunday school and also trained the choir, assisted by her husband.

Throughout both World Wars 1 and 11 she knitted and packed parcels for the troops, and also financially supported the first Camden Scout Troop for which she was awarded the scout's Helper's Badge. During World War II she acted as accompanist to the R.A.F. male choir which had been formed at Camden Aerodrome in 1943 by her husband.

Despite ill-health over the last 10 years of her life she continued to teach music until 1956. She died on 15th April 1961 and is buried in Section F045. Her

---

[24] B.V. – Blessed Virgin

Radiant Light

husband installed a window in the church in her memory in what is known as the "children's corner," Michael Brien died 18th August 1976 and is buried beside her.

Bertha Victoria Brien Memorial Window

Written in Stone

Families have chosen varying tomb styles for their loved ones and they also choose the inscriptions that are placed on them. They chose different symbols to adorn the graves which express their feelings for the family members buried in the grave. Symbolism visible within the Cemetery includes the following:-

Anchor	A Christian symbol of hope and steadfastness. It can also be an occupational symbol of occupation. A broken anchor or an anchor with a broken chain stands for the cessation of life. Wrapped in Vines – firm Christian faith Cross and Anchor - a Christian symbol referring to Christ e.g. Hebrews 6:19 "hope we have as an anchor of the soul, both sincere and steadfast"
Angel	Messengers of God
Bible or Book	Book of Life
Broken Column	Life cut short
Broken Flower	A life terminated
Circle	Eternal life – no beginning, no end
Clasped Hands	Unity and affection even in death
Corn	Rebirth, fertility
Cross	Faith and resurrection
Crown	Crown of Life – immortality, triumph over death
Crown and Cross	Christianity and victory
Dove	Holy Spirit, soul reaching peace, spirituality
Drapery	Mourning
Eye	The eye of God symbolising the omnipresence of God. Enclosed in a triangle represents the Trinity
Flowers	Broken bud or branch – an untimely or premature death Calla Lily – marriage Daisy – innocence Ivy – immortality, friendship, faithfulness Laurel – special achievement, distinction, success, triumph, heroism Lily – purity Lily and Sword – guilt and innocence Lily of the Valley – purity and humility Pansy – remembrance and humility Pomegranate – the hope of immortality and resurrection, holiness, love, hope Poppy – sleep Rose (White) – purity Rose (Red) – martyrdom Rose bud – children
Garland	Victory in death
Hands	Index finger pointing upwards – hope in heaven Holding a chain with a broken link – death of a family member Hand reaching down – the hand of God Hand reaching down and plucking a link of a chain – God bringing a soul unto himself Raised hands – praise, prayer, voice and song

Heart	Heart – love, courage and intelligence
	Flaming heart – extreme ardour
	Heart encircled with thorns – the suffering of Christ
	Heart pierced by a sword – referring to Simeon's prophecy to Mary *"a sword shall pierce through your soul"*
Hourglass	Death, the passage of time and the shortness of life
IHS	This is a monogram of the name of Jesus Christ. From the 3rd century the names of Christ were sometimes shortened, by contraction, thus IC and XC or IHS and XPS for Iesous Christos. These Greek monograms continued to be used in Latin during the Middle Ages. The first three letters in Greek spelling Jesus are "IHS." It has been interpreted as "Jesus Saviour of Mankind." (ΙΗΣ - iota-eta-sigma; short for ΙΗΣΟΥΣ).
Lamb	Christ and his sacrifice – innocence, gentleness and humility
Scroll	The scriptures
Square and Compass	Masonic sign
Urn (draped)	Sorrow, mourning
Wreath	Victory in death

Most of the early headstones are of local sandstone from the *Denbigh* quarry at Cobbitty with carved lettering. Later headstones combined white marble, set in concrete or sandstone, with lead-filled letters. The more recent headstones are of white marble or grey or red granite with embossed gold lettering or lettering etched into the stone.

Table (raised) monument in Section D as it was circa 1980. Sides of the grave have since collapsed

Coffin grave of Garlies Allinson in Section C033

Some of the older graves have not only headstones but also a footstone supplementing the headstone. The footstones usually have the initials of the person interred in the grave, as well as the year of death engrave upon them and are generally of the same shape as the headstone on a smaller scale. More recently bronze, brass or stainless steel plaques have been attached to some of the older graves.

Different headstone styles can be seen throughout the Cemetery. One of the more unusual graves is that of Garlies Allinson. This grave is an example of a coffin style grave; the sandstone has been shaped to represent a sarcophagus and on top is engraved an ornate cross. The grave of the Leuckel children is topped by a cross in the form of a birch tree with a wreath of flowers and a cloth draped over the left arm. Another grave worthy of comment is that of George Armour. It has a hunting horn embedded in the marble signifying his love of hunting.

All but two of the table (raised) monuments have collapsed due to the slope of the ground as well as ground movement. Table monuments involve a heavy ledger stone engraved with the person's details supported by short stone supports at the head and foot or on either side. None of the table monuments with side supports are still standing but there are still one of the table monuments with head and foot supports in reasonable condition despite the inscription having almost totally eroding away.

A few of the graves have either wrought or cast iron fences surrounding them. Unfortunately many of these have deteriorated or been damaged by the elements. Recently the fence on the Mitchell grave was badly damaged, and the gravestone cracked, when a branch from a large red gum fell on it.

A listing of all known inscriptions is shown below. It should be noted that most of the headstones are extremely difficult to read, and in some cases, particularly in the case of wooden memorials, have now disappeared. Less than half the graves have memorials.

Adams	B021	In loving memory of my dear huband FREDERICK ROY ADAMS died 8th December 1951 aged 53 years VERA MAUD ADAMS loved wife of Fred died 23rd August 1970 aged 67 years
	D022	In loving remembrance of JOHN GEORGE beloved husband of Annie Adams died 7th March 1932 aged 43 years late A.I.F
	D040	In loving memory of WILLIAM ANDERSON ADAMS died 20th April 1930 aged 83 years
Albury	B050	In loving remembrance of WILLIAM ALBURY, "Rosehill" Oaks, who departed this life October 24th 1883 aged 79 years "My labour is over and I must be gone, I leave you not friendless to struggle alone, be watchful and prayerful and Jesus will stay, cling close to your Saviour let Him lead the way"
Aldridge	A002	Sacred to the memory of JOSEPH ALDRIDGE who departed this life August 14th 1871 Also of MARY JANE ALDRIDGE His dearly beloved wife who died November 19th 1870. This stone is erected by the children in affectionate remembrance of their departed parents
Allan	B009	In memory of MARY EDITH ALLAN wife of George Allan of Thrunsli, Central Queensland and daughter of Edward Palmer, *Conobie* Station, Flinders River, North Queensland, great grand daughter of the Reverend Samuel Marsden born 28th December 1879 died 19th April 1939
Allen	A097[1]	Also MARY ANN ALLEN died 30th June 1854 aged 57 years
	C127	Sacred to the memory of JAMES ALLEN who departed this life at Camden March 10th 1883 aged 47 years "My God, my father, whilst I stray far from my home in lifes rough way, O teach me from my heart to say, Thy will be done!" Also BITHIA wife of the above died at Glenbrook February 6th 1931in her 93rd year "Farewell! In hope and love, in faith and peace and prayer, Till He whose home is ours above unite us there!"

---

[1] Mary Ann Allen's gravestone is on the Cranfield grave

Allinson	C033	GARLIES ALLINSON died February 7, 1859 aged 31 years youngest son of Joseph Allinson, Whitehaven, late of Singapore
Appleyard	C035	In loving memory of my dear wife & our mother, daugher & sister ELAINE JENNIFER APPLEYARD passed away 10.7.1970 aged 27 years "*At rest*"
Armour	F031	In loving memory of my dear husband and our father GEORGE ARMOUR died 23rd May 1937 aged 53 years "Through mountain ranges wild and wide no more he'll wend his horn He lived the life he wished to live a huntsmen bred and born" Also Our dear mother ISABELLA ARMOUR died 28th July, 1971 aged 86 years
Austin	E023	In loving memory of EDWIN WALTER AUSTIN died 10th April 1918 aged 29 years "*At rest*" Erected by Ellen & William Barracluff
Baldwin	D114	In loving memory of my dear husband and our father DAVID BALDWIN died December 7th 1952 aged 66 years And Our dear mother LINDA MONA CLARE BALDWIN died March 9th 1965 aged 75 years "*In God's care*"
Barry	F039	In loving memory of WILLIAM JAMES BARRY passed away 25.12.1942 aged 14 Also My dear wife & our mother & nana ALICE MAY BARRY passed away 20.8.1972 aged 63 In loving memory of our dear father, grandfather and da da died 2nd June 1981 aged 79 years
Basden	A145	Sacred to the memory of THEODOSIA BASDEN who died September 14, 1859 aged 57 years And also of RICHARD BASDEN who died January 23rd, 1870 aged 68 years
Battam	C012	Sacred to the memory of JEREMIAH BATTAM who died 31 December 1853 aged 58 years "Waken, O Lord, our drowsy sense, To walk this dangerous road! And if our souls be hurried hence, May they be found with God"
Baxter	B028	In loving memory of our dear little son and brother LANCE RICHARD BAXTER who died 12th November 1942 aged 9 weeks "Safe in the arms of Jesus"
	F028	CHARLES GEORGE BAXTER died 15th Dec 1897 Also DULCIE MARTHA BAXTER died 21 Oct 1922 "*dearly loved*" MARTHA beloved wife of GEORGE BAXTER died 20th Dec 1931 aged 72 years
Baxter	F028	GEORGE BAXTER husband of above died 21st Oct 1939 aged 81 years "*At rest*"
Bayley	B086	Also In loving memory of ALFRED J BAYLEY who died September 5th 1899 aged 34 years

Benjamin	B089	In loving memory of ETHEL daughter of F.W. & L. Benjamin died July 3 1894 aged 7 years "*Taken in love*"
Biddulph	B072[2]	Also Our aunt ELLEN BIDDULPH died 22nd April 1939
Biffin	A034	DONALD beloved son of Aaron & Christina Biffin who died February 12th 1878 aged 33 years "*Blessed are the dead which die in the Lord*" CHRISTINA the beloved wife of Aaron Biffin who died 14th June, 1889 aged 68 years "O may we stand before the Lamb, When earth and seas are fled, And hear the Judge pronounce our name, With blessings on our head" Also AARON BIFFIN Husband of the above died 18th October 1902 aged 80 years "*I heard the voice of Jesus say, come unto me and rest*"
	D161	In loving memory of ALLAN EDMOND BIFFIN died 4th April 1925 aged 22 years "*Blessed are the pure in heart for they shall see God*"
	D162	In loving memory of our dear mother & father JANE BIFFIN died 12th Oct 1942 aged 70 years And W.A.E. (ALF) BIFFIN died 31st Dec 1942 aged 73 years
	D163	In loving memory of HAROLD ERNEST dearly beloved son of Alfred & Jane Biffin died May 1897 aged 6 years "*Gone but not forgotten*" Also RONALD THOMAS loved Son of Colin & Ann Biffin died 18th Dec 1930 aged 4 years
Billett	F016	In loving memory of GEORGE ROBERT BILLETT died 6th August 1915 aged 44 years "*Peace, Perfect Peace*" SARAH BILLETT (nee JENKINS) born 6.6.1842 died 10.7.1923 THOMAS BILLETT died 20.7.1919
Blackburn	A137	Remembrance of MARY ELIZABETH WRIGHT wife of J.S. Blackburn, Daughter of J S Walker, Surgeon 25th June, 1867 aged 28 years "*Think not of smouldering dust of the foul grave the just bright wave*"
Blades	E024	In loving memory of DOUGLAS SYDNEY BLADES died 4th April 1916 aged 26 years "*At rest*" Also Our dear mother ADELAIDE beloved wife of Thomas Blades died 19th July 1929 aged 74 years Also THOMAS BLADES loving husband & father of the above died 1st June 1937 aged 87 years "*At rest*"
Blow	B114	In loving memory of MAGGIE BLOW died 29th August 1902 aged 12 years "*She is not dead but sleepeth*"

---

[2] Ellen Louisa Biddulph's gravestone is alongside that of Leonard Russell Boardman

Boardman	B071	In loving memory of our dear parents ELIZA BOARDMAN died 10th Oct 1950 aged 78 years And RAYMOND BOARDMAN died 3rd Feb 1956 aged 74 years
	B072	In loving memory of our dear father LEONARD RUSSELL BOARDMAN 7.8.1914 - 7.11.1978 *"Sadly missed by family & friends"*
Boyd	A062	In memory of ALICE BOYD died 9 of December 1856 age 4 months Also FLORENCE BOYD died 12 of December 1864 age 2 years 10 months Also WILLIAM BOYD died October 17, 1865 age 7 years & 6 months
	D141	In loving memory of RUBY BOYD (nee STONE) 29th Oct 1981 *R.I.P.*
	E066	Sacred to the memory of RICHARD BOYD died 8th January 1859 aged 58 years Also SARAH wife of the above died 5th December 1870 aged 69 years Erected by Benjamin and Ellen Boyd
Brady	B063	Sacred to the memory of MARGARET beloved wife of Samuel Brady died 23rd January 1892 aged 42 years
Braithwaite	B066	In memory of my dear sister AGNES BRAITHWAITE died December 12 1873 aged 1 year and 4 months *"In heaven by grace of God we hope to meet her there"* Erected by her loving brother John
Bransby	A128	In memory of JOHN KENNEDY REYNOLDS son of George Bransby died August 27th, 1854 aged 15 Months *"For theirs is the kingdom of heaven"*
Bridges	C189	In memory of JAMES BRIDGES died 24th June 1887 aged 61 years And MARION BRIDGES died 14th September 1887 aged 69 years Erected by their loving daughter H.C. Tomkins DANIEL BRIDGES died 9th February 1853 aged 5 months
Brien	D108	A.I.F. 7355 Gunner ALEXANDER BRIEN 5th Field Artillery Brigade 16th June, 1952 aged 64 *"dearly Loved and sadly missed by his wife Annie & Sons"* In loving memory of our dear mother ANNIE LAURA BRIEN died 9th June 1974 aged 85 *"Sadly missed by her sons and their families"* *"Rest in peace"*
	F045	In loving memory of BERTHA VICTORIA BRIEN who fell asleep in Christ April 15th, 1961 age 77 years *"For ever with the Lord"* In loving memory of MICHAEL BRIEN died 18th August, 1976 beloved husband of Bertha *"Lover and benefactor of Camden"*
Brigstocke	C110	In loving memory of EVELYN JULIA beloved wife of F. P. Brigstocke who passed away 13th July 1922
Buchan	A149	In memory of MARGARET BUCHAN died 4th October, 1897 aged 90 years

Bugden	A082[3]	Also MARY ANN ELIA BUGDEN died 5th October, 1940 aged 73 years
Burford	E059	In loving memory of THOMAS beloved Husband of Emily Burford father of Olive and Sid died 20th June 1952 aged 68 years Also EMILY BURFORD passed away 8th June 1952 aged 68 years "*Resting*"
Burrett	A067	In loving memory of TIMOTHY BURRETT who departed this life September 18th 1881 aged 51. "*Blest are the pure in heart for they shall see God*" In loving memory of TIMOTHY BURRETT who departed this life 10th June 1886 aged 28 years and 11 months Also of WILLIAM BURRETT grandfather of the above died 8th May 1883 aged 82
Butchers	C152[4]	Also JOSEPH WILLIAM BUTCHERS father of above died 19th Nov 1946 aged 66 years Also His beloved wife and our mother MARIA died 15 Dec 1959 aged 69 years "*At rest*"
Butler	A130	In loving memory of WILFRED CHARLES BUTLER died 25th February 1958 aged 71 years Also ELSIE MAY BUTLER wife of the above passed away 25th July 1864 aged 68
	C005	In loving memory of DORA beloved wife of Wilfred Charles Butler died 18th April 1917 aged 26 years "*Peace, perfect peace*"
	C196	In loving remembrance of FANNY BLANCHE beloved daughter of Charles & Lucy Butler died 29th October 1906 aged 22 years "*Gone but not forgotten*" Also MERVYN ROY BUTLER died 11th May 1914 aged 11 years Also CHARLES BUTLER father of the above died 5th November 1914 aged 60 years "*Thy will be done*" Also LUCY BUTLER mother of the above died 6th May 1937 aged 78 years In loving memory of CECIL CLARENCE BUTLER born 16.3.1897 died 18.3.1987 dearly loved husband of Laura Edith Butler A proud grand & great grandfather and Distinquished W.W.1 Veteran

---

[3] Mary Ann Eliza Bugden's gravestone is on the grave of Annie Rofe
[4] The Butchers' gravestone is on the grave of Richard Mitchell

Butler	D001	Sacred to the memory of HARRIET wife of James Butler, Mount Hunter Creek, who departed this life March 28th 1850 aged 32 years *"I shall go to her but she shall not return to me"* Also In memory of JAMES BUTLER who departed this life 13th June 1888 aged 81 years "Therefore be ye also ready for in such an hour as you think not the Son of Man cometh"
	D001	And Their son JAMES died 4th February 1934 aged 85 years And His wife ROSANNA died 30th Mar 1935 aged 85 years
	D003	SUSANNAH BUTLER died 15th July 1898 aged 76 years *"Peace, perfect peace"*
Butt	B154	Sacred to the memory of ANN wife of JACOB BUTT who departed this life on the 24th May 1872 in the 72nd year of her age *"To thee I came a sinner weak and scarce know how to pray or speak, from fear and weakness set me free, O God be merciful to me"* Also JACOB BUTT who departed this life 15th May 1878 in his 72nd year "Reject not then Thy servant Lord when I with age decay, forsake me not when all wearied my vigor fades away"
Cameron	C152	In loving memory of EILEEN[5] beloved wife of Thomas Cameron died 4th Sept 1935 aged 18 years Also Her baby DON[6]
Campbell	A056	In loving memory of DOROTHEA CAMPBELL who died September 30th, 1901 aged 78 years *"May her soul rest in peace"* Also JOSEPH CAMPBELL who died December 16th, 1871 aged 15 years
	D106	In loving memory of SARAH JANE CAMPBELL died 1st February 1953 aged 75 years
Carron	F004[7]	Also JESSIE CARRON daughter of the above died at Old Guildford 19th May, 1910 aged 76 years
Channell	C164	Sacred to the memory of ELEANOR CHANNELL The dearly beloved daughter of William and Eleanor Channell, Menangle born in the year 1869 died March 5th 1876 aged 6 years *"Suffer little children to come unto me and forbit them not for such is the kingdom of heaven"* Also GEORGE son of the above born December 14 1874 died March 7 1884

---

[5] Freda Eileen Cameron
[6] Thomas Donald Cameron
[7] Jessie Carron's gravestone is on the grave of her mother Eliza Pearson

Channell	C168	In loving memory of my dear husband WILLIAM ARTHUR CHANNELL died 16th February, 1935 aged 54 years
		And
		His wife ALICE MATILDA CHANNELL died 20th Nov 1941 aged 63 years
	C171	In memory of WILLIAM CHANNELL died Apr 27 1864 aged 73 years *"The Lord gave and the Lord hath taken away"*
		Also
		ANN wife of the above died June 13 1856 aged 43 years
		Also
		HENRY son of the above died June 10 1855 aged 1 year & 9 months
		Also
		NAOMI second wife of the above died Jan 1869 aged 49 years
	D154	Also his daughter LILY ANN CHANNELL died 18-8-59 64 years *"Always Remembered" "At rest"*
		CHANNELL HENRY THEODORE JAMES loving husband of Lillian Ann father of Leonard, Doreen & Bill passed away 31 March 1984 aged 74 years
Chapman	A138	LAZARUS CHAPMAN Native of Somersetshire England died 20th June, 1880 aged 97 years erected by his son Joseph
Cheaney	D177[8]	In loving memory of GEORGE THOMAS CHEANEY died 5th August 1861 aged 2 years
		Also
		ELIZABETH MARGARET CHEANEY died 10th November 1867
Chisholm	F001	In memorium of JAMES KINGHORNE CHISHOLM died at Gledswood 28th August 1912 aged 82 years *"He laid his right hand upon me saying unto me, fear not"* Rev. 1 17
		In remembrance ISABELLA MACARTHUR CHISHOLM died Jan 7th 1883 aged 48 years
		Also
		EDWARD GLEDSWOOD CHISHOLM her eldest son died May 13th 1935 aged 70 years
		In remembrance ISABEL EMMELINE CHISHOLM died April 11th 1876 aged 5 years *"At rest"*
		In loving memory of MARY MACARTHUR CHISHOLM who died at Gledswood 23rd October 1919 *"And there shall be no night there the Lord giveth them light"* Rev.XXII 5
	F001	Also
		ELIZABETH MARY CHISHOLM who died at Turramurra 3rd Jan 1947 aged 86 years *"The weary are at rest"*

---

[8] Gravestone now missing

Clark	B155	In memory of ELIZA daughter of James & Fanny Clark died May 25 1860 aged 5 weeks & 4 days
		Also
		FANNY wife of James Clark died March 13 1863 aged 21 years "Weep not for me my friends so dear, since its God's will to call me here, my debt is paid, my grave you see, prepare yourselves to follow me"
		In loving memory of SUSAN MARIA CLARK died 28 January 1885 aged 8 years "Sleep on dear Susie take thy rest, for God has called when he thought best. This loss is great that we sustain, in heaven we hope to meet again"
	D043	In memory of MARY ANN daughter of James and Ann Clark died Sept 8 1851 aged 8 years
		Also
		The above JAMES CLARK died May 17 1887 aged 70 years
		Also
		ANN widow of the above died January 893 aged 69 years "And God shall wipe away all tears from their eyes; and there shall be no more death"
Clifton	C199	In loving memory of PETER WAYNE CLIFTON infant twin son of Joyce & Frank born 14.3.54 passed away 15.3.54
Clinton	D113	In loving memory of JOHN WILLIAM CLINTON passed away 11-5-1967 aged 81 Yrs. beloved husband of Alice Wilson Clinton *"Peacefully sleeping"*
		Our dear mother ALICE WILSON CLINTON passed away 10-3-1975 aged 90 yrs *"In God's care"*
	F044	In loving memory of KEVIN JOHN CLINTON died 29th March 1940 aged 6 years "Peacefully sleeping"
		Also
		Our dear mother DOROTHY RUBY MAY CLINTON died 28th December 1994 - aged 79 years *"She lived for those she loved, and those she loved remember" "Re-united"*
Close	A037[9]	Also
		HENRY THOMAS CLOSE beloved husband of Mary Anne Close who died December 15th 1912 aged 55 years
		Also
		MARY ANNE relict of Henry Thomas Close and daughter of the above died 2nd April, 1947 aged 88 years *"who trusteth in the Lord, Happy is he"*
Clout	B088	In loving memory of CHARLES CLOUT who died 28th April 1885 aged 86 years "Shed not for him the bitter tears, nor dim thy eye with vain regret, Tis but the casket that lies here, the gem that filled it sparkles yet"
		Also
		AMELIA CLOUT who died August 23rd 1891 aged 72 years *"In the midst of life we are in death"*

---

[9] The Close gravestone can be found on the Biffin grave

Coker	A108	In memory of GEORGE COKER who died October 31st, 1846 aged 56 years "Lord make me know mine end, and the measure of the days, what it is that I may know how frail I am" Ps 39th vs 4
Collopie	B135	MAY MARIA COLLOPIE died 22nd October 1950 aged 47 years
Cox	E082	In memory of SOPHIA GUMBLETON wife of Thomas Cox who died 29 Oct 1844 aged 29 years "Weep not dear friends Camden's no more, I am not lost but gone before, and in good time I hope to see, my dearest friends in heaven with me"
Cracknell	D094	MARGARET BAINES CRACKNELL died 17th Oct 1953 age 22
Cranfield	A096	In loving memory of my dear wife and our mother MARY ANN CRANFIELD died 16th May, 1932 aged 61 years Also GEORGE THOMAS CRANFIELD died 17th Nov 1937 aged 75 years
	A098	Also MARY ANN CRANFIELD died 30th September, 1852 aged 31 years. Also WILLIAM CRANFIELD died 2nd September, 1860 aged 53 years
	A139	Sacred to the memory of ELIZABETH CRANFIELD who departed this life June 30 1884 aged 51 years. Also ALICE ISABELLA daughter of the above, who died April 3 1872 aged 4 years & 3 months "Dearest loved ones, we have laid thee In the peaceful graves embrace But the memory will be cherished Till we see thee face to face" Also GEORGE HENRY CRANFIELD beloved husband of the above died May 16th 1913 aged 71 years "*At rest*" Also GEORGE ROBERT CRANFIELD departed this life 31st July 1962 aged 59 years dearly loved husband of Grace and dear father of John In loving memory of our dear baby BARRY[10] son of J. & E. Cranfield who died 24th January, 1892 aged 1 year and 4 months
	A140	In loving memory of GRACE ADELINE CRANFIELD departed this life 18th August, 1967 aged 71 years "*Peace, perfect peace*" In loving memory of ROSS[11] dearly beloved youngest son of J. & E. CRANFIELD who fell asleep 13th April, 1914 aged 15 years "*Until the day breaks and all shadows flee away*"
	A141	JOHN CRANFIELD died 20th October, 1950 aged 93 years
	A142	EMMA beloved wife of John Cranfield died 23rd April, 1940 aged 81 years
	A143	In memory of our loving parents "POPPY" E.B. 31.5.1898 - 16.3.1970 And

---

[10] William Barrington Cranfield
[11] Leonard Ross Cranfield

Cranfield	A143	FRANK 9.7.1894 - 29.7.1984 CRANFIELD 　　　　Also JOHN BRYAN 11.12.1030 - 23.5.2002 loved son of the above "*So deeply loved*"
	C046	In loving memory of MAY[12] CRANFIELD beloved wife of F Cranfield died 3rd October 1920 aged 21 years "*Behind all shadows standeth God*"
	C097	In memory of RAYMOND FRANK the dearly beloved child of Thomas & Elizabeth Cranfield who died January 21st 1892 aged 2 years & 3 weeks 　　　　Also ALFRED OWEN CRANFIELD who died August 2nd 1895 aged 2 1/2 years In loving memory of THOMAS CRANFIELD died 28th August 1896 aged 51 years 　　　　Also MARY wife of the above died 9th Sept 1924 aged 73 years ARTHUR THOMAS CRANFIELD passed away March 22nd 1958 aged 78 years
	D062	A tribute of love to the memory of my dear husband FREDERICK LAURIE CRANFIELD who departed this life 10th Sept. 1920 aged 32 years "*Dearly loved sadly missed*" VERA MAY CRANFIELD his dearly beloved wife who passed away 24th July 1982 aged 95 years "*United - At peace with God thy will be done*" In loving memory of ASTLEY ARTHUR (FRED) CRANFIELD beloved younger son of the above loved brother of Cecil, killed in action R.A.A.F. over Germany 22nd September 1943 aged 24 years, buried in Becklington British Military Cemetery, Soltau, Germany
Cresford	A095	In memory of WILLIAM CRESFORD died 30th June, 1850 aged 70 years 　　　　Also JAMES CRESFORD died 1st January, 1852 aged 70 years
Critchley	C068	In loving memory of WILLIAM CRITCHLEY died 22nd June 1912 aged 18 years "*Peace, perfect peace*" 　　　　And Our beloved mother MARY CRITCHLEY 3rd July 1951 "*At rest*"
Croaker	E073	JANE FRANCES CROAKER died 8.8.1973 aged 69
Cross	A017	In memory of CHARLES son of Charles & Mary Cross
Cummins	E101	In memory of our beloved son WILLIAM RICHARD CUMMINS died 12th Aug 1925 aged 2 years & 10 months 　　　　Also JOAN PATRICIA died 13th Aug 1932 aged 1 year, 8 months

---

[12] Edith May Cranfield

Curry	D121	In loving memory of GEORGE GUYATT CURRY died 14th Jan 1948 aged 76 years Also His beloved wife MARY died 8th June 1951 aged 76 years *"Abide with me"*
Cuthel	D117	In loving memory of ROBERT CUTHEL died 21st Nov 1948 aged 73 years *"Lead kindly light"*
	D144	In loving memory of SARAH ANN CUTHEL died 15th Dec 1907 aged 32 years & 10 months "Asleep in Jesus" "Not dead to us, we loved her dear, not lost but gone before, she lives with us in memory still and will for ever more" Also JEAN ALEXANDRA BLANCHE CUTHEL daughter of Sarah Ann Cuthel died 27th Jan 1923 aged 20 years
Darby	F064	In loving memory of MADELINE RUTH DARBY who departed this life November 6th 1943 aged 63 years Also Her husband HERBERT HENRY DARBY died July 8th 1944 aged 65 years *"At rest"*
Dawson	A129	In loving memory of WILLIAM DAWSON died 3rd June 1895 aged 85 years. SARAH DAWSON died 17th September 1893 aged 79 years. PRUDHOE JAMES DAWSON died 13th July 1859 aged 2 years. To the Memory of THOMAS DAWSON of Brooks Flat, Camden who died March 4th 1893 aged 72 years Also ELIZABETH DAWSON wife of the above who died May 11th, 1877 aged 54 years Also WILLIAM Son of the above who died July 11th, 1856 aged 9 weeks Also JANE daughter of the above who died September 10th, 1922 aged 69 years. *"At rest"* Also THOMAS Son of the above who died October 7th 1925 aged 76 years
	B055	In loving memory of OCTAVIE ELIZABETH infant daughter of John & Mary Dawson who died June 13 1893 aged 8 months *"mother's darling babe has gone to dwell with Him who gave"* In loving memory of my beloved husband and our dear father JOHN DAWSON who departed this life 10th October 1927 aged 70 years *"Forever with the Lord"* Also Our dear mother MARY DAWSON passed away 29th June 1944 aged 79 years *"Peace, perfect peace"* In loving memory of our dear sister DAISY VICTORIA DAWSON passed away 16th June 1976 aged 75 yrs Also Our beloved uncle LINCOLN GEORGE NORTON DAWSON passed away 18th Sept 1983 aged 80 yrs *"Sadly missed by family & friends"*

Dawson	B075	In loving memory of CHARLES DAWSON died 12th April 1917 aged 63 years
		Also
		MARY beloved wife of the above died 27th August 1931 aged 76 years "*Peace, perfect peace*"
		In loving memory of WILFRED DAWSON died 11th December 1889 aged 5 Weeks
	B075	Also
		MARION DAWSON died 6th October 1892 aged 4 months "*At rest*"
		In loving memory of CHARLES DAWSON died 26th June 1953 aged 66 years
	B158[13]	In loving memory of JOHN THOMAS DAWSON died 16th May 1967 aged 73 years
	C084	In loving memory of my dear wife & our loved mother HAZEL MAY SYLVIA DAWSON passed away 4th June 1962 aged 53 years
		And
		Our dear father FREDERICK WILLIAM DAWSON passed away 29th July 1973 aged 67 years "*Abide with me*"
Day	B110	In memory of DAPHNE daughter of S B Day born 29th Aug 1891 died 25th March 1910 "*Nearer my God to Thee*"
		Also
		SYDNEY BOLDEN DAY father of the above died 2nd Jan 1924 aged 67 years
De Zoete	B153	To the sacred memory of CHARLES SEPTIMUS DE ZOETE born the 27th September 1857 died the 13th September 1904 "*Come unto me and I will give you rest*"
Dengate	B062	In loving memory of my dear husband FREDERICK JAMES DENGATE died 8th September 1901 aged 62 years
		Also
		ELISA FLORIST beloved wife of the above died 24th July 1908 aged 69 years
		Also
		FRANK HERCULES DENGATE died 19th July 1951 aged 75 years
		MABEL VICTORIA DENGATE died 12th July 1968 aged 86 years mother of Morton
		Also
		MORTON HERCULES DENGATE died 30th Aug 1982 aged 77 years loved son of Frank & Mabel
	B135	"To the memory of the descendants of Frank and Frances Dengate"
		In loving memory of FRANCES ANN dearly beloved wife of Frank Dengate died 19th Aug 1924 aged 63 years
		Also
		FRANK DENGATE died 26th Oct 1929 aged 69 years In loving memory of FRANK CALMSLEY DENGATE 1898 - 1984
		IDA MARY DENGATE (nee DOWLE) 1905 - 1988
		ARTHUR DRURY DENGATE died 4th November 1957 aged 62 years

---

[13] Headstone now missing

Dengate	D089	In loving memory of ELIZA FLORIST dearly beloved daughter of Fred and Eliza Dengate aged 19 years Also His grandson JOHN EDWARD DENGATE who died June 1874 aged 1 year and 3 months Also WILLIE aged 7 months Also GEORGE aged 11 days "*Thy will be done*"
	D146	In loving memory of my dear husband EDWARD JOHN DENGATE died 8th May 1944 aged 78 years And His beloved wife & our loving mother EMMA DENGATE died 10th June 1952 aged 84 years
	D157	In loving memory of my dear husband EDWIN DENGATE who passed away 18th August 1924 in his 82nd year Also AMELIA ELIZABETH beloved wife of the above passed away 6th March 1937 in her 89th year "*Peace, perfect peace*"
	E114	In loving memory of JOHN DENGATE died February 5th 1920 aged 72 years
Derriman	A022	In memory of WILLIAM DERRIMAN died 23rd August 1891 aged 47 years MARY ANN DERRIMAN died 19th March 1925 aged 76 years ARTHUR DERRIMAN died 7th September 1943 aged 68 years CHARLES DERRIMAN died 14th August 1960 aged 83 years STELLA DERRIMAN died 31st July 1963 aged 74 years
	A026	In loving memory of ALBERT EDWARD DERRIMAN passed away 7th April 1966 aged 83 years
Dobson	A050	In memory of ANNIE beloved wife of the Rev. Simmons Dobson died Nov 5th 1873 aged 27 years "*Weep not, she is not dead but sleepeth*"
Douglas	A006	In loving memory of ANGUS GRAHAM DOUGLAS died 14th May 1946 aged 55 years And EMILY MAUD beloved wife of the above died 12th June 1948 aged 54 years "*Until the dawn breaks*" In loving memory of IAN GRAHAM DOUGLASS born 11th May 1933 died 28th December 1994 husband of Helen, father of Jocelyn, Grace & Bronwyn, brother of Mavis & Angus "*At peace at last*" ANGUS GRAHAM DOUGLAS JNR husband of Gloria father of Jamie 9.12.1920 - 16.4.1978 "*Re-united in God's care*"
Douglass	A047	In memory of HENRY GRATTON DOUGLASS who during a residence of about forty years held various high office within the Colony and was at all times an active supporter of its educational and benevolent institutions some of which he aided in establishing. Also In memory of HESTER his estimable and attached wife

Douglass		This stone is here placed by a few friends. Doctor Douglass died in Sydney on 1st December 1865 in his 75th year and his wife at Douglass Park in this county on 6th June 1863 aged 68 years
Doust	A053	In loving memory of AMY DOUST died 27th January 1949 aged 37 years "*Abide with me*"
	B128	In memory of RACHEL ABIGAIL beloved wife of A. J. Doust died March 23 1895 aged 34 years In memory of ELLEN GRACE beloved wife of A. J. Doust died Jan 9 1893 aged 37 years Also ALICE JULIA died Jan 29 1893 aged 3 weeks
Dowle	B129	In loving memory of CHRISTINA & FRED DOWLE died 19.12.53 & 29.8.53 aged 79 & 81 years beloved aunt & uncle of Florrie & Ivy "*Abide with me*" In loving memory of AMY & JOHN DOWLE AMY died 6.6.1970 aged 87 years JOHN died 12.9.1970 aged 89 years "*Re-united*"
	C112	In loving memory of FRANK DOUGLAS DOWLE beloved husband of Mildred our dear father & grand pop passed away 21st Nov 1964 aged 68 "*At rest*" Also His beloved wife MILDRED passed away 9th June 1968 aged 70 "*Forever with the Lord*"
Driscoll	F047	In loving memory of KEVIN WAYNE DRISCOLL passed away 9th March 1938 aged 5 weeks In loving memory of RONALD JOSEPH DRISCOLL loved husband of Verna, Loving father of Kevin, Fay, Val & Denis passed away 21 September 1999 aged 83 years "*At peace*"
	F061	In loving memory of LILLIAN beloved wife of D Driscoll passed away 15th August 1946 aged 67 years Also Our dear father DENNIS JOSEPH DRISCOLL passed away 10th August 1955 aged 84 years "*At rest*"
Druitt	B112	In loving memory of EMMA WALLWORTH DRUITT died 17th July 1938 aged 87 years In loving memory of ROBERT HENRY DRUITT son of the late Ven Archdeacon Druitt died 30th September 1899 aged 49 years "*Father in Thy gracious keeping leave we now Thy servant sleeping*"
Drury	B135	In loving memory of GEORGE DRURY died 15th February 1920 aged 80 years
Duck	F058	In loving memory of my dear wife and our mother GERTRUDE MARY DUCK died 11th Sept 1942 aged 48 years HERBERT WILLIAM DUCK died 7th December 1975 aged 91 years
Dunk	A134	In memory of JESSE DUNK. Born 22nd April 1787 Sussex England, died 15th June 1860 Camden Australia. *Without your journey*

		we would not be here. Our thanks. The Dunk family (Shirley 2009 Camden)
Dunk	C177	MILLICENT IRENE (MILLIE) dearly loved and only daughter of George & Jane Dunk died 23rd February 1915 aged 25 years *"Forever with the Lord"*
		JANIE darling wife of E.G. Dunk
		Also
		GEORGE loving husband and father of above died 10th June 1939 aged 74 years
Eagles	E061	In loving memory of our dearest son SIDNEY JAMES EAGLES died 15th May 1920 aged 3½ months *"Our bud in heaven"*
Eastwood	C093[14]	Also
		His mother CHARLOTTE EASTWOOD 16.31913 - 10.7.2006
Eirth	F040	In loving memory of EILEEN MARY darling wife of Mark Eirth who passed away 31st July 1938 aged 31 years *"God saw what was before her and what she had to bear and smiling down upon her He took her in His care"*
Ellis	A055	In loving memory of WILLIAM CHARLES ELLIS died 12th December, 1884 aged 4 years
		Also
		MARGUERITE MAUD ELLIS died 2nd May 1921 aged 43 years *"Resting"*
	B105	In loving memory of MARGARET ELLIS died 27th April 1921 aged 71 years
		Also
		SAMUEL ELLIS beloved husband of the above aged 76 years *"At rest"* Eleanor, Paul, Harold
		Also
		SAMUEL ERNEST son of the above died 28th February 1939 aged 61 years
Entwistle	A015	In loving memory of THOMAS ENTWISTLE died 27th April 1894 aged 28 years
		Also
		MARIA ENTWISTLE beloved sister of the above died 10th January 1919 aged 48 years *"Peace, Perfect Peace"*
Erwin	B070	In loving memory of THOMAS ERWIN died 21st July 1940 aged 77 years
	B070	Also
		His beloved wife MARY LYDIA ERWIN died 18h July 1954 aged 87 years
Fell	A151	Here are deposited the ashes of JOHN SIMPSON FELL who died August 18th, 1927 great grandson of the above beloved husband of Lilian, eldest son of John Wilson and Margaret Clark Fell aged 33 years

---

[14] Charlotte Eastwood's gravestone is on the grave of Melville Alfred Peachey

Ferguson	C002	In loving remembrance of FRANCIS FERGUSON died Sep 8 1892 aged 68 years Also ARTHUR BRUCE son of above, beloved husband of Edith C Ferguson died August 11th 1940 aged 60 years SARAH CAMP FERGUSON died July 20 1876 aged 53 years STANLEY HENRY SHEPHERD FERGUSON died May 30, 1875 aged 10 years BEATRICE GERTRUDE FERGUSON died Sep 22 1885 aged 2 years SEPTIMUS LESLIE FERGUSON died May 24 1886 aged 4 years & 6 months In loving memory of ROBERT "BRUCE" FERGUSON OAM born 11th May 1916, died 25th April 2008 And His dearly loved wife LILIAN "MARY" FERGUSON (nee SANDERS) born 4th August 1916 died 16th October 1995 "*Much respected servants of the community of Camden*"
	C002	In memory of CAMPBELL JOHN FERGUSON born 26th February 1857 died 27th September 1927 beloved husband of Mary (nee Jones), second son of Francis Ferguson, father of Stanley Nigel Ferguson (1881 - 1957) grandfather of Robert Bruce Ferguson and Hazel Joan Murray
Finch	F063	In loving memory of my dear husband & our dad EDWARD C FINCH passed away 24th October 1954 aged 54 years
Finlay	B104	In loving memory of LILY FINLAY who passed away 2th Nov 1954 aged 49 years ever remembered by her loving husband Billy
Fleming	B120	In loving memory of our dear son & brother ROBERT MATTHEW FLEMING died 17th June 1954 aged 13½ years MAY ELIZABETH FLEMING died 7.1.1963 aged 48 years WILLIAM (JOCK) FLEMING died 25.81973 aged 70 years
Ford	B135	FANNY ALICE FORD died 26th Feb 1982 aged 87 years
Fordham	B025 D014	RUBY FORDHAM 9.3.42 aged 48 CAROLINE FORDHAM 23.9.44 aged 78 JOHN FORDHAM 15.5.52 aged 84
Foreman	C037	In loving memory of our dear brother, mother & father ROBERT HENRY FOREMAN died 1st Nov 1964 aged 88 years "*God has them in His keeping, we have them in our hearts*" "*At rest*"
Foster	E079	In loving memory of EDENSOR FOSTER Bank Top, Kingsley, Eng. died 2nd Oct 1922 aged 43 years "*Rest in peace*"
Franklin	A019	In loving memory of my dear husband FREDERICK GEORGE FRANKLIN passed away 13th February 1963 "*I have fought the good fight, I have finished the course, I have kept the faith*" MARGARET ROSE beloved wife of the above died 21st August 1975 "*At rest*"
	A079	In loving remembrance of LOUISA the beloved wife of John Franklin died August 17th, 1882 aged 34 years. "I leave this world without a

		fear, save for the friends I held dear. To heal their sorrows Lord descend and to the friendless prove a friend"
		Also
Franklin		JOHN FRANKLIN died 2nd July, 1926 aged 79 years.
		Also
		JANE FRANKLIN relict of the above died 10th July, 1929 aged 76 years
	E035	In loving memory of ISABELLA FRANKLIN died 27th Feb 1918 aged 27 years
		In loving memory of MARY LEES FRANKLIN died 19th Sept 1940
		In loving memory of LEONORE MABEL FRANKLIN died 28th Oct 1952 aged 73 years
Freestone	B032	In loving memory of EDWARD PERCY ROBERTS FREESTONE died 24th August 1931 aged 60 years
		And also
		His beloved wife ANNA RUSSELL FREESTONE died 8th July 1946 aged 75 years
Fryer	B084	In loving memory of SARAH beloved wife of John Fryer died 7th July 1885 aged 34 years "*I go to prepare a place for you*"
Fuller	C071	In loving memory of THELMA AMELIA beloved wife of Charles Fuller died 18th August 1945 aged 36 years
		Her dear husband & our father CHARLES B W FULLER died 8th September 1964 aged 57 years "*Resting*"
	E051[15]	Sacred to the memory of SHARLOT FULLER (died 27 March 1858 aged 27 years
		Also
		MARY ANN FULLER aged 11 months
		FRANCIS FULLER aged 10 months
		HENERY FULLER died aged 8 months
Fussell	B026	In loving memory of ANTHONY IAN FUSSELL died 21st May 1942 aged 2 years and 5 months
Gammage	D154	In loving memory of our dear father WILLIAM ABRAHAM GAMMAGE died 3rd July 1932 aged 79 years
Gardner	A099	REX[16] beloved eldest son of G. & F. J. Gardner born 1893 died 1907 erected by his loving Aunt Kate.
		PRIVATE V.C. GARDNER 54th Battalion A.I.F. died in France 19.4.1918 aged 21 years.
		FRANCES JEAN beloved mother of the above died 31st March, 1937 "Till with the morn those angel faces smile which I had loved and lost awhile"
Garrard	B056	In loving memory of CHARLES AUGUST GARRARD who died 24th June 1900 aged 44 years

---

[15] Frances Charlotte Fuller-note correction to the name from Sharlet to Charlot
[16] Reginald Gardner

Giles	B014	Erected by Catherine Giles in memory of her beloved husband JAMES who died February 25th 1876 aged 42 years "Jesus said to her I am the resurrection and the life, he that believeth in me though he were dead yet shall he live" John X1, XXV Here also lies our only and beloved child JIMMY who died June 16th 1876 aged 3 years and 2 months *"Lie safe in the fold"*
Gill	F047	In loving memory of ELVY FLORENCE GILL (nee JENKINS) 27.11.1916 – 24.4.2002 aged 86 years Loved and loving wife of DONALD KEITH GILL 27.10,1925 – 26.9.2003 aged 77 years loved and loving parents of Greg born 10.10.10.1947, Peter born 8.11.1954, Lindy born 8.11.1955
Gillespie	B149	In loving remembrance of our dear son WILLIE GILLESPIE died 18th July 1899 aged 14 years In loving remembrance of our dear son JOHN WILLIAM GILLESPIE died 10th Oct 1905 aged 18 years EMILY GILLESPIE died 3rd Oct 1936 aged 65 years JOHN JOSEPH GILLESPIE died 14th Nov 1922 aged 63 years
Gilliat	B106	In loving memory of FREDERIC GILLIAT late of Hourncastle, England Obiit[17] August 14th 1886 aged 49 years "R.I.P."
Gittoes	B137	In loving memory of WILLIAM GITTOES who died 6th Feb 1884 aged 62 years Also
	B137	MARY GITTOES wife of the above who died 8th Feb 1887 aged 53 years "They are gone but not forgotten, never shall their memory fade, sweetest thoughts shall ever linger, round the spot where they are laid"
Glover	A004	FRANK GLOVER beloved husband of Madge and father of Frank and Joyce born at Olton, Birmingham, England 1889 died 1947 MADGE GLOVER beloved wife, dear mother of the above died 9th August 1969 aged 74 years *"Forever with the Lord at rest"*
Gray	C197	Sacred to the memory of WILLIAM SIMPSON GRAY who departed this life November 11th 1859 aged 32 years *"Death is swallowed up in victory"*
Greenfield	A100	Sacred to the memory of MARY ANN wife of James Greenfield of Narellan who departed this life 24th August, 1845 aged 35 years *"Weep not for me my husband dear, I am not dead but sleeping here, My debt is paid, my grave you see, Prepare yourself to follow me"*
Gregory	B102	In loving memory of our dear brother NOEL WILLIAM GREGORY who passed away 17th September 1937 aged 13 years "Dear Noel we sadly miss your cheerful smile and ever thoughtfulness. Far too short did God permit your golden heart to us. God giveth his beloved rest midst trees and birds he loved so much"
Grigg	C072	In loving memory of HENRY JOHN GRIGG died 24th Sept 1902 aged 68 years

---

[17] He or she died

Grigg		Also ANNIE GRIGG died 2nd June 1914 aged 80 years
Gwynne	B081	Beloved memory of the Revd. EDWARD HENLEY ACTON GWYNNE B.A. died 30th June 1890 aged 74 years
	B081	Also CORNELIA his wife died 24th March 1915 aged 67 years
Haigh	B022	In loving memory of V.L.B. HAIGH M.C. beloved husband of Leila Haigh
Haisell	D079	Sacred to the memory of WILLIAM HAISELL who died May 30th 1854 aged 12 years and 6 Months "Farewell dear son thy race is finished, thy painful days are past. The life of glory has begun and shall forever last"
Hall	C122	Here rest the ashes of FLORENCE EDITH HALL nee RIX wife of Charles T Hall who passed on 28 Oct 1942 aged 72 years "*Dearly beloved*" Also CHARLES THOMAS HALL who departed this life August 7th 1945 in his 80th year
	C156	Also HARRIET beloved wife of M.S. Hall and daughter of above died 31st October 1907 aged 48 years "*At rest*"
	D158	Erected by Margaret Hall In memory of her beloved husband WILLIAM killed by a falling tree on the 7th May 1868 aged 40 years "*The hue of his cheek and lips decayed, around his mouth a sweet smile played, they looked and he was dead*"
Hansen	A001	In loving memory of my dear husband and our father LARS CHRISTIAN HANSEN born Kallundborg, Denmark 10th June 1855 died 26th June 1936 Also Our dear mother SOPHIE wife of the above born Horsens, Denmark 6th November 1862 died 1st May 1945
Harris	B115	Also CATHERINE beloved youngest daughter of A & H M Harris and granddaughter of the above died 20th April 1929 aged 20 years
	D188	Sacred to the memory of JAMES HARRIS who died at *Camden Park* January 16th 1853 aged 25 years
Harrison	C059	Sacred to the memory of CHRISTIANA infant daughter of David and Martha Harrison died March 23 1855 aged 5 months
Hawkey	C076	In loving memory of LUCY beloved wife of Arthur Hawkey died 29th October 1914 aged 54 years Also RICHARD JOHN beloved son of the above killed in action in Palestine 27th March 1918 aged 24 years Also ARTHUR BURTON HAWKEY beloved husband of the above died 6th January 1935 aged 63 years

Hawkey	C126	EDITH MARY HAWKEY died 28th May 1966 aged 79 years
In loving memory of FANNY RUNDLE HAWKEY passed away 7th August 1935 aged 70 years "*At rest*"
Also
MARY ADA HAWKEY died 16 March 1954 aged 87 years
In affectionate remembrance of our dear father RICHARD HAWKEY who died Aug 15th 1901 aged 65 years "*Thy will be done*"
In affectionate remembrance of MARY ANN beloved wife of Richard Hawkey who died 29th September 1887 aged 50 years
Also
PRUDENCE ANN & FLORIST ELIZABETH daughters of the above who died young "*Blessed are the dead which die in the Lord*"
	D130	In loving memory of ROSE PEARL dearly beloved wife of Edward Hawkey departed this life 11th Nov 1923 aged 31 years "*At rest*"
Also
Her beloved husband EDWARD HAWKEY died 21st Feb 1954 aged 58 years
	D131	In memory of a loved husband and father RICHARD ERNEST HAWKEY passed away 21st July 1952 aged 78 years
Also
BEATRICE MARY his beloved wife died 7th August 1960 aged 80 "*In sure and certain hope of the resurrection to eternal life*"
	D137	In beloved Memory of WILLIAM HAWKEY passed away 14th March 1939 aged 63 years
And
ANNIE HAWKEY who passed away 22nd March 1939 aged 54 years
Hayter	D183	In loving remembrance of MARY HAYTER the beloved wife of James Hayter who departed this life 7th Jan 1886 aged 42 years
Also
	D183	EDWARD JAMES son of the above who died in infancy "*Blessed are the pure in heart for they shall see God*"
Hayward	A109	LORNA ALICE HAYWARD 1915-1990 "*Fear no more the heat of the sun*" Erected by L.A. Hayward ggdaughter 1980
Also
Her parents WILLIAM C HAYWARD 1889-1967
FLORENCE ALICE HAYWARD nee HOBBS 1891-1969
Heighington	D164	In loving memory of GEORGE FREDERICK HEIGHINGTON died 10th August 1909 aged 58 years Erected by his beloved wife & family
Also
JANE beloved wife of the above died 23rd Sept 1923 aged 75 years
Also
Beloved son JACK[18] died 18.4.37 aged 49
Also
Their beloved son EDWARD died 28.10.1958 aged 68
In loving memory of GEORGE DANIEL HEIGHINGTON died 20.5.46 died 20.5.46 aged 21 years 6 months
Also

---

[18] John William Heighington

Heighington		Our darling JIM[19] died 20.11.46 aged 19 years 5 months "*In God's care*"
Hellings	E064	In loving memory of ERNEST WYNNE HELLINGS died 30th Sept 1932 aged 60 years
Hemmens	E015	ALBERT ERNEST HEMMENS [BERT] died 23rd May 1916 aged 43 years "*At rest*" IDA MARTHA wife of the above died 16th May 1946 aged 64 years
Herbert	A046[20]	Sacred to the memory of KEZIA the beloved wife of Thomas Herbert of Narellan who departed this life June 1st 1872 aged 60 years "*Farewell, dear husband, my days are past, I loved you while my life did last, no more sorrow for me take but love my children for my sake*"
Hewitt	D180	In loving memory of a dear husband and father REGINALD ERIC HEWITT who passed away 24th August 1950 aged 56 years "*Abide with me*" In loving memory of RUBY RHODA HEWITT loved mother & grandmother died 27 Sept. 1989 aged 96 years
Hilder	A139[21]	Also Dear little JACK only son of J. & C. Hilder who left us 10th July, 1911 aged 4 years "*We loved them much but Jesus loved them best*"
	D034	SARAH JANE HILDER died 5th Sept 1907 aged 51 years GEORGE HILDER died 12th Dec 1854 aged 18 years WILLIAM J HILDER died 21st Nov 1891 aged 32 years HARRIET HILDER died 22nd Aug 1917 aged 63 years JAMES HILDER died 8th June 1901 aged 87 years PHILA[22] HILDER wife of the above died 18th Nov 1869
	D035	Erected by their children In loving remembrance of MOSES HILDER died June 7th 1868 aged 60 years Also ELIZABETH HILDER wife of the above died Dec 11th 1881 aged 68 years "*Their toils are past, their work is done, and they are fully blest. They fought the fight, the victory won, and entered into rest*"
	E098	In loving memory of FLORENCE LOTTIE HILDER died 4th April 1937 aged 53 years
Hill	D073	THELMA IRENE HILL (nee BARRETT) passed away 4th August 1970 beloved mother of Donell, grandmother of Desleigh Anne "*R.I.P.*"
	E033[23]	"*R.I.P.*" Dad CYRIL HILL died 30.11.83 aged 75 years
Hillier	B079	In loving memory of RICHARD HILLIER died Oct 24th 1891 aged 82 years Also SARAH LOUISA beloved wife of the above died Sep 28 1898 aged 77 years "*Blessed are the pure in heart for they shall see God*" "*At rest*"

---

[19] James Deamer Heighington
[20] The other Herbert graves and headstones have been covered over
[21] This gravestone is on the Cranfield grave
[22] Philadelphia Hilder
[23] Original wooden cross no longer visible

Hillier		Also AMY HILLIER died 1st June 1903 aged 58 years In loving memory of RICHARD HILLIER died 9th June 1908 aged 61 years
Hinde	A012	OLIVER HINDE MARY HAMILTON HINDE
Hindes	B058	In loving memory of FRED beloved son of R.G. & M. Hindes August 2nd 1913 aged 29 years
	B058	Also MARGARET HINDES died 15th June 1930 aged 74 years Also RICHARD GEORGE HINDES died 28th September 1942 aged 86 years
	C079	In memory of FREDERICK A HINDES died 3rd Oct 1905 aged 74 years ANN R HINDES died 18th May 1905 aged 80 years HERBERT A HINDES died 6th May 1892 aged 27 years *"Thy will be done"*
Hobbs	A107	Sacred to the memory of MARY EMELINE infant daughter of Thomas and May Hobbs who died May 1st 1852 aged 9 months. Also One who died in infancy October 9th, 1854
	A109	THOMAS HOBBS farmer & storekeeper of Sussex Eng. 25 years in N.S.W. husband of H. Rofe[24] & M. Coker[25]
Hodge	D146	In loving memory of MAUD dearly beloved wife of Philip Benjamin Hodge died 4th December 1953 aged 80 years Also EDNA EMMA and ERIC VICTOR loved children of the above PHILIP BENJAMIN HODGE died 20th May 1979 age 102 years
Holdsworth	D094	CRYSTOBEL EILEEN HOLDSWORTH died 1.12.72 GERARD BAINES HOLDSWORTH died 19th July 1934 aged 3 years PEARL ALEXANDRIA HOLDSWORTH died 9th August 1924 aged 34 ROY DOBSON HOLDSWORTH died 25th April 1950 age 61 In loving memory of JOE[26] & ALICE HOLDSWORTH *"Re-united"*
	E116	In loving memory of FLORENCE AGNES beloved wife of Edwin Holdsworth died 25th April 1931 aged 31 years Also EDWIN JOSEPH HOLDSWORTH died 22nd April 1954 aged 53 years
Hopson	C137	In loving memory of our dear mother father & brothers CHARLES HOPSON died 18-10-1914 aged 77 DORCAS HOPSON died 17-8-1919 aged 73

---

[24] Harriet Rofe
[25] Mary Coker nee Dawson
[26] Ernest John Holdsworth

Hopson		LLOYD EDWARD beloved husband of Ethel Dowle[27] died 19-6-1955 aged 59 HERBERT HOPSON died 28-10-1906 aged 27 WILLIAM HOPSON died 9-11-1907 aged 41 ARTHUR HOPSON died 28-7-1953 aged 80 "*Peace, perfect peace*"
Hourn	B101	In fond remembrance of ALICE youngest daughter of John and Ruth Hourn who died 15th June 1882 aged 2 years "*Angels beckoned far away and Jesus bid her come*" Also RUTH HOURN mother of the above who died 6 April 1884 aged 62 years "Though lost to sight her memory still lives in hearts that knew her worth"
Hughes	A010	In memory of EDWARD CHARLES LAWRY the beloved husband of Emmie Hughes born 28th November 1856 died 14th August 1902 Also SARAH EMILY ANNETTE HUGHES died 1st September 1909 aged 55 years dearly beloved daughter of Mrs. E. R. McMullen, Moreton Park "*Peace, Perfect Peace*" Also EMMIE MARY HUGHES beloved wife of above died 2nd June 1919 aged 63 years "*The beloved of the Lord shall dwell in safety*" In loving memory of HENRY CLARENCE HUGHES youngest son of Ellen R. McMullen who died at Moreton Park on 12th day of October 1904 aged 42 years "*Gone from us but not forgotten, never shall thy memory fade, loving thoughts shall ever linger round the spot where thou art laid*" In loving memory of EVELYN FORREST the dearly beloved infant daughter of E.C. and E.M. Hughes born 4th August 1892 died 31st October 1893 "*The Lord gave and the Lord hath taken away, Blessed be the name of the Lord*"
Hulme	B084[28]	And The ashes of her daughter SARAH JANE HULME died 20th December 1930 aged 65 year
Inglis	C038	Sacred to the memory of LOUISA ANN INGLIS who departed this life 9th February 1858 aged 11 months
Ings	E113	In loving memory of our dear father RICHARD INGS died 29th Dec 1955 aged 87 years Our dear mother MARY ANN died 2nd June 1934 aged 76
James	C070	In loving memory of DUDLEY JOHN beloved infant son of W.J. & A.K. James died 17th Nov 1914
Jarrett	C032	STEPHEN JARRETT died 8th June 1870 aged 75 years Also LOUISA JARRETT died 24th August 1886 aged 82 years natives of Lydd, Kent, England

---

[27] Emily May Hopson nee Dowle
[28] This gravestone is on the Fryer/McDowall grave

Jenkins	A058	In loving memory of my dear husband and our father ARTHUR D. JENKINS died 28th June 1928 aged 56 years In loving memory of our dear mother LUCY JENKINS died 25th January 1955 aged 85 years WILLIAM JENKINS died 1875 ELIZA (TULLY) JENKINS died 1902 married at Sydney 2nd October 1838 "*Pioneers of the Camden/Picton area*"
	C049	In loving memory of WILLIAM JAMES JENKINS died 26th December 1911 aged 49 years "*Lord all pitying Jesu blest, grant him Thine eternal rest*"
	D115	In loving memory of my dear husband & our father HERCULES JENKINS died 13.5.1950 aged 42 years
	D194	ADA - Mrs Jenkins 1 August 1956 aged 93
	E057	In loving memory of SYLVESTER REUBEN JENKINS born Oct 13th 1872 passed peacefully away Aug 16th 1944 "*Sleep on beloved*" Also EMILY CAROLINE JENKINS wife of above passed away 22nd Feb 1964 aged 87 years
	E073	Also SHIRLEY JENKINS died 28.8.1927 aged 19 mths sadly missed by Lila
	F015	In loving memory of JOHN JENKINS died 24th Nov 1913 aged 69 years Also SUSANNAH beloved wife of the above died 12th Jan 1936 aged 85 years "*Peace, Perfect Peace*"
	F049	In loving memory of CHARLES HERCULES JENKINS passed away 9th August 1950 aged 70 years Also MINNIE ELIZABETH wife of the above passed away 1st December 1958 in her 74th year "*At rest*"
	F053	In loving memory of WALLACE CONRAD ROFE JENKINS late 1st Batt A.I.F. died 12th Oct 1938 aged 40 years JESSIE MILDRED JENKINS died 3rd March 1991 aged 93 years
	F059	THOMAS EDWIN JENKINS ELIZABETH ALICE JENKINS (nee BUTCHERS)
Johnson	C051	"*I will ransom them from the power of the grave*" In loving memory of JOHN JOHNSON who died August 24 1891 aged 63 years Also SUSAN His wife who died June 29 1889 aged 59 years Also WALTER who died July 9 1879 aged 12 years Also SUSAN & GEORGE who died in their infancy children of the above
Kaffie	B127	In memory of HENRY KAFFIE died 1st Sept. 1918 aged 75 years "*At rest*"
Kemp	A094	In memory of CHARLES KEMP died 13th April, 1853 aged 38 years Also CHARLES GEORGE son of the above died 24th February, 1854 aged 6 years

Kemp		Also MARY widow of the above Charles Kemp died 21st June, 1880 aged 77 years Also MARY JANE KEMP daughter of the above died 15th May, 1910 aged 58 years
Kendall	E016	MARY CONSTANCE HASSELL beloved wife of Robert Kendall died 31st July 1915 aged 24 years "*At rest*"
Kent	F039	In loving memory of BERYL JOYCE KENT (BARRY) 16.7.1927 – 18.6.2009 "*Loved by all*"
Kettley	B108	HARRIET KETTLEY GEORGE KETTLEY
King	B152	CECIL J KING M.A. Rector of St. Johns Camden for 34 years called to higher service Easter April 18th 1938 in his 75th year "*Near to each other, nearer yet to Him, we are united in the life divine*"
	B152	In loving memory of A MAY KING beloved wife of Cecil John King rector of Camden who passed to her rest on October 12th 1945 COPLAND KING M.A. Priest New Guinea Mission 1891-1915 died 5.10.1918 aged 55 years (*also on cross*) C.K. Obiit[29] 5.10.18 Ætat[30] 55 years
Knox	A051[31]	And ADA ELIZA JANE KNOX died February 6th, 1957 aged 82 years widow of James Knox and granddaughter of the above "*Remembered*"
Kowald	A053[32]	Also ELLEN KOWALD loving mother of Amy died 17th November 1964 aged 83 years
Kyle	B123	In memory of LATITIA beloved wife of W Kyle died Dec 29th 1894 aged 56 years
Lakeman	A102	Sacred to the memory of JOHN LAKEMAN born September 3rd, 1811 drowned May 8th, 1869
	A103	In memory of HANNAH LAKEMAN born September 4th, 1841 died May 23rd, 1845
Leacock	B005	In memory of CHARLES GEORGE LEACOCK died 22nd December 1887 aged 42 years Also His third daughter JESSIE HELENA departed 7th March 1933 aged 58 "*Passed from death into life having loved the brethren*" Also JANET FLORENCE LEACOCK wife and mother of above died 24th October 1941 aged 93 years "*Awaiting the day of resurection*"

---

[29] He or she died
[30] L *aetatis*, gen. of *aetas*, life, age
[31] This gravestone is on the Marks grave
[32] This gravestone is on the Doust grave

Leuckel	D166	Sacred to the memory of our beloved son CHRISTIAN LEUCKEL who died 23rd of March 1888 aged 29 years Also MARTIN aged 4 years ANNA aged 5 years BERNARD aged 5 years ELIZABETH aged 7 years Erected by their loving parents Christian and Margaret Leuckel *"May their souls rest in peace"*
Lilley	C017	Sacred to the memory of ARTHUR LILLEY of Upper Tooting, Surrey, England who died at Menangle 2[0-9]nd June 1886 in his 31st year *"Spare him Lord, all-pitying, Jesu blest, Grant him thine eternal rest!"*
Little	A135	In loving memory of my dear husband JAMES DIXON LITTLE died 9th July 1940 aged 51 years Also VERA MAY LITTLE died 19th December 1957 aged 52 years
	C002	In memory of SYDNEY FERGUSON LITTLE 11th July 1983
	E102	In loving memory of ALFRED DENISON LITTLE who passed away 24th Feb 1936 aged 68 years Also MARGARET ELIZABETH LITTLE died 8th May 1958 *"At rest"*
Lock	D184	In loving memory of HENRY LOCK who died April 7th 1882 aged 72 years For 29 years Sexton of St. Johns Church Camden Also DAVID died Jan 17th 1881 aged 28 years Also AMY died Nov 13th 1859 aged 15 months beloved children of Henry and Sarah Lock *"Thy will be done"*
Lovell	C086	In memory of SAMUEL LOVELL died 29th Jun 1923 aged 69 years foundation member of Morning Star Lodge Camden Erected by the members of No. 515 Manchester Unity I.O.O.F.
Low	D179	MERCY LOW (Massy Law) b. 1826 Newport, Essex, England d. 6.4.1861 *R.I.P.*
Lowe	A111	In loving memory of EDWIN FREDERICK LOWE of Deptford, Clarence Town died 10th January, 1917 aged 64 years. Also Our dear sons BRUCE WHYSALL died in infancy. Also ERIC LYNDON A.I.F. wounded at GALLIPOLI died in London 10th September 1915 aged 19 years *"Alls well"*
	C181	In loving memory of CATHERINE ANN LOWE of Booral died 14th February 1906 aged 61 years
Luker	B016	In memory of CHARLES LUKER died 22nd October 1891 aged 57 years MARY ANN LUKER died 5th September 1881 aged 35 WILLIAM LUKER died 17th July 1870 aged 68

Luker		MARTHA LUKER died 18th August 1885 aged 79 *"May they rest in peace"*
Lusted	A144	In memory of ELIZABETH LUSTED wife of Edward Lusted who died 11th November, 1864 aged 38 years Also of ANNIE LUSTED daughter of the above died 4 January, 1865 aged 5 months. Also of EDWARD LUSTED who died 25th February, 1877 aged 53 years "Yea though I walk through the valley of the shadow of death I will fear no evil for Thou art with me, Thy rod and Thy staff they comfort me" Psalm XXIII
Lye	D185	F L 1888 E L 1891 A L 1893
Mahoney	F032	In loving memory of JAMES MAHONEY died 6th June 1940 aged 79 years And His beloved wife ADA E MAHONEY died 26th Aug 1948 aged 79 years
Marden	B041	DORCAS ANNE MARDEN died 2nd Feb 1980 *"The Lord is my shepherd"*
	E035	In loving memory of PHOEBE MARDEN died 16th Nov 1953 aged 46 years
	F036	In loving memory of ADA GRACE MARDEN died 2nd Oct 1928 aged 44 years Also HERBERT JESSE MARDEN died 30th April 1942 aged 61 years
	F067	In loving memory of ERNEST ALLEN MARDEN, Marion Vale, Werombi died 18.1.58 aged 75 years Also ELSIE MAY wife of the above died 22.7.62 aged 81 years In loving memory of my dear husband & our father RONALD ERNEST MARDEN who died 17th August 1971 aged years
Marks	A051	In memory of THOMAS MARKS died October 11th, 1874 aged 87 years. Also ELIZA his beloved wife died August 11th 1883 aged 77 years
Martin	B019	In memory of FREDERIC JOHN MARTIN born 6th December 1856 died 2nd September 1861 And of WALTER CECIL MARTIN born 24th March 1861 died 10th June 1866 Also In loving memory of their parents HONOR MARTIN died 26th September 1908 aged 84 years And JOHN BENSON MARTIN died 2nd September 1908 aged 89 years

Martin	B019	Also
		ELEANOR GERTRUDE MARTIN died 13th June 1941 aged 78 years
		Also
		HENRIETTA MARIA MARTIN died 28th May 1945 aged 87 years
	F003	In memory of ALEXANDER MARTIN Commander R.N. died 7th September 1868 aged 84 He was early and actively employed, having joined the Service in 1795 In which year he took part in Cornwallis's action. He was present at the battles of Camperdown and Trafalagar and in many minor engagements
		Also
		SARAH wife of the above died 2nd October 1884 aged 96 years
Martyn	B024	In loving memory of PERCY MARTYN who passed away 21st February 1941 aged 70 years
Matthews	B078	In loving memory of BENJAMIN MATTHEWS died December 29th 1895 aged 64 years
McClung	A061	In loving memory of my beloved husband and our dear father WILLIAM AUBREY McCLUNG who departed this life 29th May, 1949 aged 74 years
		And
		Our dear mother SARAH GRACE McCLUNG who departed this life 30th January 1958 aged 78 years "*At rest*"
McDonald	C105	In loving memory of REBECCA MARY McDONALD died 10th June 1919 aged 62 years "*Peace, perfect peace*"
		In loving memory of EDWIN VICTOR McDONALD died 23rd April 1929 aged 31 years
McDowall	B084[33]	And
		Her youngest daughter SARAH MAY McDOWALL died 21st January 1960 aged 74 years
	E106	In loving memory of MAJORIE beloved wife of Rees McDowall and daughter of A.H. & I. Mitchell died 27th March 1927 aged 29 years
McEwan	A040	In loving memory of JAMES A. McEWAN died 24th October 1938 aged 68 years
		Also
		SUSAN wife of the above died 28th March 1945 aged 68 years "*At rest*"
	B001	In loving memory of IDA beloved wife of Alfred C. McEwan died 29th August 1919 aged 36 years "*After much suffering*" "*At rest*"
		Also
		ALFRED CHARLES McEWAN died 18th April 1947 aged 68 years
	B002	In loving memory of HENRY McEWAN died 2nd June 1931 aged 57 years "*Peace, Perfect Peace*"
		In loving memory of WILLIAM WALKER McEWAN died September 11th, 1896 aged 64 years
		Also children of the above
		ANNIE died February 10th 1873 aged 10 months

---

[33] This gravestone is on the Fryer grave

McEwan		WILLIAM died January 7th 1884 aged 15 years
		ANNIE BARBARA died February 23rd 1887 aged 11 years
	B002	In loving memory of RACHEL beloved wife of William W. McEwan died 2nd April 1928 aged 92 years
	C101	In loving memory of ALFRED KEITH McEWAN passed away 31st July 1961 aged 62 years
		Our dear mother MURIEL AMY McEWAN passed away 28th May 1974 aged 66 years
		In loving memory of JAMES VICTOR McEWAN beloved son of James & Susan passed away 18.2.1975 aged 69 years
McGrath	E020	In loving memory of ALFRED GEORGE beloved Son of E. & H. McGrath died 18th Sept 1915 aged 3 years "*Safe in the arms of Jesus*"
		In loving memory of PTE ERNEST H McGRATH died of injuries in Egypt 26th May 1941 aged 31 years Erected by his loving wife Heather and baby Fay "*Always in our thoughts*"
		In loving memory of HANNAH FRANCES McGRATH died 14th Nov 1960 aged 73 years "*At rest*"
		ERNEST MILLINGTON McGRATH died 7th April 1974 aged 86 years "*At rest*"
McGregor	C005	Also MARY beloved wife of JOHN McGREGOR died 29th Jan 1927
McIntyre	F057	In loving memory of our dear Son and our dear brother ARNOLD McINTYRE called home 22nd Aug 1942 aged 15 years & 10 months "*Forever with the Lord*"
McKechnie	E026	In loving memory of ROSE ANNE McKECHNIE died 9th February 1917 aged 42 years "*At rest*"
		LEONARD J McKECHNIE born 1907 died 1967 sadly missed father of Heather "*R.I.P.*"
McKenzie	C167	In loving memory of my dear husband ALEXANDER JOHN McKENZIE died 21st Sept 1922 aged 61 years
		MARGARETTA McKENZIE dearly loved wife of above died 19th June 1942 aged 81 years "*At rest*"
McLeod	E112	In loving memory of JAMES McLEOD died 21st January 1927 aged 64 years
		LAURA McLEOD died 11th March 1962 aged 86
		Our devoted mother NELLIE JEAN EVANS died 8th December 1992 aged 84
		In loving memory of FREDERICK JAMES McLEOD 1.7.1912 - 11.3.2002 "*At peace*"
	F022	Our dear mother ELIZABETH McLEOD who departed this life 24th Sept 1922
		NP618 MAJOR N. T. McLEOD Royal Aust. Artillery 7th October 1969 aged 82
		Our dear father NORMAN McLEOD who departed this life 4th Oct 1922
		Also
		MARTHE MABEL beloved wife of Norman McLeod died 5th Feb 1962 aged 73 years "*At rest*"

McMinn	B008	In loving memory of ALEXANDER WATSON the dearly beloved eldest son of John Thomas and Anne McMinn who died 12th August 1895 aged 25 years *"The Lord gave and the Lord hath taken away, Blessed be the name of the Lord"* Job 1 Chap 21 verse Also
	B008	JOHN THOMAS McMINN father of the above who died 7th July 1913 aged 79 years *"Thy will be done"* In loving memory of MARY AGNES McMINN who departed this life 31st October 1914 aged 29 years *"Peace, Perfect Peace"* In loving memory of ANNE beloved wife of John Thomas McMinn who died 8th June 1935 aged 88 years Also SAMUEL beloved brother of the above who died 4th March 1922 aged 48 years *"At rest"* Also MILDRED MABEL beloved wife of the above who died 11th May 1960 aged 78 *"Abide with me"* In loving memory of ANNE beloved wife of John Thomas McMinn who died 8th June 1935 aged 88 years *"Nearer my God to Thee"* Also LEWIS AUSTIN beloved son of the above who died 5th November 1955 aged 76 years *"Abide with me"*
	B041	In loving memory of a beloved wife and mother ELEANOR MAUD McMINN who passed away 23rd May 1962 aged 75 years *"For those who live in faith and love there is a glorious rest above"* ROBERT DAVID McMINN dearly loved husband of the above departed this life 10th May 1971 aged 93 years *"In God's care"*
	B042	In loving memory of my dear husband and my father JOHN THOMAS McMINN who passed away on 1st October 1933 aged 58 Also His wife and my dear mother GEORGINA BLANCH McMINN who passed away on 29th January 1875 *"The Lord gave and the Lord hath taken away, blessed be the name of the Lord"* *"At rest"*
McMullen	A010[34]	Also ELLEN ROSETTA McMULLEN died 3rd April 1914 aged 87 years In loving memory of OSWALD ROBERT HERBERT infant son of Franklin and Ellen McMullen who died at Moreton Park 14th March 1877 aged 1 year and 3 months
McNiven	B130	In memory of MALCOLM McNIVEN 1851 - 1937 JOHN McNIVEN 1841 - 1906 And ELLEN McNIVEN his wife 1848 – 1807
	D194	MINNIE - Mrs M McNIVEN 1 May 1959 aged 92
McWilliam	B034	In loving memory of JANET McWILLIAM died 6th May 1938 aged 97 years And

---

[34] The McMullen gravestones are on the Hughes grave

McWilliam		MARY JESSIE ORR McWILLIAM died 30th October 1961 aged 83 years
Mead	C062	In loving memory of WILLIAM MEAD died 20th Sept 1923 aged 69 years *"Peace, perfect peace"* Also MILDRED ANNE daughter of W & C.A. Mead died 28th Oct 1944 CHARLOTTE ANN MEAD wife of William Mead died 29.8.1952 aged 89
Mead	F011	In loving memory of ALBERT EDWARD MEAD 1902 - 1982 GLADYS IRENE MEAD 1912 - 1986 loved always by Ted, Valda & family
Miles	C173	In loving memory of a loving wife and mother MABEL IRENE (MAY) MILES died 26.9.27 aged 35 years *"To live in hearts"*
Miller	A148	Sacred to the memory of AMOS MILLER who died May 30, 1895 aged 82 years Also JOANNA beloved wife of the above who died August 30, 1875 aged 58 years Also their children AMOS CHRISTOPHER aged 3 weeks and 3 days And FLORENCE AGNES aged 3 months Also JOHN MILLER who died October 26th, 1876 aged 61 years *"There remaineth the refuge a rest to the people of God"*
	F065	In loving memory of my dear husband and our father JAMES LOVELL MILLER died 11th March 1944 aged 56 years *"Ever remembered"*
Mills	B027	In loving memory of SARAH ANN MILLS died 9th June 1942 aged 41 years Also WILLIAM MILLS died 8th July 1946 aged 79 years Also GEORGE GRIFFIN MILLS died of Wounds 16th April 1918 aged 21 years
	B038	In loving memory of our little son ALLEN JAMES MILLS who passed away 1st June 1936 aged 8 days HOWARD JAMES MILLS passed away 9.1.1998 aged 87 years WINIFRED MILLS passed away 2.8.1998 aged 84 years *"Always in our hearts"*
	D082	JAMES E MILLS 1874-1934 Also His wife MARGARETTA 1882-1964
Minell	A016	In memory of KATE MINELL died June 18th 1858 aged 7 months
Mitchell	A013	In memory of JAMES STUART MITCHELL born March 1 1851 died 9th March 1857 aged 6 years and 9 days In loving remembrance of ANNA MARIA MITCHELL died 20th November 1879 aged 66 years *"Thy will be done"*

Mitchell	C153	In loving memory of RICHARD MITCHELL died 25th March 1903 aged 46 years
Also
ELIZA MITCHELL died 2nd Sept 1911 aged 17 years
Also
MARY ANN beloved wife and mother of the above died 27th Sept 1940 aged 74 years *"Too dearly loved to be forgotten"*
	E105	In loving memory of ANDREW HUGH MITCHELL died 6th Jan 1939 aged 74
Also
	E105	LOUISA MITCHELL beloved wife of the above died 27th March 1943 aged 67 years
Monk	B003	Sacred to the memory of LEAH the beloved daughter of Lenhard and Christina Monk who departed this life the 27th day of August 1878 aged 21 years *"Weep not my friends and parents dear, I am not dead but sleeping here. My pain has gone. My grave you see, once done prepare to follow"*
Also
LEONARD MONK father of the above died 29th December 1897 aged 73 years "Gone from us but not forgotten, Never shall thy memory fade, Loving thoughts shall ever linger, Round the spot where thou art laid"
Also
CHRISTINA FREDERICA wife of the above died 17th December 1911 aged 78 years *"Too far away for sight or speech but not too far for thoughts to reach"*
In memory of CHRISTINA MONK who passed away 13th October 1939 aged 65 years *"Forever with the Lord"*
In loving memory of JOHN MONK who departed this life 9th February 1940 aged 86 years *"At rest"*
Montgomery	B036	In memory of my dear husband THOMAS JOHN MONTGOMERY who passed away June 28th 1935 *"Abide with me"*
Moore	C038	Sacred to the memory of ANNIE the beloved wife of E.L. Moore of Molles Main who departed this life Sept 10th 1868 *"She sought the Lord in youth and death And promised him with her latest breath"*
Also
BARRINGTON MOORE her 8th son who died Feb 20th 1860 aged 10 months and 3 days
Also
EDWARD LUUMAS[35] her 9th son who died March 25th 1867 aged 4 years and 2 months
Sacred to the memory of EDWARD LUUMAS MOORE who died at Badgally 9th February 1887 in his 65th year "Looking unto Jesus" Heb. XII: 2 "Praise my soul the King of heaven, to His feet thy tribute bring. Ransomed, healed, restored, forgiven, who like thee His praise should sing"
Also

---

[35] Note: correct spelling is Lomas not Luumas

Moore		FRANCES MARGARET MOORE wife of the above who died June 5th 1901 aged 59 years *"Peace, perfect peace"*
		Also
		ESSINGTON MOORE son of the above died 27th Nov 1937 aged 56 years
	E060	In loving memory of DORA MOORE died 2nd July 1925 after 7 years *"At rest"*
Morgan	A068	Sacred to the memory of WILLIAM STONEHAM MORGAN late of Levuka, Fiji died at Camden June 28th, 1876 in the 30th year of his age *"Believe in the Lord Jesus Christ and though will be saved"*
Moses	A046[36]	Also
		ROSE the beloved granddaughter of the above aged 3 years and 6 months
Mulley	E038	In loving memory of CHARLES MULLEY died 3rd Nov 1918 aged 47 years *"I heard the voice of Jesus say come unto me and rest" "Peace Perfect Peace"*
		Also
		ALICE MARY died 8th April 1949 aged 56 years
		Also
		MARY JANE MULLEY beloved wife of above died 16th March 1943 aged 81 years *"Our loss is great, we'll not complain But trust in God to meet again"* Erected by their loving family
	E039	In loving memory of JOSEPH GORDON MULLEY died 20th Feb 1920 aged 25 years *"Thy will be done"* erected by his loving parents
	E040	In loving memory of our dear father JAMES MULLEY passed away 13th June 1936 aged 72 years
		Also
		MATILDA MULLEY passed away 6th June 1942 aged 68 years *"At rest"* erected by their loving family
Murdoch	A049	In loving memory of MARGARET ISABELLA MURDOCH passed away 13th August 1950 aged 69 years.
		In loving memory of ROBERT WILLIAM MURDOCH passed away 22nd June 1954 aged 72 years
		In loving memory of AMELIA MURDOCH passed away 28.10.74 aged 71 years
Nash	A115	Sacred to the memory of ELIZABETH wife of Joseph Nash who departed this life March 28th, 1847 aged 52 years *"I trust in Him who stands between The father's wrath and me; Jesu, thou great eternal Mean, I look for all from Thee"*
Neile	C191	SARAH ANN NEILE died 4th January 1876 aged 32 years
Neve	A014	In loving memory of WILLIAM NEVE died 17th November 1910 aged 50 years
		Also
		SARAH ELLEN beloved wife of the above died 29th October 1938 aged 80 years

---

[36] The gravestone is on the grave of Kezia Herbert

New	A072	In loving memory of our dear father and brother WILLIAM THOMAS NEW died 24th January, 1938 aged 79 years
Also
Our dear mother and Grandmother MARY JANE NEW died 16th May, 1869
	A074	In loving memory of CECIL WILFRED NEW 10.11.1897 - 5.8.1956 EDITH DORA NEW 2.7.1900 - 2.8.1981
ERNEST. JOHN NEW 6.3.1928 - 10.2.1932
RONALD VERNON NEW 25.8.1929 - 7.2.1942 "*Always remembered*"
	A075	In memory of Mum & Dad SARAH NEW 27.8.1861 - 25.8.1934
WILLIAM HENRY NEW 13.6.1857 - 1.1.1939
	B045	In loving memory of TREVOR third son of C. & M. New born 13th April 1891 died 21st October 1891
STANLEY NEW died 19th August 1971 aged 85 years
In remembrance of MARY A.R. NEW died 16th July 1935 aged 71 years
Also
CHARLES NEW beloved husband of the above died 26th July 1937 aged 73 years
MARGARET FLORENCE NEW wife of Stanley New died 28th May 1980
	B094	In loving memory of JULIA NEW died 26th Dec 1946 aged 80 years
Also
CHARLES E NEW husband of the above died 17th July 1848 aged 80 years, 29 years Verger of St. John's Camden "*At rest*"
	B156	In loving memory of FREDA ETHEL died 18th Feb 1924 aged 17 died 18th Feb 1924 aged 17
PHYLLIS EDNA died 19th Sep 1939 aged 36 beloved daughters of Norman & Elsie New
	C078	In loving memory of JOHN NEW died 12th Jan 1922 aged 75 years
Also
SARAH NEW wife of the above died 13th June 1927 aged 82 years "*Silently remembered*"
	D129	In loving memory of ELIZABETH NEW died 1.10.1949 aged 74 years "*Peace, perfect peace*"
Nicholson	D152	In memory of RICHARD NICHOLSON died 17th Sept 1883 aged 65 years
Also
DAVID NICHOLSON his cousin died 8th Feb 1883 aged 77 years
Also
MARY ANN wife of the above David Nicholson died 8th August 1880 aged 75 years
Nixon	B039	In remembrance of ADA ISABEL NIXON died 16th April 1935 aged 48 years
Her beloved husband LESLIE EDWARD NIXON died 26th May 1966 aged 81 years
	E094	In loving memory of FRED NIXON died 11th March 1920
Also
ELIZABETH NIXON died 10th June 1924 aged 66 years

Nixon		Also CECIL son of the above died 4th July 1945 aged 63 years
Noakes	C155	JAMES NOAKES born Udimore, Sussex, England 1803 arrived aboard "Augusta Jessie" 1837 with wife Eliza (Masters) and family employed at Brownlow Hill, died Camden 18 May 1874
	C156	In loving memory of ALFRED NOAKES killed by a tree 13th June 1861 aged 26 years
Nolan	B047	In loving memory of VERA dearly loved wife of GEORGE NOLAN who passed away 22nd September 1934 aged 31 years Also infant twin sons FIRTH aged 3 days PETER aged 7 days "Free from earthly care and sorrow lying now in peaceful rest, where kind hands have gently laid her, with her babes upon her breast" WAYNE infant son of George & Essie Nolan Also ESSIE NOLAN died 21.1.1962 aged 50
Ottery	C026	In memory of LIZZIE OTTERY (ELIZABETH) died 8th July 1915 aged 35 years *"Peaceful be thy silent slumbers"* In loving memory of EDWIN OTTERY died 21st June 1919 aged 74 years His beloved wife MARY ANN OTTERY died 2nd Oct 1929 aged 82 years *"Peace, perfect peace"*
Palmer	B009	In loving memory of EDWARD THOMPSON PALMER born Parsonstown, Ireland died 14th April 1879 aged 67 years *"I know my Redeemer liveth"*
	E046	In memory of BARBARA JUNE loved daughter of Richard & Ivy Palmer 10.9.52 aged 17 years *"Sadly missed"*
Parcell	A116	In loving memory of EDITH PEARL much beloved wife of S. A. Parcell who departed this life 2th October, 1960 And SAMUEL ALFRED PARCELL passed away 5th January, 1972
Parker	F013	In loving memory of ERSKINE CHARLES P PARKER died 17th September 1931 aged 84 years In loving memory of EMILY MARY beloved wife of E. C. P. Parker died 12th October 1922 Also ANNE PARKER died 7th November 1945 aged 33 years Also ALBERT PARKER infant son of the above died 1893
Parnell	E011	Sacred to the memory of MARY ANN PARNELL wife of Matthew James Parnell J.P. and daughter of Revd Edward Rogers formerly of Camden, Born 26th August 1848 died 27th March 1917 aged 68 years *"Come unto me all ye that travail and are heavy laden and I will give you rest"* MATTHEW JAMES PARNELL died 6th August 1926 aged 79 years

Parsons	B069	In loving memory of EVA AGNES MERCY infant daughter of John Kerbey Parsons M.D. and his wife Isabelle, died 22nd Oct 1865 aged 4 months "*Thy will be done*"
Patterson	B067	In loving memory of my dear wife CATHERINE PATTERSON died 2nd April 1910 aged 47 years Also RUBY LILLIAN died 3rd September 1899 aged 5 months Also HENRY PATTERSON died 11th July 1929 aged 66 years "*At rest*" ETHEL ADELINE PATTERSON died 16th July 1970 aged 84 years
Paul	A125	In loving memory of THOMAS GILES PAUL M.C. Rector of the Parish of Camden 1927-1943 died 24th December 1943 aged 60 years
Paxton	C112	In loving memory of PHYLLIS LENA PAXTON beloved wife of Les, dear mother & ya ya passed away 22nd Oct 2005 aged 79 years And Her beloved husband LESLIE JOHN PAXTON dear father & Pa passed away 14th August 2008 aged 86 years "*Both at rest*"
Peachey	C035	EMILY ELIZABETH PEACHEY died 17th August 1972 aged 87 years
	C093	A tribute of love to our dear son MELVILLE ALFRED PEACHEY died 3rd Oct 1938 aged 3 yrs 11 months
Pearson	F004	In memory of ELIZA widow of James Pearson Esq. died 26th May, 1879 aged 76 "*I waited patiently for the Lord and the Lord inclined unto me and heard my cry*"
Peat	D022	Also ANNIE PEAT died 25th Jan 1958 aged 65 years
Peel	A054	Sacred to the memory of MARYANN PEEL who departed this life January 17 A.D.1870 aged 12 years. "Weep not dear friends, lament no more, I am not here but gone before, and in good time there to see my dearest friends in heaven with me" Also ELIZABETH the beloved wife of Richard Peel who died December 25th 1884 aged 47 years Also RICHARD PEEL who died April 8th, 1903 aged 71 years
Perkins	B030	In loving memory of my dear husband HAROLD EDWARD PERKINS died 12th March 1952 aged 53 years "*He will be our guide*" ELIZA ADELAIDE PEARL PERKINS passed away 21.8.1994 aged 93 years "*An angel with God*"
	B037	In loving memory of my dear wife and our dear mother JESSIE ADELAIDE PERKINS who passed away 18th January 1945 Also Our dear father EDWARD CHARLES PERKINS who passed away 22nd February 1954 aged 81 years "*Forever with the Lord*"

Perry	A059	14887 FLIGHT SERGEANT I. G. PERRY Royal Australian Air Force 8th February 1949 aged 41 dearly loved and missed by wife Floss and children Helen and Margo
Pinkerton	C174	In loving memory of FREDERICK JAMES (MICK) PINKERTON died 29th August 1927 in his 22nd year "*To live in hearts we leave behind. Is not to die.*"
	C175	In remembrance of ny dear husband JAMES FREDERICK JOHN PINKERTON died 14th July 1936 aged 58 years Also AMY wife of the Above died 28th September 1970
	F058	RUBY MAY PINKERTON nee DUCK born Ipswich 6.5.1914 died Camden 6.3.1994 mother of Terry & Roger "*Sweet are the memories silently kept, the ones that loved you will never forget*"
Platt	C021	In loving memory of WILLIAM PLATT died 29th August 1853 aged 38 years "*We part to meet again*"
	D074	In loving memory of ELIZABETH PLATT[37] wife of John Platt died 9th August 1884 Also GEORGE PLATT son of the above died 2 July 1852 aged 4 years Also JOHN beloved husband of the above who died August 19th 1896 aged 79 years
Pocketts	D076	In memory of JAMES POCKETTS died 7th August 1852 aged 41 years
Pollock	A021	To the memory of ELIZABETH POLLOCK who departed this life February 4th, 1860 aged 56 years leaving nine children to deplore their loss "*Weep not for me my children dear, I am not dead but sleeping here, Return then home no trouble make, but love each other for my sake*"
Poole	D003	In loving memory of SUSANNAH POOLE died 26th June 1854 aged 7 years "*mother and daughter re-united*"
	D083	In loving memory of my dear husband and our father GEORGE POOLE died 23rd Nov 1899 aged 54 years Also ESTHER wife of the above died 25th Dec 1923 aged 74 years "*He giveth his beloved sleep*" SGT JOHN RICHARDSON POOLE 1st Light Horse Regt died 5th Nov 1916 at Shorncliffe England from wounds received in France aged 30 years
	D112	In loving memory of my dear husband and our father FRANK POOLE died 6th July 1946 aged 61 years MATHA POOLE died 10th June 1976 in her 94th year "*At rest*"
	F008	JOHN WILLIAM POOLE died 24th August 1926 aged 75 years FANNY beloved wife of John W. Poole died 7th March 1916 aged 55 years "*Thy will be done*" In loving memory of ELSIE FANNY POOLE died 19th February 1921 aged 33 years

---

[37] Mary Elizabeth Platt

Poole		ARTHUR POOLE died 19th Nov. 1963 husband of Lillian
LILLIAN LOUISE POOLE died 17th Nov. 1994 aged 93 years
Porter	B115	In loving memory of GEORGE ALEXANDER PORTER died 23rd February 1897 aged 61 years
Also
CATHERINE beloved wife of the above died 7th December 1936 in her 90th year
	A029	In memory of JAMES POTTER died 3rd February 1861 aged 32 years
Also
HANNAH POTTER died 28th December 1866 aged 71 years
Preshaw	B007	In loving memory of GEORGE OGILVY PRESHAW died 28th November 1890 aged 51 years
Also
ANNA MARIA beloved wife of the above died 4th December 1919 aged 77 years "*Peace, Perfect Peace*"
Prosser	A057	In loving memory of JAMES HENRY PROSSER born (Grosmont Wales) February 21st, 1885 died May 23rd, 1962 "*At rest*"
ANNIE WINIFRED PROSSER nee TAYLOR – plaque now missing [born 1888 Wales died April 4, 1975 Camden]
Quigley	E058	In loving memory of our dear parents GEORGE QUIGLEY died 12.12.1959 aged 73
And
MARGARET QUIGLEY died 28.9.1963 aged 74 "*Abide with me*"
Rankin	B083	In loving remembrance of ELIZABETH beloved wife of James D. Rankin died 15th November 1898 aged 33 years "Had He asked us well we know we should cry, O spare this blow Yes, with streaming eyes should pray Lord we love her, let her stay"
Also
JAMES DOWNIE RANKIN husband of the above died 18th May 1902 aged 41 years
Rapley	C109	In loving memory of THOMAS beloved husband of Emma Rapley passed away 20th May 1974 aged 66 years "*Thy will be done*"
Also
His beloved wife EMMA died 27th July 1945 aged 87 years "*At rest*"
Also
Only son of the above WILLIAM RAPLEY died 17th May 1961 aged 64 years
	E115	In loving memory of RAPLEY
CECIL 15.2.1901 - 3.1.1964
ERIC 8.1.1933 - 31.8.1978
BARBARA died 19.1.1927 aged 10 Months
MARY 19.71904 - 6.12.1999 beloved wife & mother
	E117	In loving memory of my husband, and our dear father WILLIAM RAPLEY passed away 4th April 1943 aged 74 years
Also
Our dear mother MARY JANE RAPLEY passed away 8th October 1951 aged 74 years "*At rest*"

Rapley	E118	In loving memory of E.M. TED RAPLEY late 8th Div killed in accident 29th Sept 1947 aged 36 years Erected by his mother, brothers & sisters VICTOR NEVILLE RAPLEY brother of the above loved youngest son of William and Jane Rapley died 5th August 1979 aged 66 years
Ravaillon	A005	In memory of ELIZA RAVAILLION 1871-1947 JOHN RAVAILLION 1866-1955 dedicated by Mavis & Ian
Ray	A092	MILTON RAY 18/3/1926 – 16/11/2009 *"Forever in our hearts"*
Redmond	B122	Sacred to the memory of FRANCES ELIZABETH REDMOND died 5th April 1895 *"I know that my Redeemer liveth"*
Reeves	F007	In loving memory of HENRY POLLOCK REEVES died 26th November, 1900 aged 69 years Also ANN beloved wife of the above died 12th October, 1922 aged 84 years
Reynolds	E080	A tribute of love to my dear husband WILLIAM HENRY REYNOLDS died 9th April 1926 aged 57 years *"Safe in the arms of Jesus, safe on His gentle breast, There by His love oer-shaded sweetly my soul shall rest"* Also ELLEN LOUISE REYNOLDS died 6th September 1957 aged 82 years "Always remembered by her loving son Eric, daughter-in-law Majories and children Annette, Kathleen & Thomas"
Richardson	C020[38]	Also THOMAS DOCKERY RICHARDSON died 14th February 1903 aged 73 years Also ANN MARIA RICHARDSON wife of the above died 29th June 1907 aged 87 years
Rideout	F024	In loving memory of ARTHUR RIDEOUT died 17th November 1936 aged 65 years FLORENCE JANET RIDEOUT died 18th May 1937 aged 61 years Also LAWRENCE ARTHUR RIDEOUT died 18th November 1968 aged 57
	B031	To the Sacred Memory of WILLIAM HENRY RIX died 6th August, 1956 aged 88 years *"At rest"*
	B065	In loving memory of our dear mother & our dear father ELLEN ANDERSON RIX died 18th August 1967 aged 84 years And ALBERT EDWARD RIX died 20th May 1968 aged 86 years *"At rest"*

---

[38] The gravestone is on the Platt grave

Rix	C123	In loving memory of ELEANOR SNEDSDELL RIX died 1st Feb 1896 aged 58 years "*R.I.P. Thy will be done*" Also JOHN RIX beloved husband of the above died 22nd Nov 1922 aged 90 years
	C125	Sacred to the memory of the Rev. ARTHUR G RIX Priest, late Rector of St. John's Church of England Balmain North died 30th December 1953 aged 72 years "*Eternal rest*"
Roberts	C183	Sacred to the memory of ELIZABETH JANE infant daughter of Robert and Elizabeth Roberts who died on the 18th of January 1866 aged 10 days "*This open bud, so young and fair, called hence by early doom, just came to show how sweet a flower in Paradise would bloom*"
	C185	Sacred to the memory of ROBERT the eldest son of Robert and Elizabeth Roberts who departed this life 3rd July 1876 aged 16 years "*Safe in the arms of Jesus*" Also ELIZABETH mother of the above died 28th December 1904 aged 75 years Also ROBERT RICHARD father of the above died 7th October 1905 aged 73 years "*Resting*"
Rofe	A081	In memory of THOMAS ROFE late of Robertsbridge Salehurst, Sussex died May 24th, 1854 aged 19 years
	A084	In loving memory of WILLIAM ROFE died January 17th, 1896 aged 73 years Also GEORGE SPENCER son of the above died February 6th, 1878 aged 16 years Also WALTER CHARLES ROFE died 15th June, 1948 aged 76 years Also ARTHUR ALBERT ROFE died 7th June, 1951 aged 77 years
	B073	In loving memory of my dear husband and our dear father ERNEST EDWARD ROFE passed away 4th Oct 1967 aged 88 years "*At rest*" Our dearest mother RUBY MYRA ROFE died 7th January 1976 aged 86 years "*At rest*"
	D132	In memory of our dearly beloved sister LINA wife of the late W Rofe passed away 18th March 1950 aged 66 years
	F020	In loving memory of ESTHER ELLEN beloved wife of William Rofe died 4th July 1914 aged 55 years "*At rest*"
	F029	In loving memory of my dear husband JOHN STUART ROFE died 9th Oct 1930 aged 66 years "*Nearer my God to Thee*" Also In memory of our dear mother ELEANOR died 13th December 1949 aged 79 years Also Their beloved son CLYDE STUART ROFE died 1st Nov 1934 aged 43 years "*Sadly missed*"

Rofe	F037	In loving memory of RUPERT ROFE 22nd Sept 1980 aged 87 GARNET ROFE 20th May 1991 aged 74 ADA ROFE 11th May 1974 aged 85 BETTY ROFE 29th May 2006 aged 85
Rogers	B021	In loving memory of my dear wife and our mother ADA ROGERS who passed away 13th June 1936 aged 64 years
Rootes	A117	In memory of JAMES son of Sivyer and Mary Rootes of Camden died 13 August 1850 aged 20 years "*We lay thee here in hope the Lamb once slain will rise and we shall see thee once again in Paradise*"
	A118	In memory of JOHN son of Sivyer and Mary Rootes of Camden died 14 March 1848 aged 21 years "A Christian's body rests beneath, his hope in life, his hope in death was God, our Saviour, hope divine, ask thy soul reader is it thine"
	A120	In memory of SIVYER ROOTES died July 31 1852 Also of SIVYER ROOTES died March 25th 1883 aged 83 years "Mortals be dumb what great ire dares dispute his awful will ask no account of his affairs but tremble and be still"
	A121	In memory of HENRY son of Sivyer and Mary Rootes of Camden died 18th February, 1856 aged 28 years "Why mourn my soul by parting fled oer the dark river of the dead to Cannan's happy shore, rather as to the day when God hath wiped the tears away to meet and mourn no more"
	A122	In memory of MARY wife of Sivyer Rootes of Camden died December 14th 1858 aged 57 years "Speak ye who stood around her in that hour when faint and pale she breathed a farewell sigh, when hope's full bud was bursting into flower, when light, when heaven was dawning in her eye, he smiled and rain and death defied struggled to say her last goodbye and died"
Rose	D171	In loving memory of ANGUS MARK ROSE died 19th Feb 1931 aged 70 years "*Till we meet again*" Also JANE ROSE beloved wife of Above died 18th April 1941 aged 79 years "*Peace, perfect peace*" Erected by his fond wife & family
Rouland	D169	Our dear dad & gramps VICTOR HENRY ROULAND died 7th Sept 2001 aged 85 years "*Hoo Roo*" DAPHNE HAZEL ROULAND (nee STARR) died 11th March 1990 aged 70 years "*Loved by all*"
Rowe	F038	In loving memory of WILLIAM ROWE passed away 12.8.1938 aged 68 And EMILY MAUDE ROWE passed away 14.11.1949 aged 66
Rummell	B086	In loving memory of AMY beloved wife of William Rummell who departed this life September 9th 1895 aged 39 years "*At rest*"

Ryder	C149	In loving memory of JOSEPH HENRY RYDER died 27th July 1940 aged 80 years Also BERTHA MARIA wife of the above died 22nd Oct 1940 aged 70 years Also ERNEST. JOHN son of the above died 17th August 1915 aged 15 years *"Peace, perfect peace"*
	C150	Sacred to the memory of THOMAS RYDER who departed this life August 14 1892 aged 72 years *"My hopes rest on the infallibility of the promises of God"* Also PHRONESSOR infant daughter of the above died July 8 1873 aged 9 weeks Also SUSANNAH wife of Thomas Ryder died 15 June 1902 aged 78 years *"At rest"*
Sams	D172	In loving memory of ANNA MARIA the beloved wife of James Sams died 25th Oct 1883 aged 47 years *"Weep not my loving friends so dear, since its God's will to call me here. My debt is paid, my grave you see, prepare yourselves to follow me"* Also MARY ANN daughter of the above died 7th Nov 1861 aged 2 months Likewise MARIA MATILDA died 11th Aug 1866 aged 4 months Also
	D172	JAMES SAMS died 24th July 1916 aged 85 years Also JANE SAMS died 14th Jan 1918 aged 73 years
Sawyers	E020	In loving memory of ROY SAWYERS 2nd A.I.F. passed away 10.12.2002 - aged 90 years loved husband of Pat. Dear father of Leonie, Rodney, Debbie and his grandchildren *"Loved and remembered always At rest"*
Scott	A069	Sacred to the memory of ELIZABETH JULIANNA SCOTT died November 27th, 1858 aged 33 years
	B035	In loving memory of CHARLES HERBERT SCOTT passed away 30.6.1932 aged 44 years *"At rest"* Also His beloved wife JOSEPHINE passed away 10.5.1964 aged 75 years
Seymour	E070	Sacred to the memory of GEORGE SEYMOUR of The Oakes who departed this life 30th August 1853 aged 37 years *"He was a loving husband, a kind father, and a faithful friend"*
Sharpe	D111	In memory of EILEEN RUBY PEACE dearly loved wife of Stephen John Sharpe died 21st February 1941 aged 22 years

Sharpe	E002	In loving memory of my dear wife MARTHA SHARPE died 7th Nov 1921 aged 69 years *"Peace, perfect peace"* Also JOHN beloved husband of the above died 7th Nov 1921 aged 84 years *"Thy will be done"*
	F025	And My dearest friend MARTHA JANE SHARPE died 9th March 1960 aged 80 *"A friend in need is a friend indeed"* HELEN EDITH SHARPE died 13th August 1916 aged 29 years *"At rest"* Also SARAH SHARPE died 21st January 1938 aged 89 years *"Mother resting"*
	F026	In loving memory of dad THOMAS HERBERT SHARPE died 5.7.1941 age 54 years Mum LILIAN MAY SHARPE died 29.6.1952 age 58 years And LEONIE MAY SHARPE granddaughter of above died 31.5.1959 age 9 months
Sheather	E087	In loving memory of our dear Brother WILLIAM HENRY SHEATHER passed away 23rd August 1968 aged 81 years *"Loved by all who knew him"*
	E088	In loving memory of GEORGE SHEATHER died 15.8.1976 aged 80 years *"R.I.P."*
	E089	In loving memory of ANNIE HELENA SHEATHER died 16th February 1959 aged 62 *"At rest"*
	E090	In loving memory of EDWARD SHEATHER died 23rd May 1958 aged 81 years *"Never forgotten"*
	E091	In loving memory of my dear wife CHARLOTTE SHEATHER died 15th Jan 1887 aged 51 years Also
	E091	JAMES SHEATHER died 2nd June 1895 aged 73 years *"At rest"*
Sheil	A010	Memory everlasting of LILLIAN MAUDE SHEIL
Shepherd	D051	In loving memory of MARY ANN SHEPHERD died 2nd Aug 1931 aged 67 years *"At rest"*
Shipman	A129	ELIZABETH SHIPMAN died 29th November 1867 aged 85 years
Shoobridge	E006	In loving memory of my dear wife HANNAH MARIA SHOOBRIDGE died 18th Oct 1916 aged 60 years *"Peace, perfect peace"* ROBERT SHOOBRIDGE beloved husband of the above died 16th July 1931 aged 80 years
Siddins	F012	HAIDEE F. M. SIDDINS died 9th September 1914 aged 40 years *"Her children rise up and call her blessed, her husband also, and he praiseth her. Let her own works praise her in the gates."* Also ALFRED SIDDINS beloved husband of the above died 17th January 1919 aged 54 years *"Father into Thy gracious keeping leave we now Thy servant sleeping"*

Sidman	F006	In loving memory of WILLIAM SIDMAN died 21st February 1918 aged 70 years And HONOR SIDMAN died 24th February 1938 aged 87 years In loving memory of NANCY DOROTHEA SIDMAN who fell asleep 31st July 1922 aged 15 months MABEL SIDMAN died 13th September 1916 JESSIE SIDMAN passed away 11th August 1982 aged 100 years ROBERT ALFRED SIDMAN died 10th October 1964
	F062	In loving memory of my dear husband & our father CHARLES WARRANE SIDMAN who passed away 12th Oct 1945 aged 54 years Also Our dear mother HARRIET DORA SIDMAN who passed away 14th Sept 1985 aged 88 years
Simpson	A150	In memory of JANET GRACE beloved child of Ebenezer Simpson and Jane his wife born June 28th, 1868 died January 5th, 1870 Also EBENEZER born December 12th, 1871 died July 12th, 1875 "*Of such is the kingdom of heaven*" Also GRACE died August 25th, 1877 aged 3 years and 5 months
	A151	Sacred to the memory of EBENEZER SIMPSON died January 16th, 1855 aged 59 years Also His loving wife SARAH who died May 7th, 1878 aged 81 years
Sluman	D037	In loving remembrance of ALFRED EDWIN SLUMAN died 30th March 1909 aged 79 years Also His wife SARAH ANN died 15th August 1918 aged 80 years
	D038	In loving memory of ELIZABETH KATHERINE SLUMAN died 2nd January 1916 "*Peace, perfect peace*"
Small	B149	In memory of LILLIAN SMALL Born .8194 died 15.3.1947 In memory of EDITH ELIZA SMALL died 17.3.1971 aged 79 years
	C087	In loving memory of PERCY ROBERT SMALL died 3rd June 1901 aged 10 months
	C091	In loving memory of GRACE VERA daughter of E. and K.B. Small died 12th Dec 1893 aged 5 months "*Taken in love*" Also NOELINE DAPHNE daughter of the above died 5th Jan 1895 aged 4 months & 2 weeks "*God knows best*" "*At rest*"
	C094	In loving memory of AGNES SMALL who passed away July 17 1956 aged 70 years "*At rest*" In memory of our dear father EDWIN SMALL who died 3rd August 1925 aged 80 years "*Asleep in Jesus*" In memory of ELIZABETH beloved wife of Edwin Small who died 29th November 1899 aged 52 years "Through all pain at times she'd smile, a smile of heavenly birth, and when the angels called her home she smiled farewell to earth. Heaven retaineth now our treasure, Earth

		the lonely casket keeps; And the sunbeams love to linger Where our sainted mother sleeps."
Small	D047	In loving memory of LOTTIE SMALL passed away 21.4.1958
	D142	In loving memory of JAMES second son of James & Mary Ann Small who was accidentally killed on the 14th Aug 1906 aged 47 years *"Thy will be done"*
		In loving memory of MARY ANN beloved wife of James Small died 13th Sept 1923 aged 88 years *"She hath done what she could"*
		In loving memory of JAMES SMALL died 18th Sept 1920 aged 86 years *"Abide with me"*
Smith	B107	In loving memory of JOHN HOLBROW SMITH died 4th July 1921 aged 93 years *"Nearer my God to Thee"*
	C107	In loving memory of AMELIA SMITH died 18th Aug 1912 aged 35 years *"Peace, perfect peace"*
		SERGT REX SMITH[39] died in Egypt 19th June 1915 from wounds received in the Dardenelles aged 36 years
	C136	In loving memory of WILLIAM SMITH died 19th September 1934 aged 69 years
		Also
		ARTHUR DALE SMITH son of the above died 14th June 1959
		ANNIE DALE SMITH passed away 19th December 1960 age 86 years
	D150	In loving memory of JOHANNA SMITH died 10th September 1883 aged 36 years
		Also
		GEORGE SMITH died 15th July 1905 aged 61 years "Long days and nights he bore in pain, to wait for cure was all in vain. But God alone, who thought it best, did ease his pain and gave him rest"
	D155	In memory of CLARA infant daughter of Charles & Elizabeth Smith who departed this life the 9th of March 1859 aged seven months
		Also of
		CHARLES SMITH who died 23rd of June 1876 aged 62 years
	E006[40]	Also
		ELIZABETH ANN SMITH beloved daughter of the above died 1st July 1919 aged 43 years *"Asleep in Jesus"*
	F019	In loving memory of RUBY SMITH passed away 23.1.1968 aged 62 years
		KEVIN SMITH passed away 29.1.1935 aged 4 years
Sparkes	F050	In loving memory of MARY relict of David Sparkes daughter of Martha & Frank Poole died 12th Sept 1948 aged 30 years *"At rest"*
Spicer	D033	In loving memory of HERBERT STANLEY SPICER passed away 19th December 1979 aged 74 years
		In loving memory of EUNICE MARGARET (DOON) SPICER loving wife of Herbert, parents of Dimity & Priscilla 1.9.09 - 12.4.83

---

[39] Reginald Sydney Smith
[40] This gravestone is on the Shoobridge grave

Stanner	F017	In loving memory of my dear husband and our father ALBERT STEPHEN STANNER died 3rd May 1924 aged 76 years And ELLEN STANNER died 28th October 1942 aged 84 years *"At rest"*
Starr	C042	In memory of W & E STARR and DESCENDANTS Also WILLIAM STARR grandson of the above aged 6 months
	D169	In loving memory of FLORENCE MABEL STARR departed this life 31st July 1939 aged 43 years Also CHARLES EDWIN STARR died 26th October 1959 aged 71 years
	D181	In loving memory of LESLIE GEORGE beloved youngest son of W. & S. Starr died 1st March 1916 aged 24 years *"Patient sufferer. At rest"* Also WILLIAM beloved father of the above died 31st Oct 1925 aged 79 years Also SELINA beloved of the above died 10th Aug 1937 aged 82 years
Stevens	B136	In loving memory of THOMAS STEVENS son of John & Mary Ann Sevens passed away 31st May 1935 aged 78 years *"Peace, perfect peace with loved ones far away"* In loving memory of MARY ANN STEVENS beloved wife of John Stevens died 8th October 1900 aged 69 years *"Peace, perfect peace"* In loving memory of EMILY STEVENS died 15th April 1952 aged 74 years ELEANOR STEVENS died 24th Jan 1960 aged 86 years *"Thy will be done"* In loving memory of my dearly beloved husband JOHN STEVENS who departed this life 22nd August 1889 aged 64 years Also ROBERT and ELIAS sons of the above who died in their infancy
Stewart	B017	Here in peace and Christian hope rests the body of JAMES STEWART son of James Stewart Esq. of Rollands Plains who was struck down by the hand of a maniac at *Camden Park* on 5th January 1872 aged 25 years. He was a dearly loved and loving son and brother and was greatly respected, his many friends have raised this tribute to his memory
Stokes	D189	In loving memory of MARIE LOUISE STOKES died 12th July 1911 aged 62 years *"Behind all shadows standeth God"*
Stone	D139	In loving memory of ALFRED FRANCIS STONE died 22.7.1918 aged 40 MINNIE STONE died 21.9.1963 aged 81
Street	D081	EDRIC HENRY STREET born 10th December 1864 died 24th December 1923

Stuckey	B060	In loving memory of ELGAR STUCKEY died 6th July 1899 aged 75 years Also AMY wife of the above died 12th May 1915 aged 91 years
	B061	In loving memory of JOSIAH STUCKEY died 1st September 1941 aged 78 years And SARAH wife of the above died 13th August 1946 aged 83 years
	F014	In loving memory of our darling daughter SHIRLEY E STUCKEY who passed away 3rd Dec 1934 aged 8 years & 6 Months "*Our angel gone home*"
	F014	LYNNETTE ALICE[41] sister of Shirley 23.3.1962 aged 21 years LYN STUCKEY[42] beloved daughter of Alice & Fred left her body 23.3.62 - aged 21 years "Lyn's body died, she did not. She shares my senses still. Until my body lies aside then we'll re-unite in spirit, As God created us: all of us" her beloved bethrothed Terry Hogan, Cairns, April 1996 In loving memory of my dear husband and our father FREDERICK H STUCKEY died 19th July 1948 aged 54 years ALICE KATHERLINE STUCKEY nee MAHONEY 10.10.1898 - 5.10.1989 aged 90 years beloved wife of Fred, mother of Shirley & Lynette. Ashes lie at St. James Church, Menangle, her birth place
Sutton	B132	In memory of SARAH TRIGG SUTTON wife of John Sutton Hornsby daughter of James Jacklin Royston, Camb. England born 18th June 1841 died 4th Feb 1892
	E032	CHARLES JOHN SUTTON died 7th July 1922 aged 35 year "*A patient sufferer*" "*At rest*" WALTER H SUTTON died 6.7.1963 aged 51 years "*Sleep in peace*" HENRY SUTTON died 13.9.65 aged 83 years "*At rest*"
Taplin	A024	In memory of AMY TAPLIN died 31st October 1905 aged 26 years Erected by the members of St. Johns choir and the Guild of St. Faith In loving memory of EDWIN R. TAPLIN who passed away 23rd January 1968 aged 74 years beloved husband of Vera and loved father of Neta
	A024	In loving memory of VERA MAY TAPLIN who passed away 23rd August 1965 aged 70 remembered always by her husband Ted, daughter Neta
	B059	In loving memory of my dear husband & our father WILLIAM JOHN TAPLIN died 11th April 1936 aged 65 years And Our dear mother GERTRUDE ELEANOR TAPLIN died 1st March 1964 in her 90th year
	C121	In loving memory of my dear husband TRAVIS R TAPLIN died 30th March 1926 aged 31 years

---

[41] Original headstone (still visible) installed in 1962
[42] Additional headstone installed in 1996

Tarman	C138	In loving memory of THOMAS TARMAN died 30th August 1899 aged 77 years Also HANNAH MARIA beloved wife of the above died 5th October 1918 aged 93 years
Tate	A136	In loving memory of our dear husband & father CECIL TATE died 26th May 1940 aged 54 years Also The beloved wife of the above THERESA TATE died 4th October 1955 In loving memory of our devoted husband and son FLT.SGT. COLIN TATE killed in air operation over Germany 30th January, 1944
Teasdale	E056	In loving memory of THOMAS GEORGE TEASDALE a beloved husband & father died 4th Nov 1924 aged 61 years *"At rest"*
Templeman	B023	In loving memory of THOMAS TEMPLEMAN died 3rd October 1940 aged 66 years Also ANNIE TEMPLEMAN wife of the above died 10th September 1948 aged 63 years erected by his loving wife & family
Terry	A106	In loving memory of HENRY CLARKE TERRY beloved husband of Albine Edna Terry who passed away 8th July, 1925. Also ALBINE EDNA TERRY who passed away 5th April, 1847
Thompson	A076	Sacred to the memory of EDWARD THOMPSON who departed this life June 6th, 1892 aged 76 years *"Thou hast given him his hearts desire and has not withholden the request of his lips"* Ps XXI, 2
	A123	Sacred to the memory of MARY THOMPSON who departed this life July 22nd 1884 aged 66 years Also of EDWARD THOMPSON died September 7, 1852 aged 6 years Likewise MARGARET died November 4, 1854 aged 14 months
	A123	Also EDWARD THOMPSON Did April 20th, 1887 aged 32 years Also of ROSE wife of JOHN THOMPSON died September 8th, 1902 aged 64 years
	B020	Sacred to the memory of FREDERICK PERCY RAYMOND ERNEST ELEANOR ADA
	B020	GERTRUDE ETHEL Beloved children of Henry and Anne Thompson Also of HENRY THOMPSON who died July 29th 1871 aged 51 years Also ANNE wife of Henry Thompson died at Burwood February 20th 1912 aged 87 years

Thompson		Also CHARLES AUGUSTUS THOMPSON son of the above and beloved husband of Emma Thompson died 26th August 1929 aged 82 years
Thorn	B105	Treasured memory of MARY JANE THORN departed 12th April 1960 aged 7 years
	C054	In loving memory of my dear wife and daughter EILEEN MAY THORN died 31st July 1980 aged 63 years LURLENE EILEEN THORN died 14th Jan 1958 aged 18 years ERIC JOHN L THORN died 6th April 1985
	D133	In loving memory of my father ALLAN THORN died 6th June 1924 aged 77 years
Tickner	D085	Sacred to the memory of PETER TICKNER of Camden died September 23 1854 aged 38 years "Be ye also ready for in such an hour as ye think not the Son of Man cometh" Matthew XXIV: 42 "We will trust his soul has found a home among the faithful blest, where the wicked cease from troubling and the weary are at rest"
	D086	To the memory of SARAH TICKNER died June 7 1860 aged 75 years "A wife most kind, a mother dear, a faithful friend lies buried here. When Christ shall come we trust she'll have a full rising from the grave" 'Watch therefore for we know not what our the Lord doth come" Matthew XXIV: 42
	D087	Sacred to the memory of EDWARD TICKNER died 14 October 1864 aged 75 years "We shall go to him but he will not return to us" "Break not the rest aye sleep in peace, from henceforth shall their sorrows cease and though we deeply mourn our loss like them we too must bear the cross"
	D088	Sacred to the memory of JOHN TICKNER who died on the 9th of March 1875 aged 56 years
Tomkins	D031	In loving memory of EDNA TAMAR TOMKINS departed 26th July 1965 aged 57 beloved wife of Eric and loved mother of Graham, Patricia and Helen In loving memory of ERIC GEORGE TOMKINS Departed 8.1.1989 aged 80 beloved husband of Edna (Dec'd) and loving father of Graham, Patricia & Helen (dec'd) *"Both in God's care"*
	D075	In loving memory of our darling baby DULCIE IRIS TOMKINS died 15th May 1912 aged 13½ months *"Now she waits for us above, resting in the Saviours love"* Also JOSEPH TOMKINS died 22nd January 1949 aged 80 years Also MARGARET ROSE ISABELLA beloved wife of the above died 23rd April 1957 aged 82 years *"At rest"* GLADYS IRENE TOMKINS passed away 6th July 1976 aged 71 years
Tomlin	A020[43]	ERNEST F TOMLIN died 23.3.64

---

[43] Original marker, a wooden cross, no longer visible

Tornaghi	A010[44]	Also ALLAN NELSON TORNAGHI died 23rd February 1913 aged 4 months *"A bud in heaven"* Also
	A010	GLADYS MURIEL beloved wife of Leoni Angelo Tornaghi died 24th October 1919 aged 29 years *"Ti Rivedero in Cielo"*
Tulloh	F010	In loving memory of ARCHIBALD TULLOH died 20th July 1938 aged 68 years *"At rest"* In loving memory of CECIL JOHN TULLOH passed away 10th December 1989 And SELINA JOYCE COMERFORD TULLOH passed away 23rd December 1995
Turk	A027	In loving memory of DESOLIE TURK passed away 5th June 1992 aged 71 years beloved wife of Harvey & mother of Bronwyn, Rick & Peter
Turner	D031[45]	Also JOSEPH H. W. TURNER loved husband of Eliza Ann called home 19th May 1960 aged 78 years *"At rest"*
	D032	In loving memory of ELIZA ANN beloved wife of Joseph H Turner died 25th Feb 1916 aged 33 years Also Darling MAVIS (BUB) daughter of the above called home 9th Sept 1944 aged 31 years *"Peace, perfect peace"*
Vaughan	F054	In loving memory of ROMA VAUGHAN loving wife of John and only darling child of Vera & Alex Sluice fell asleep Aug 11th 1940 aged 25 years *"Peacefully sleeping"* Erected by mother & father
Veness	A038	W. A. VENESS passed away 22 July 1969 *"Rest in peace"*
	A078	In loving memory of MINNIE LOUISA CHRISTINA beloved daughter of W. & M.L. Veness died 4th March, 1918 aged 19 years *"At rest"* WILLIAM ERNEST VENESS passed away 25th May, 1948 aged 74 years. MARY LOUISA VENESS passed away 20th August, 1956 aged 77 years
	B013	In loving memory of my dear husband and our dear father JOHN EDWARD VENESS who passed away 8th March 1941 aged 61 years And His wife MARTHA ABIGAIL VENESS who passed away 16th December 1972 aged 91 years
Vicary	F018	In loving memory of EMILY BLANCHE MAY VICARY passed away 24th July 1935 aged 49 years And WALTER HERBERT VICARY passed away 14th January 1948 aged 67 years *"Resting"*

---

[44] The Tornaghi gravestone is on the Hughes grave
[45] The Turner gravestone is on the Tomkins grave

Vincen	C044	In memory of JANE VINCEN who died Nov 15 1871 aged 62 years "Farewell dear husband, all my days are past, I loved you well while life did last. No more sorrow for me take but love my kindred for my sake" And Her beloved husband GEORGE VINCEN who died Dec 29 1890 aged 89 years
Wade	A074	ERNEST LEON WADE 12.11.1915 - 9.1.2005 A.I.F.
Wallace	B148	In loving memory of Rev.THOMAS VESIAU WALLACE M.A. T.C.D. died 26 Nov 1915 aged 27 years
Walshe	E103	In loving memory of our dear father EUSTACE VARIAN WALSHE who passed away 30.11.37 Also Our dear mother CAROLINE LOUISA WALSHE who joined him 12.5.47
Wasson	C065	In loving memory of THOMAS BARNES WASSON died 21st April 1865 aged 30 years Also JANE[46] beloved wife of the above died 22nd August 1910 aged 72 years. "*At rest*"
	C157	In loving memory of CLARRY WASSON[47] died 3rd Aug 1923 aged 24 years "*So dearly loved and sadly missed*"
Waters	A080	In loving memory of ELIZABETH WATERS died 29th December, 1888 aged 32 years "*Nothing in my hands I bring simply to Thy cross I cling*" In loving memory of JOHN WATERS died 23rd March, 1882 aged 34 years Also of MAUD ELIZABETH died 10th July, 1885 aged 6 years Also of LUCY ELLEN died 22nd May, 1883 aged 2 years children of the above. In loving memory of CHARLES WATERS died 17th April, 1885 "*Thy will be done*" Also of LUCY wife of the above died 19th March, 1889 aged 69 years years "*Blessed are the pure in heart for they shall see God*"
Waterworth	C172	In loving memory of JAMES EDWIN WATERWORTH died 2nd Aug 1911 aged 53 years Also MARY ANN ELIZABETH beloved wife of the above died 8th Oct 1935 aged 78 years

---

[46] Sarah Jane Wasson
[47] Clarence John James Wasson

Watson	D021	In loving memory of WALTER (SNOWY) WATSON beloved husband of Ethel died June 4th, 1944 aged 64 years *"Till we meet again"* Also His beloved wife ETHEL died 26th October 1977 aged 96
	D033	In loving memory of GEORGE beloved husband of Eliza Watson died 29th Dec 1917 aged 63 years. Also ELIZA ANN WATSON beloved wife of the above died 6th Jan 1923 aged 77 years Also VICTOR who died in infancy
	D167	In memory of WILLIAM GEORGE WATSON died 23rd March 1944 aged 65 years *"To live in the hearts of those we love is not to die"*
	D178	FRED WATSON died 6.2.1946 - 57 years MATHA WATSON 30.8.1981 - 86 yrs *"R.I.P."*
	E120	In memory of JOHN WATSON who died 25th Oct 1852 aged 26 *"At rest"*
Webb	B048	In loving memory of CHARLES HENRY WEBB died 21st January 1954 aged 72 years Also His loving wife MATILDA died 25th July 1960 aged 74 years *"Always loved and remembered"*
Wedmore	F060	In loving memory of my dear husband & our father JAMES HENRY WEDMORE died 24th March 1951 aged 82 And Our dear mother MAUDE MARY WEDMORE died 15th March 1961 aged 82 parents of Norman, Eric & John *"At rest"*
Weiberle	C117	In loving memory of ROSE ELLEN WEIBERLE died 23rd February 1913 aged 48 years *"Nearer my God to Thee"*
West	B121	FRANCIS JAMES WEST died 4th Feb 1912 aged 69 years FRANCIS WILLIAM WEST M.B. C.H.M. died 20th October 932 aged 58 years And His wife ADELINE LYDIA died 11th September 1954
Wheeler	C159	In loving memory of my beloved husband & our father JAMES WHEELER passed away 7th March 1953 aged 76 years And His beloved wife & our mother AMY SARAH died 11th Nov 1961, aged 86 *"Beyond the sunset"*
	C199	In loving memory of MAJORIE RUTH WHEELER died 16th May 1914 aged 6 years
	C200	Erected by His Comrades & the Citizens of Camden To the Memory of PRIVATE CECIL CLAUDE WHEELER 4th Battalion A.I.F. Wounded Polygon Wood, France 20th September 1917 Invalided to Australia And died of wounds 29th March 1927 aged 32 years *"Loves Last Token"* Erected by his wife A loving tribute from G Darran
	D002	In loving memory of CAROLINE WHEELER died 25th August 1891 aged 89 years

Wheeler		Also JAMES WHEELER died 13th January 1893 aged 80 years Also GEORGE WHEELER died 30th September 1914 aged 75 years Also ANNIE WHEELER died 8th September 1922 aged 79 years
	D194	In loving memory of SAMUEL WHEELER died 30th May 1909 aged 94 years Also ANNIE wife of the above died 5th August 1941 aged 97 years And SARAH LUCY WHEELER died 23rd July 1920 aged 54 years
	D197	"*At rest*" In loving memory of JOHN WHEELER who died 16th Oct 1905 aged 79 years Also
	D197	FANNY wife of the Above died 4th June 1912 aged 80 years "The Lord is my shepherd I shall not want, Thought I walk through the valley of death I will fear no evil for Thou art with me"
	E001	ETHEL FLORIST WHEELER beloved daughter of Bertha & Ray Wheeer died 2nd May 1925 aged 6 years
	F023	In loving memory of our dear mother MARY ANN WHEELER passed away 15th March, 1932 Age 64 years In "*Abide with me*" Loving Memory of our dear father EDMUND WHEELER passed away 21st June 1941 aged 78 years "*Nearer my God to Thee*"
	F035	In loving memory of DOROTHY WHEELER died 15.11.31 aged 8 years In memory of a loving wife STELLA A WHEELER died 27.8.37 "*Called to higher service*"
	F066	In loving memory of CLARA GRACE WHEELER died 14th May 1945 aged 61 years And GEORGE THOMAS WHEELER dearly loved husband of the above died 27th May 955 aged 74 years
White	C135	In loving memory of ROSA beloved wife of REUBEN WHITE late of Brownlow Hill died 10th February 1016 aged 44 years "*At rest*"
Whiteman	C008	Sacred to the memory of MARY WHITEMAN wife of Thomas Whiteman died 18th Nov 1849
Whitfield	B043	In loving memory of my dear husband CLAUDE WILLIAM WHITFIELD passed away 20th December 2001, aged 87 years "*At rest*" Also His beloved wife RUBY GWYNNETH MAY WHITFIELD passed away 3rd November 2003 aged 83 years "*Sadly missed*"
Wilkinson	A113	This tomb was erected by WILLIAM WILKINSON of Elderslie In memory of his wife ANNE who departed this life 11th April, 1847 aged 30 years. Also His infant daughter CHARLOTTE who departed this life 29th May, 1847 aged 1 year and 8 days

Williams	B077	In loving memory of HARRY & NELLIE died in infancy beloved children of Edward and May Evelina Williams Also L.CPL. JOHN EDWARD WILLIAMS eldest son of the above killed in action in France 2nd April 1917 aged 23 years *"Greater love hath no man than this"* Also EDWARD WILLIAMS died 18th March 1946 aged 83 years
	B077	And MARY EVELINA WILLIAMS died 22nd November 1947 aged 81 years
Willoughby	F025	In loving memory of my dear wife ALICE MAY WILLOUGHBY who passed away 7th May 1942 aged 60 years *"God be with you till we meet again"*
Wills	C069	In loving memory of my dear husband & our father ALFRED JOHN ERNEST WILLS died 9th June 1928 aged 60 years
Wilson	D090	In loving memory of MARY ANN WILSON who departed this life 10th March 1898 aged 79 years "Dearest loved one we have laid thee in the peaceful graves embrace but the memory wll be cherished until we see thy heavenly face"
Windred	F030	In loving memory of ALBERT VICTOR WINDRED died 29th May 1931 aged 37 years And His beloved wife THELMA GLADYS died 8th August 1951 aged 51 years
	F030	In loving memory of our darling son & my brother IAN ALBERT WINDRED died 3rd Jan 1959 aged 8 years
Wood	A145	Also GEORGE RICHARD WOOD teacher of the infant school Christ Church, Sydney and also clerk of that Church who died April 17, 1860 aged 30 years
	C034	In loving memory of JOHNATHAN[48] WOOD who passed away 27th March 1881 aged 77 years beloved husband of Harriet nee Haines & loving grandfather & great grandfather *"A true pioneer"*
York	D176	In loving memory of JAMES YORK died 26th May 1926 aged 65 years In loving memory of JOHN YORK died 29th Sept 1911 aged 78 years
Zglinicki	B091	In loving memory of MAXAMILIAN VON ZGLINICKI who Departed this life 19th Jan 1898 aged 71 years *"Thy will be done"*

---

[48] Spelling error – should read Jonathan Wood

Plans

The following plans give an indication as to the overall layout of the cemetery.

View of cemetery from eastern side of church – the Douglass grave is to the right

Cross shaped like a birch tree with drapery – the Leuckel children's grave

Plans

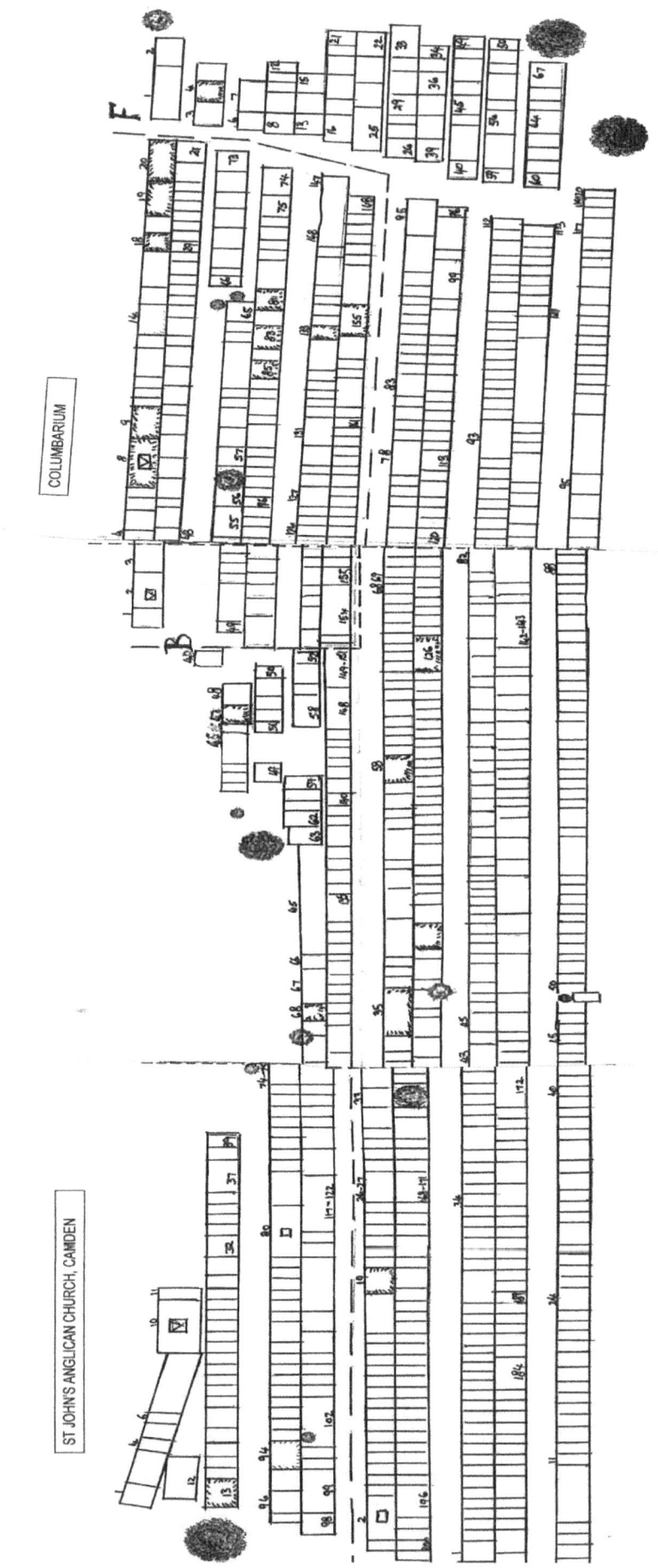

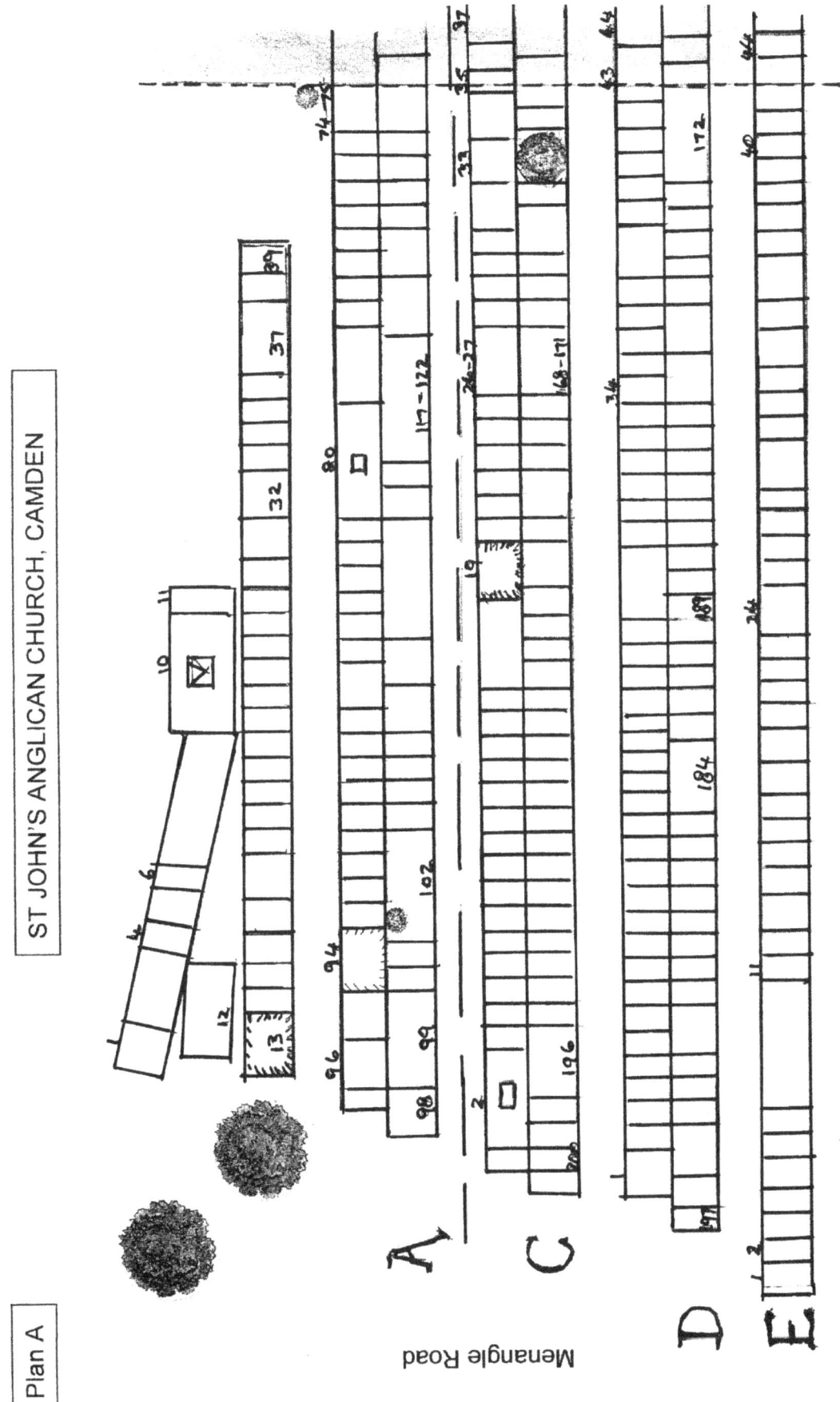

Plans

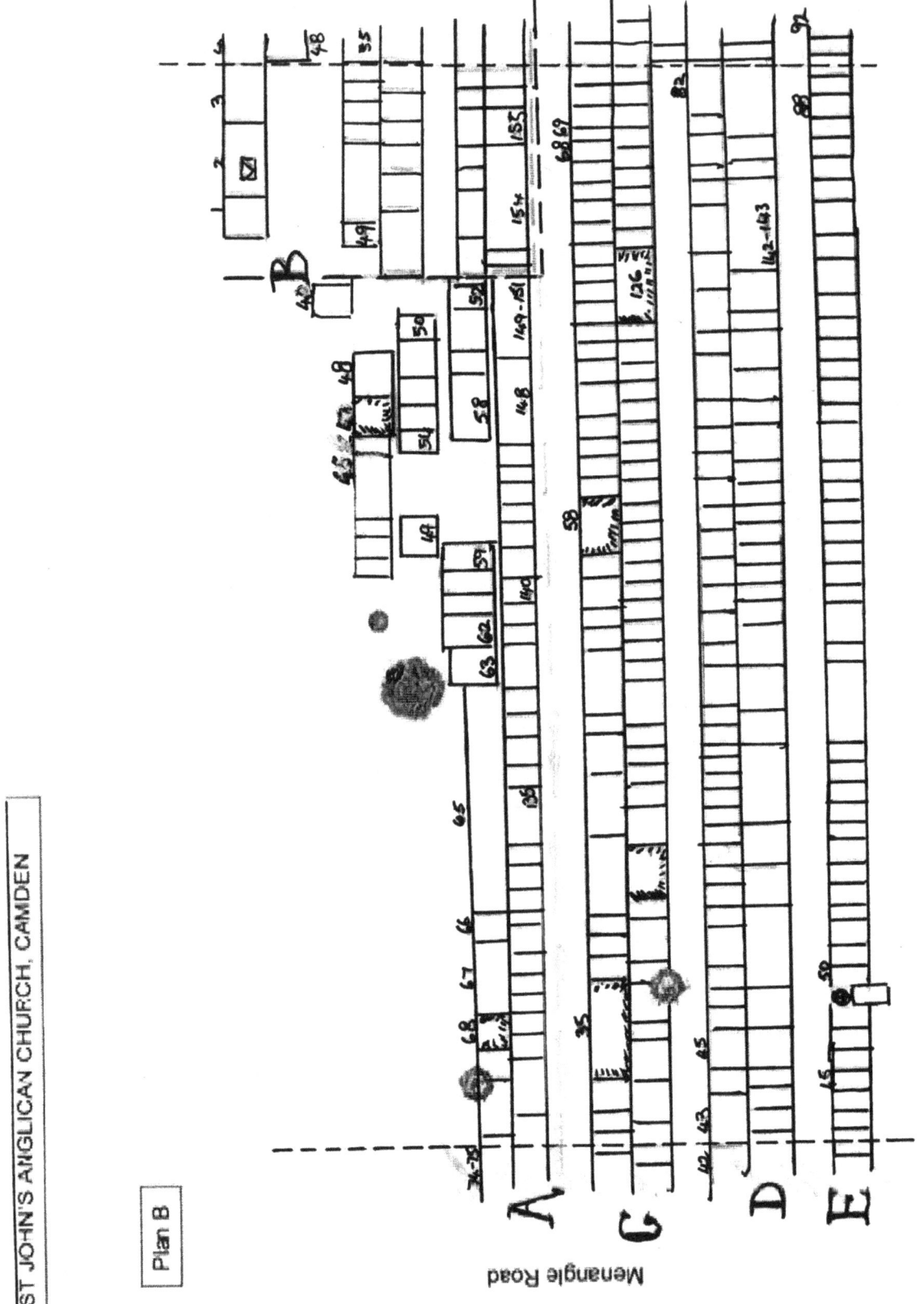

216

Plans

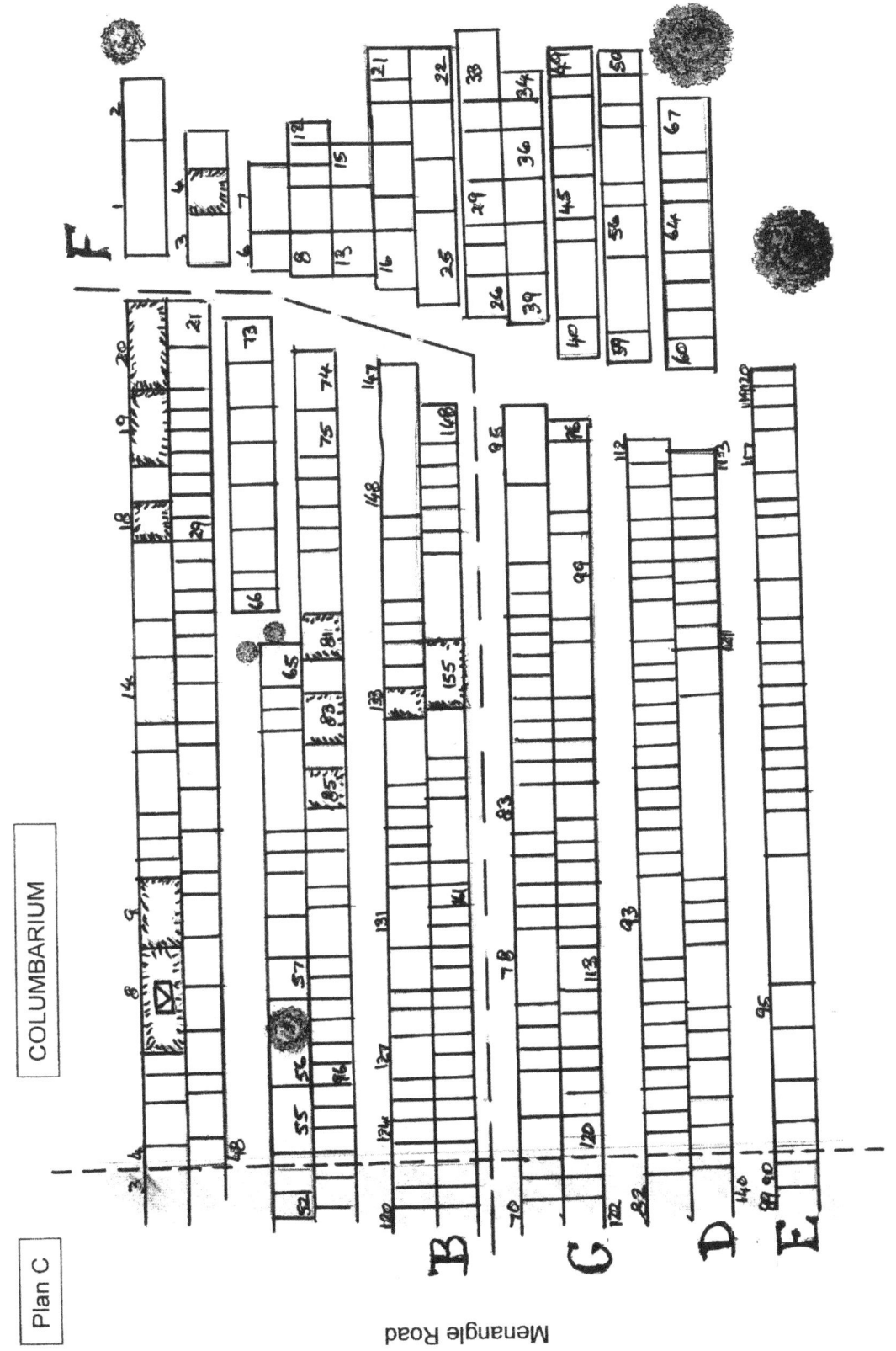

Plan C

Plans

St John's has created an interactive version of the plans on their website. In January 2022, the URL was https://map.chronicle.rip/St-John-Camden-Anglican-Cemetery

Bibliography

A Giant for Jesus (The Story of Silas Gill) – Eric G. Clancy

A Short History of Blood Transfusion – Phil Learoyd: Scientific & Technical Training Manager – Lead DDR – Leeds Blood Centre

Barker, Frederic (1808-1881) – K. J. Cable - Australian Dictionary of Biography, Volume 3, Melbourne University Press, 1969, pp 90-94

Bootbarrie (1768-1833) - Macquarie University – www.lib.mq.edu.au

Bounty Immigrants from Dorset – Weeks – John W. Weeks

Bungaree (- 1830) - F. D. McCarthy, Australian Dictionary of Biography, Volume 1, Melbourne University Press, 1966, p. 177.

Camden Advertiser, Camden, 1936-2007

Camden Characters – J D Wrigley (ed.) - Camden Historical Society, Camden, 1990.

Camden Crier, Camden.

Camden District – A History to the 1840s – P. J. Mylrea: Camden Historical Society

Camden – Farm and Village Life in Early N.S.W. – Alan Atkinson - Oxford University Press 2nd edition 1992

Camden News, Camden, 1895-1982

Camden Wollondilly Advertiser, Camden.

Campbelltown News, Campbelltown.

Carron, William (1821-1876) – Australian Dictionary of Biography – L.A. Gilbert -Volume 3, Melbourne University Press, 1969, pp 360-361.

Census of New South Wales November 1828 ed. by Malcolm R Sainty & Keith A Johnson – Library of Australian History Sydney 1980

Colonial Landscapes of the Cumberland Plain and Camden, N.S.W., 2000 – Colleen Morris & Geoffrey Britton for the National Trust of Australia (N.S.W.)

Commander Alexander Martin, R.N. - Memoir, by one of his Sons - Camden News 21st August 1898

District Reporter, Camden, 1998-2010

Douglass, Henry Grattan (1790-1865) - Australian Dictionary of Biography - K.B. Noad - Volume 1, Melbourne University Press, 1966, pp 314-316.

Early Colonial Scandals – The Turbulent Times of Samuel Marsden - Bill Wannan: Landsdowne 1972

Elizabeth Macarthur and Her World – Hazel King - Sydney: Sydney University Press, 1980.

Bibliography

Emigration to N.S.W. – The Saturday Magazine 11th May 1839

From Tartan to Wattle the descendants of Richard & Sarah Boyd - compiled by Val Garner & Jeanette Robertson

God's Acre: the religious values of cemeteries – Lisa Murray: National Trust Magazine May-July 2008

Gothick Taste in the Colony of New South Wales – Joan Kerr, James Broadbent: Davod Ell Press, in association with the Elizabeth Bay House Trust

History of Parramatta Hospital to 1988 – catal0ogue.nla.gov.au/Record/569670

Historic Organs of N.S.W. – Graeme D. Rushworth: Hale & Iremonger

I Remain the Kid, as Ever. Cobbitty Public School – Cobbitty Child Anzac Committee

James Macarthur, Colonial Conservative (1798 – 1867) – John Manning Ward - Sydney University Press, Sydney: 1981

Kanakas in Central Queensland – Toni Philipoom – CQ Family History Association Inc

King, Copland (1863-1918) – Australian Dictionary of Biography – Ian Stuart - Volume 9, Melbourne University Press, 1983,

King, Philip Gidley (1758-1808) – Australian Dictionary of Biography – A.G.L. Shaw - Volume 2, Melbourne University Press, 1967, pp 55-61.

King, Philip Gidley (1817-1904) – Australian Dictionary of Biography – Frank O'Grady - Volume 5, Melbourne University Press, 1974, pp 29-30.

King, Phillip Parker (1791-1856) – Australian Dictionary of Biography, Volume 2, Melbourne University Press, 1967, pp 61-64

King, Robert Lethbridge (1823-1897) – Australian Dictionary of Biography – K. J. Cable - Volume 5, Melbourne University Press, 1974, pp 30-31.

Macarthur, Elizabeth (1766 – 1850) – Australian Dictionary of Biography - Volume 2, Melbourne University Press, 1967, pp 144-147 – Jill Conway

Macarthur, Hannibal Hawkins (1788-1861) – Australian Dictionary of Biography – Bede Nairn - Volume 2, Melbourne University Press, 1967, pp 147-149.

Macarthur, James (1798 – 1867) – Australian Dictionary of Biography - Volume 2, Melbourne University Press, 1967, pp 149-153 – J D Heydon

Macarthur Papers

Macarthur-Onslow, Francis Arthur (1879 – 1938) – Australian Dictionary of Biography - Volume 10, Melbourne University Press, 1986, pp 196-198. – G.P. Walsh

Macarthur-Onslow, George Macleay (1875 – 1931) – Australian Dictionary of Biography - Volume 10, Melbourne University Press, 1986, pp 196-198. – G.P. Walsh

Macarthur-Onslow, James William (1867 – 1946) – Australian Dictionary of Biography - Volume 10, Melbourne University Press, 1986, pp 196-198. – G.P. Walsh

My Recollections - William Russell (of the Gandangara)

Bibliography

Narrative of an Expedition Undertaken Under the Direction of the Late Mr. Assistant Surveyor E.B. Kennedy, for the Exploration of the Country Lying Between Rockingham and Cape York - William Carron

National Archives

News From a Country Village, Camden 1847-52 – Reports made by Charles Tompson Jnr. to the Sydney Morning Herald while Clerk of Petty Sessions

North Head, Sydney, New South Wales – Australia's National Heritage

Parliament of N.S.W. archives.

Place Names of the Camden Area – Camden Historical Society/Camden Area Family History Society

Reminiscences – J B M – reprint from the Camden Times 1883 – 1884 Published by A J Doust, Times Office, Camden

Shipwrecks on the UK – Australia Run - Encyclopaedia of Australian Shipwrecks Oceans Enterprises, 303 Commercial Road, Yarram, Vic 3971, Australia

Some Came Early, Some Came Late – Nancy Phelan: Macmillan of Australia

Spinks Standard Catalogue of British Orders Decorations & Medals – A R. Litherland & B. T. Simpkin: Spinks & Son Ltd.

Stained Glass – Michael Archer: Mitchell Beazley, London

State Records N.S.W. Sz1046; Fich 3276

Stories in Stone: A field guide to Cemetery symbolism and iconography – Douglas Keister: Gibbs Smith

Sydney Gazette – 1841 - 1872

Sydney Morning Herald – 1841 - 2010

The Best of Back Then – John Wrigley: Camden Historical Society

The Buchans of Camden – Helen Ruth Dicker

The Colonial Hospital 1818 to 1848 - Governor Macquarie - Parramatta - John Watts

The Darug and Their Neighbours –James Kohen: Darug Link in association with the Blacktown & District Historical Society

The Dharawal and Gandangara in Colonial Campbelltown, New South Wales 1788 – 1830 – Carol Liston – Aboriginal History, Vol 12: 1988: pages 49 - 62

The Forgotten Men of a Forgotten War – Colin Sproule

The Life and Letters of Admiral Cornwallis - G. Cornwallis-West

The Royal George – Ancestor, Summer 1987

The Voyage of the Beagle – James Taylor: Conway Maritime Press

Bibliography

The Wheelers of Camden – Linda Anne Powell

They Worked at *Camden Park* – Brian Burnett, Richard Nixon, John Wrigley: Camden Historical Society

Thomas Herbert's World – Jeanne Chiddle Stacey

Through English Eyes - Extracts from the journal of John Gould Veitch during a trip to the Australian Colonies" – Colleen Morris, page 11 "Australian Garden History, Vol 5 No 6 May/June 1994.

Valley of Wealth – Ian Frederick Welsh: Mini-Publishing

Index

Aborigines
  Barrett
    James, 32
    Margaret, 32
    Mary Matilda, 32
    Richard Jnr., 32
  Boodbury, 31, 32
  Bootbarrie, 32
  Bungaree, 70
  Cubbich Barta, 31, 32, 35
  Dharawal, 31, 33
  Gandangara, 31
  Guribunger, 26, 32, 35
  Nanny, 17, 32, 35
  Susan Sophaline, 32
  Tharawal, 31, 33
Adams
  Catherine Jane, 129
  John George, 112, 113
Agricultural Bureau Women's Club, 87
Agricultural Department, 101
Aidman, Robert Alfred, 123
Allinson , Garlies, 51, 158
Ames, Stanley, 29
Anderson, Ethel May, 80
Antill
  Captain John Macquarie, 124
  Major Henry Colden, 39
Armidale Light Horse, 117
Armour
  George, 83, 84, 158
  George William, 83
Australian Agricultural Co., 70
Australian Clubs, 110
Australian Forces
  Boer War
    "A" Squadron of the Mounted Rifles, 124
    1st Light Horse Brigade, 111
    2nd Australian Light Horse, 120
    2nd Light Horse Regiment, 111
    2nd Mounted Rifles, 124
    2nd N.S.W. Mounted Rifles, 112
    3rd N.S.W. Imperial Bushmen, 124
    5th Battalion of the Australian Commonwealth Horse, 111
    7th Division, 111
    Australian Light Horse, 116, 127
    Camden Mounted Rifles, 103, 123
    Picton Half Company of Mounted Rifles, 124
  WWI
    1st Australian Light Horse, 125
    1st Battalion Australian Light Horse, 120
    1st Infantry Battalion, 116
    1st Light Horse, 111, 112, 113, 123, 124, 195
    1st Light Horse Regiment, 112, 113, 124
    2nd Battalion A.I.F, 123
    2nd Brigade HQ Australian Field Artillery, 116
    2nd Light Horse, 111, 118, 119
    2nd Remount Unit, 114
    3rd Battalion A.I.F., 113
    3rd Field Company Engineers., 123
    4th Battalion A.I.F, 120, 210
    4th Infantry Battalion A.I.F, 125
    5th Field Artillery Brigade, 113
    5th Light Horse Brigade, 119
    6th Australian Light Horse A.I.F., 116
    6th Battalion, Headquarters (Australian Army Medical Corps), 121
    7th Light Horse, 109, 118, 119
    9th Light Horse Regiment, 118
    17th Battalion A.I.F., 117
    18th Battalion A.I.F, 113, 117
    49th Battalion A.I.F., 114
    54th Battalion A.I.F., 114, 175
    Sea Transport Service of the A.I.F., 112
  WWII
    2/15th Field Regiment A.I.F., 127
    7th Recovery Section, 2/3 AFD W/shops AAOC, 126
    14th Field Company., 128
    39th Battalion, 126
    53rd battalions, 126

Index

55th Battalion, 126
R.A.A.F, 125, 127, 128, 129
Swan Military Barracks, 127
Australian Jockey, 110
Australian Newspaper, 25, 47
Australian Nursery, 64
Avery, William, 94
Awards
    Camden Citizen's Award, 126

Barker, Bishop Frederic, 64, 71
Barrett, Richard, 26, 32, 35
Barry, William James, 82
Basden, Richard, 22
Bathurst, Earl Henry, 40
Battle of Camperdown, 44
Battle of Trafalgar, 44
Battle of Waterloo, 24
Bayley, Alfred John, 54
Beck, Constable, 54
Betts, Clara Susan, 49
Biffin, William Alfred Ernest, 84
Blackett, Edmond, 25
Blandon, Murray, 33
Blow, Maggie, 80
Boardman, Emma. *See* Dengate, Emma
Boer War, 109, 110, 111, 112, 118, 124
Boyd
    Alice, 80
    Florence, 80
    Richard, 35, 93, 97
    Robert, 80, 93, 94, 95
    William, 35, 97
    William Jnr., 80
Brain, Percy Sidney Raymond, 113
Breton, Colonel Henry William, 39
Brien
    Alexander, 113
    Michael Charles Louis, 155
British Forces
    Boer War
        7th Dragoon Guards, 110
    Chitral Campaign
        1st Battalion King's Royal Rifle Corps, 111
        11th Hussars, 111
        Royal Artillery, 111
    Crimea War, 147
    Maori War, 57
    Napoleon
        18th Regiment, 39
        99th Regiment, 80
    WWI
        16th Queen's Lancers, 118
        London Regiment (Princess Louise's Kensington Battalion, 117

Broughton
    Bishop, 22, 47, 71, 98, 140
    Bishop William Grant, 46
Bryant, Thomas, 102
Buchan
    Margaret, 23
    William, 23
Buchan, Margaret, 23
Butler
    James, 35, 55
    Susannah, 55
Butt, Jacob, 65
Byrne, Constable Thomas, 54

Camden A.H. & I. Society, 65, 68, 84, 86, 89, 101, 114, 120
Camden Ambulance, 127
Camden Bowling Club, 153
Camden Bush Fire Brigade, 91
Camden Council, 56, 57, 58, 73, 74, 101, 119, 126
Camden Cricket Club, 86, 127
Camden Cricket Team, 126
Camden District Tennis Association, 126
Camden Football and Rifle Club, 86
Camden Historical Society, 26, 64, 91, 104, 122
Camden Parents and Citizens Association, 90
Camden Park private cemetery, 111
Camden Post Office, 66
Camden Probus Club, 91
Camden Progress Association, 101
Camden Rifle Club, 85, 116
Camden Saw Mills, 77
Camden School of Arts, 51, 64, 74
Camden Scout Troop, 155
Camden Show, 17, 67, 74, 78, 91
Camden Show Society, 74, 91
Camden Vale Milk Co., 110
Camden Volunteer Fire Brigade, 90
Camden, Earl, 31
Campbelltown Bowling Club, 123
Carron
    Jessie, 73
    William, 73
Casson, Elias, 98

Index

Cemeteries
    Bundanoon Cemetery, 37
    Caestre Military Cemetery, France, 116
    Cairo War Memorial Cemetery, 124
    Camden General Cemetery, 27, 89, 106
    Camden Park private cemetery, 110, 112, 119, 144, 147
    Camden Roman Catholic Cemetery, 27
    Cemetery at St. John's Camden, 60
    Chatby War Memorial Cemetery in Egypt., 125
    Damascus British War Memorial Cemetery in Syria, 116
    Eastern Cemetery, Boulogne, France, 114
    Heilly Station Cemetery Mericourt-L'Abbe France, 114
    Namps-au-Val British Cemetery Rouen (Somme), 117
    Nunhead (All Saints) Cemetery London, 117
    Parade Ground Cemetery at Gallipoli, 120
    Sendgrove, Surrey, England, 149
    Shorncliffe Military Cemetery Kent, England, 123
    Shrapnel Valley Cemetery Anzac, 120
    South Head Cemetery, 49
    St. John's Cemetery, 17, 39
    St. Paul's Church Cemetery Cobbitty, 48
    St. Sever Cemetery Extension, Rouen, 115
    St. Thomas's Cemetery, Narellan, 36
    Villers-Bretonneux, France, 113, 125
Channell, William Arthur, 107
Chesham, Hilton John, 113
China Opium War, 47
Chisholm
    Dr. Edward, 95
    James Kinghorne, 84
Churches
    All Saints Sutton Forrest, 51
    Camden Methodist Church, 77, 114
    Congregational Church, 55
    Holy Trinity Church, Sydney, 71, 72
    Methodist Church, 155
    Middle, 22
    Newcastle Cathedral, 121
    Oldham Street Presbyterian Church, 47
    St. Andrew's Presbyterian Church, Newcastle, 153
    St. Andrews Cathedral, Sydney, 75
    St. Anne's Ryde, 48
    St. George the Martyr, Southwark, Surrey, 52
    St. James Anglican Church Menangle, 89
    St. James Church, Menangle, 74, 205
    St. James, King Street, 47
    St. James' Church, Menangle, 87
    St. John's Camden, 25, 55, 60, 65, 68, 70, 71, 80, 94, 91, 101
    St. John's Church Balmain North, 86
    St. John's Church Parramatta, 70
    St. John's, Parramatta, 36, 37, 41
    St. Luke's Anglican Church, Liverpool, 47
    St. Mary's Cathedral, 50, 73
    St. Nicholas' Church, Liverpool, 47
    St. Paul's Church Cobbitty, 57
    St. Paul's Cobbitty, 124
    St. Paul's Westbrook, 85
    St. Paul's, Mount Hunter, 84
    St. Peter's Church Campbelltown, 36, 37, 155
    St. Peters Church, Theresa Park, 84
    St. Phillip's Church Hill, 70
    Wesleyan Chapel Cawdor, 100
    Westbrook Church. *See* churches St. Paul's Mount Hunter
    Westbrook Church, 101
Clarke, James Coleman, 114
Clayton & Bell, 134, 140, 142, 144, 147, 149
Clinton, John William, 153
Close, Henry Thomas, 73
Coker, George, 36
Collingwood Smith, William, 149
Collins, James, 54
Connolly, Patrick, 54
Cornwallis, Sir William, 44
Couch, Henry Turbet Harvey. *See* Sutton, Henry Turbet Harvey
Cox
    Sophia, 60
    Thomas, 60
Cranfield
    Astley Arthur, 125
    Bertha Victoria. *See* Brien, Bertha Victoria
    Leonard Ross, 81
    Mary Ann, 62
    Mary Jane. *See* Dawson, Mary Jane
    Thomas, 100
Critchley, William Leslie, 103
Crookston, Dr., 82

Index

Cross, Thomas, 54

Cuckow
    George. *See* Coker, George
    George Cuckow. *See* Coker, George
    Thomas, 36
Cunningham, John, 21
Cycle Club, 116
Cycling Club, 86

Dabinett, George, 37
Dairy Farmers' Co-operative Milk Co., 110
Darwin, Charles, 70
Davies, Llewella, 26, 122
Dawson
    Mary, 36, 85, 100, 169
    Mary Jane, 85
    Thomas, 56, 66
Death, Thomas, 54
Dengate
    Edward John, 85, 114
    Emma, 85
    Frederick, 99
Department of Agriculture, 126
Derriman, William, 65
Donahue
    Hilda, 130
Donohue, John, 106
Doodey, Eliza. *See* Pearson, Eliza
Douglass, Henry Grattan, 39, 43
Downes, Frederick Arthur, 84
Doyle
    Sergeant Douglas, 131
    Sergeant Douglas Brian, 129
    Sergeant Francis Joseph, 129
Druitt, Robert Henry, 101
Dunk, Jesse, 62

Earl, Dorothea. *See* Campbell, Dorothea
Ellis, Samuel, 68
English
    Henry (known as Dusty), 104
    Herbert Thomas, 26, 27
    James, 26, 36
    James Joseph, 32
    Len, 17, 27, 104

Fairall, William, 62
Ferguson
    Francis, 64, 125, 174
    Robert Bruce, 125, 174
Flinders, Matthew, 70
Forrest, Rev. Robert, 25, 70

Fullagar
    Henrietta Maria, 45, 51
    Sarah Smith, 46
Furner, Major Mr. W.C., 66

Gardner, Reginald George, 81
Gibbs, Catherine Elizabeth, 52
Gibson
    Chief Constable, James, 80
    William, 80
Goal
    Berrima, 50
    Campbelltown, 50
    Cockatoo Island, 53
    Greenock Gaol, 35
    Parramatta Gaol, 98
    Port Macquarie, 36, 41, 50
    Sydney Gaol, 50
Goodluck, Joseph, 24, 52
Gordon, William, 49, 56
Governors
    Bourke, 21, 46, 59
    Brisbane Sir Thomas, 40, 42
    Darling, Ralph, 42, 46
    Gipps, Sir George, 42
    Hunter, Captain John, 69
    King, Philip Gidley, 31, 69
    Macquarie, Lachlan, 21, 31, 37, 40
    Philip, 35
Gumbleton, Sophia. *See* Cox, Sophia
Gunn
    Bertie Stewart, 106
    George Drummond, 32

Haigh, Victor Louis Bosker, 115
Hall
    Dr. James, 41
    William, 100
Handel
    Alfred Charles, 134, 136, 138
    Philip, 134
Hawkey
    John, 103, 110
    Richard, 67, 109, 178
    Richard John, 116
Haynes, Harriet, 37
Heighington, George Frederick, 103
Henders Margaret. *See* Buchan, Margaret
Herbert
    Kezia, 37
    Thomas, 37, 179

Index

Higgins, Sergeant Robert, 36
Hinde, Oliver, 66
Hindes, Richard George, 85
Hoare Town, 40
Hoare, Samuel, 40
Hobbs, Thomas, 36, 67
Hodge, Philip Benjamin, 74, 180
Home Farm, 26, 49, 93
Hopson
 Charles, 74, 75, 86
 Fanny. *See* Wheeler, Fanny
 William Henry, 86
Hospital Women's Auxiliary, 122
Hospitals
 Beverley Park Orthopaedic Hospital at Campbelltown, 153
 Camden Hospital, 68, 74, 81, 90, 102, 103, 104, 105, 106, 107, 127
 Carrington Hospital, 101
 Carrington Nursing Home, 58
 Coast Hospital, 72
 Colonial General Hospital at Parramatta, 40
 Fever Hospital and Infirmary at Cahir, Tipperary, 40
 King George Hospital London, 117
 Masonic Hospital at Ashfield, 117
 Prince Henry Hospital, 72
 Prince of Wales Hospital at Randwick, 125
 Seamen's Hospital Le Havre, 42
 Sydney Hospital, 42, 71, 90
 Windemere Private Hospital, 76
 Windsor District Hospital, 122
Hotels
 Arnold's Public House, 94
 Camden Inn, 23, 24, 52
 Camden Vale Inn, 26
 Hennessy's Hotel, 105
 Merino Tavern, 52
 Plough and Harrow, 17, 94, 100
 Red Cow, Parramatta, 52
 Royal Hotel, 52, 75
 White House Inn at Parramatta, 52
Hourn, Ellen. *See* Stanner, Ellen
Hovell, Captain William Hilton, 39
Howe, Robert, 42
Hughes
 Ellen Rosetta. *See* McMullen, Ellen Rosetta
 Henry Clarendon, 76
 James Terry, 46
 Samuel Terry, 75, 76

Hume, James, 21
Hurd, Captain Thomas, 70

Jenkins, Wallace Conrad Rofe, 116
Jiminy, 33
Johnson, Leicester, 155
Jones, Adeline Lydia, 90

Kaffie, Henry, 33, 34
Kanaka, 33
Kelly, Thomas, 37
Kernohan, Dr. Elizabeth, 28
Kettley, George Edward, 75
King
 Anna Maria, 69, 70
 Philip Gidley, 31, 69, 70
 Philip Gidley (the younger), 70
 Philip Parker, 69, 70, 140
 Rev. Cecil John, 24, 27, 28, 50, 69, 71, 78, 85, 136, 138
 Rev. Cecil John, 24, 27, 28, 50, 69
 Rev. Copland, 69, 71, 72, 136
 Robert Lethbridge, 70, 71
Kingsford Smith, Charles, 90

Lacey, James, 22
Lakeman, John, 52, 54
Lawson, William, 41
LeFevre, John, 24, 133
Lester, Flying Officer Geoffrey Hugh, 129
Lethbridge
 Christopher, 70, 140
 Harriet, 70
Light, Captain Francis, 51
Linn, Eliza Jane. *See* Rapley, Eliza Jane
Little, Kevin, 135, 155
Liversey, William Calbraith, 116
Local Government Investment Board, 126
Lodges
 Abbotsford Lodge, 50, 65, 101
 Camden Lodge, 50, 65, 68, 89
 Masonic Lodge, 89
 Royal Order of Foresters, 67, 68, 85
 Sons and Daughters of Temperance, 77
 Sons of Temperance, 74, 88, 89
Lord Howe Island, 73
Lowe
 Agnes Elizabeth, 86
 Eric Lyndon, 86, 116
Lych Gate, 26, 85, 104

Macarthur
 Elizabeth, 21

227

Index

Emily, 22, 149
Hannibal, 41, 46, 69, 70, 111
Hannibal Hawkins, 41, 46, 69
James, 22, 25, 46, 53, 69, 85, 93, 97, 144, 147, 149
John, 21, 31, 35, 37, 39, 69, 144
Mrs. Elizabeth Snr., 21
William, 48, 56, 57, 60, 64, 87, 93, 94, 110, 133, 134, 140
Macarthur Park, 73, 109, 124
Macarthur-Onslow
    Annette, 26, 149
    Arthur William, 118
    Brigadier General George Macleay, 109, 135, 151
    Elizabeth, 110, 111, 118
    Elizabeth Jnr., 25, 26, 89, 149
    Francis Arthur, 110
    George Macleay, 110, 118
    James William, 111
    Sibella, 112
Macdonald, Alice Wilson, 153
Macgregor, Sir William, 72
Mackenzie, Roderick Murcheson, 71
MacLaren, Rev. Albert, 72
Macleay
    Alexander, 46, 73, 142, 147
    Sir George, 55, 142
    Sir William, 112
    William, 46, 147
Marsden, Rev. Samuel, 41, 49
Martens, Conrad, 149
Martin
    Alexander, 39, 43, 51
    Jeremiah, 97
    John Benson, 51, 115
Marton, Alexander, 44
McAlister, Lieutenant, 39
McGrath, Ernest Henry, 126, 128
McLeod
    Norman Thomas, 127
    Walter, 101
McMahon, John, 94
McMinn, John Thomas, 66, 188
McMullen
    Ellen Rosetta, 75, 76, 103
    Franklin, 75
Medals
    Chitral Medal, 111
    CMG, 118, 119, 151
    Commonwealth Recognition Award for Senior Australians, 91
    DSO, 118, 119, 121, 151
    Long Service Medal, 90
    Malakand clasp, 111
    Military Cross, 120, 121
    Military General Services Medal, 63
    Naval General Services Medal, 45
    OAM, 26, 122, 125, 126, 174
    Order of the Nile, 119
    Queen's Medal, 90, 110, 111
    VD, 118, 119, 151
Meehan, James, 31
Mellon, Charles John. *See* Sutton, Charles John
Mills
    George, 94, 117
    George Griffen Roy, 117
Mitchell
    Richard, 102
    Sir Thomas, 64, 75
Molle, Captain George, 39
Monk
    John, 57
    John Leonard, 65
Moor, Stephen, 135, 153
Moore
    Edward Lomas, 75, 76, 117
    Essington, 117
Moran, Rev. John Fleming, 71
Morgan, William Stoneham, 33
Moses, Rosannah, 37
Mounted Rifles, N.S.W., 110, 111, 118, 120
Munck, Johann Leonhard. *See* Monk, John Leonard
Murphy, Hester, 40

N.S.W. Corps, 69
Napoleonic Wars, 44, 59
Newton, George, 54
Nixon
    Frederick, 105
    Frederick, 105
    Richard (Dick), 26, 29
    Richard (Dick), 22
Norfolk Island, 69
North Cawdor Estate, 56

Onslow
    Arthur Alexander Walton, 110, 111, 118, 147, 149
    Arthur John, 103
    Captain Arthur, 95, 147, 149
Onslow Thompson
    Astley John, 103, 109, 119

228

Index

Major Astley John, 89
Oxley
   Captain John, 39
   John, 49, 52, 62

Pallier, Mr., 54
Palmer
   Edward (Ned), 49
   Edward Thompson, 48, 49, 94
   Mary Edith, 49
   Ned. *See* Palmer, Edward (Ned)
Pansy, 91, 157
Patrick
   David, 29
   Rev. Alan, 28, 29
Paul
   Frank Henderson, 120
   Rev. Thomas Giles, 120, 138
Pearson
   James, 47, 73, 194
   Jessie. *See* Carron, Jessie
   Rev. Thomas, 47
Pellatt & Co, 134
Pellatt, Frederick, 134
Peninsular War, 39, 62
Percival, Spencer, 39
Perry, Ivo Garnett, 127
Phelan, Nancy, 26
Philip, Captain Arthur, 69
Places
   Brownlow Hill, 57, 65, 66, 77, 78, 84, 102, 117, 123
   Burragorang Valley, 125, 129, 130
   Cawdor, 24, 32, 48, 56, 62, 64, 65, 77, 78, 85, 86, 89, 99, 103, 114
   Cobbitty, 63, 67, 68, 89, 98, 99, 123, 124, 158
   Cobbitty Paddocks, 68, 98, 99, 123
   Elderslie, 49, 54, 62, 63, 68, 75, 81, 86, 94, 102, 113, 114, 211
   Kirkham Lane, 113
   Menangle, 37, 67, 68, 74, 82, 87, 100, 104, 113, 164, 184
   Mount Hunter, 24, 55, 57, 58, 62, 66, 78, 84, 100, 102, 125, 127, 164
   Narellan, 37, 39, 98, 106, 117, 176, 179
   Nattai, 130, 153
   Picton, 37, 39, 50, 51, 65, 81, 85, 88, 112, 117, 124, 127, 182
   Razorback, 67, 81, 85, 99, 114
   Theresa Park, 44, 84, 103, 123
   Westbrook, 24, 56, 57, 85, 101, 127
   Westbrook Creek, 24
   Werombi, 77, 84, 112, 117, 129, 130, 185
Platt, William, 62
Police
   Boat, 54
   Camden Police, 82, 107, 127
   Mounted Constabulary, 66
   Mounted Police, 50
   N.S.W. Police, 50
   Queensland Police, 50
Poole
   George, 55, 57, 123
   John, 55, 57, 109
   John Lambert Richardson, 123
Porteus, Sergeant, 107
Potts, Joseph Compton, 25
Powell & Sons (Whitefriars) Ltd, 134, 151
Powell, Harry James, 134, 135
Price, Anna Maria, 62
Properties
   Albion House, 75
   Alpha Cottage, 51
   Badgally, 76, 190
   Belgenny Cottage, 67
   Booligal Station, 76
   Brockley Vale, 57
   Brooks Flat, 56, 66, 169
   Brownlow Hill, 46, 73, 84, 142
   Calf Farm, 88
   Camberfield, 67, 99
   Camden Park Estate Pty. Ltd., 110, 111, 119, 120
   Camden Park, 17, 21, 24, 26, 31, 32, 36, 39, 49, 55, 56, 57, 60, 62, 63, 64, 65, 67, 70, 73, 75, 84, 85, 89, 93, 94, 97, 98, 99, 101, 103, 107, 110, 111, 112, 116, 144, 147, 149, 177, 204
   Camelot, 113
   Camperdown, 39, 44, 46, 186
   Chatsworth House, 64
   Clifton, 39
   Conobie, 49
   Daisy Vale, 85
   Denbigh, 23, 158
   Domain Lodge, 73
   Dunheved, 70
   Elderslie House, 113
   Elderslie, 39, 49
   Elizabeth Bay House, 73, 112
   Elizabeth Farm, 24, 35, 37, 144
   Erringhi, 116
   Fernleigh, 68
   Freshfields, 67, 89

Index

Funnell's Farm, 99
Gilbulla, 112
Gledswood, 76, 84
Glendarulen, 55
Glenmore, 73
Hardwick., 75
Harrington Grove, 23, 39
Herbert's Hill, 37
Hoare, 39, 40
Home Farm, 93, 94, 97
Jarvisfield, 39
Kameruka, 101
Kirkham, 39, 62, 105
Logan Downs Station, 66, 67
Macaria, 56, 90
Manar, 118
Mander, 33
Maryland Station, 90
Matahli Farm, 36
May Farm, 80, 101
Molles Main, 39, 76, 190
Moreton Park, 33, 75, 76, 77, 181, 188
Mount Hercules, 85, 99, 114
Nangus Station, 93
Narellan Grange, 39
Narrigo, 42
Nepean Towers, 64, 75, 124
Oatenleigh, 114
Oran Park, 117
Osterleigh, 85
Park Hall, 64, 124
Passchendale, 123
Pilton Estate, 89
Pleasant View Farm, 55
Ravenswood, 39
Redbank, 37
Richfield, 99
Smidmore's Paddock, 67
Springfield, 48, 49
St. Helen's Station, 89
Studley Park, 56, 155
Theresa Park, 46, 75
Thrunsli, 49
Toganmain, 142
Vermont, 46, 63
Westwood, 46
Woodburn, 84

Queen Victoria's Diamond Jubilee, 103, 111
Quigley, George, 123

Rapley
   Edwin Morton, 127
   Thomas, 65, 77
   William, 77, 127
Ray
   Milton, 27
   Milton Brettel, 90
Raymond
   Honoria Australia, 70
   James, 70
Red Cross, 57, 58, 85, 86, 87, 122
Reeves, Henry Pollock, 64
Richardson
   James, 37
   Susannah. *See* Butlr, Susannah
   Thomas Dockery, 62
Rideout, James, 77
Rix, Rev. Arthur George, 86
Robinson, Jane Emily, 48
Rofe, William, 62, 198
Rogers, Anthony, 54
Roll of Honour, 109, 113, 114, 115, 116, 117, 118, 120, 125
Rootes, Sivyer, 27, 199
Rossitter, Thomas James, 104
Rotolactor, 67
Rowsell, Rev. Harold A.C., 71
Royal Agricultural Society, 43
Royal Botanic Gardens, 72, 73
Rumsby, Ann, 41
Ruwald, Cyril, 26

Sawyers, Roy, 128
Schools
   All Saints School, Higher Walton Lancashire, 116
   Army training school, 155
   Australian College of Theology, 72
   Barker College Sydney, 117
   Cambridge, 54
   Camden Grammar School, 49, 56, 155
   Camden Public School, 85, 90
   Church & School Corporation, 46
   Church of England Denominational School at St. John's Camden, 64
   Classical and Commercial School, 56
   Cranbrook School, 125
   Edinburgh University, 117
   Exeter College, Oxford, 110
   Female Orphan School at Parramatta, 47
   Fort Street, 86
   King's and Queen's College of Physicians of Ireland, 40

Index

Kings School Parramatta, 128
Mater-Dei Special School, 153
Merton College, Oxford University, 121
Milsons Point Public School, 120
Moore Theological College, 71
Normal Central School of Art (South Kensington Museum), 149
Reading College, 120
Richmond Infants School, 122
Rugby, 110, 119
Rugby School, England, 118
St. Andrew's Cathedral School, 86
St. John's College, Cambridge, 70
St. John's College, Melbourne, 121
Sydney Grammar School, 71, 111, 128
Sydney University, 43, 71, 90
The King's School, Parramatta, 70
Toowoomba Grammar School, 90
Trinity College, Cambridge, 111
Trinity College, Dublin, 40
Westbrook, 127

Scott
    Archdeacon Thomas H., 47
    Gilbert, 25

Shadforth, Lieutenant Thomas, 39
Sharpe, Sarah, 93, 94
Sheather, Augusta Maria, 93

Sheldrick
    Frederick George, 105
    Frederick John, 105

Ships
    Annie Wilson, 66
    Asia, 37
    Augustus Jersey, 62
    Brothers, 60, 70, 99
    Brothers, 76
    Bussorah Merchant, 60
    Canton, 56
    Caroline, 51
    Chevert, 147
    China, 47
    China, 47, 73
    Coptic, 57
    Cospatrick, 60
    Deveron, 47
    Duncan, 23
    Earl Gray, 102
    Earl Grey, 42, 98
    Eliza, 64, 68
    Florist, 99
    Herald, 147
    Hibernia, 60
    HMAT Ceramic, 116
    HMAT Euripides, 113
    HMAT Hororata, 121
    HMAT Star of Victoria, 114, 120, 123
    HMAT Suffolk, 116
    HMAT Themistocles, 113
    HMAT Warilda, 125
    HMS Adventure, 70
    HMS Beagle, 70
    HMS Gordon, 69
    HMS Howe, 147
    HMS Sirius, 69
    HMS Victory, 45, 52
    Indrapura, 121
    John Barry, 73
    John Bright, 64
    John Denniston, 48
    John, 46
    Julianna, 60, 62
    Kanowna, 125
    Lady Ann, 65
    Layton, 24, 65, 78
    Lord Eldon, 35
    Mangles, 37
    Maria Ann, 41
    Marquis of Hastings, 63
    Mary Hay, 60
    Mermaid, 36, 70
    Montrose, 118
    Morayshire, 60, 62
    Neptune, 62
    Nithsdale, 35
    Pitt, 37
    Plantagenet, 67
    RMS Orontes, 114
    RMS Osterley, 112
    Royal Admiral, 36
    Royal George, 22, 60, 93
    Shankamore, 63
    Speke, 40
    SS Makarini, 123
    Switzerland, 66
    Sydney Cove, 37
    Thalia, 102
    The Peru, 50
    Waterloo, 60
    Wilson, 65, 77, 153, 173, 212

Shoobridge, Gladys May, 106

Sidman
    Charles Warrane, 123
    George, 58
    George Victor, 123
    Jessie, 57
    Mabel, 57

Index

  William, 57, 123
Simpson, Ebenezer, 24, 202
Small, James, 103, 203
Smith
  Carlton, 110, 112
  Reginald (Rex) Sydney, 124
Solomon, John, 33
Spice, Jonathon, 79
St. Andrew's Cathedral, 70
St. James Mothers Union, 85, 86, 87
Starr, Jennings, 100
Stewart, James, 93, 94, 95, 204
Stuckey, Elgar, 77
Stuckey, Joan, 77
Sturt, Charles, 142
Sutton
  Brett, 30
  Charles John, 87
  Walter Henry, 88
Sydney Botanic Gardens. *See* Royal Botanic Gardens
Sydney Royal Show, 83

Tanner, Ellen, 87
Taplin
  Henry, 103
  William John, 77
Tate, Colin, 128
Taylor, Elizabeth, 42
Teague, Lieutenant Horace Albert, 129
Thompson
  Charles, 78
  Charles Augustus, 54, 56
  Henry, 55, 74, 98, 206
Thompson's Flour Mill, 23, 25, 54
Thorn, Elias, 79
Tickner, John, 67, 99
Tingcombe, Rev. Henry, 23, 70, 95, 122, 140
Toc H, 121, 122
Tompson, Charles Jnr., 79, 97
Tornaghi, Keith Angelo, 103
Tritton, Gladys May. *See* Shoobridge, Gladys May

Unnamed Infant, 81
Unstead, Lieutenant Cecil Joseph, 129

Vaux, Joan, 65
Veitch, John Gould, 64, 222
Veness
  John Edward, 89
  Robert, 79

Volunteer Air Observer Corp, 129

Wade, Ernest Leon, 128
Watkins, Mary Ann Eleanor, 98
Watson
  George, 66, 88
  George, 88
  James, 36
  Thomas, 98, 99
Wedd, Stephen, 28, 29
Weeks, Benjamin, 99, 100
Wentworth, William Charles, 42, 43, 46, 63
West
  Dr., 33, 34, 56, 81, 102, 103, 104, 105, 106
  Dr. Francis William, 33, 89
  Dr. George, 89, 90
  Francis James, 33, 89, 90
  Francis William, 33, 90
  Rev. John, 60
Westbrook Cricket Club, 127
Wheatley, William, 55
Wheeler
  Cecil Claude, 125
  Fanny, 65
  George, 78
  James, 101
  John, 55
  John William, 65
  Jonathan, 24, 65, 78
  Samuel Edward Albert, 25
Wheeler
  Fanny, 65
  George, 78
White
  Adelaide Maria, 71
  Rufus, 65
Whitefriars Glass Company, 134, 151
Whiteman
  Charles Thomas, 49
  Spencer, 24
Whysall, Agnes Elizabeth. *See* Lowe, Agnes Elizabeth
Williams, John Edward, 125
Wilton, William Langworthy, 99
Wollondilly Shire Council, 104, 119
Wood, Jonathan, 37
Woods
  Joseph, 52
  Mary Ann, 52
Woore, Lt. Thomas, 23, 25, 39

World War I, 57, 83, 86, 109, 110, 112, 118, 121, 123, 125, 127, 155
World War II, 28, 58, 90, 109, 122, 125, 127, 155

Wright, James, 94
Wrigley, John, 26, 51, 64, 122

Zglinicki, Maximillian von, 50

Draped urn, Ferguson grave Section C02

www.ingramcontent.com/pod-product-compliance
Lightning Source LLC
Chambersburg PA
CBHW041713290426
44110CB00024B/2823